SECRETS OF
THE WORLD'S
UNDISCOVERED
TREASURES

Also by Lionel and Patricia Fanthorpe

Lionel and Patricia Fanthorpe

SECRETS OF THE WORLD'S UNDISCOVERED TREASURES

DUNDURN PRESS
TORONTO

Copy Editor: Andrea Waters
Design: Erin Mallory
Printer: Friesens

Library and Archives Canada Cataloguing in Publication

Fanthorpe, R. Lionel
    Secrets of the world's undiscovered treasures / by Lionel and Patricia Fanthorpe.

Includes bibliographical references.
ISBN 978-1-55002-938-3

    1. Treasure troves. I. Fanthorpe, Patricia II. Title.

G525.F35 2009   904   C2009-900099-7

1 2 3 4 5   13 12 11 10 09

We acknowledge the support of the **Canada Council for the Arts** and the **Ontario Arts Council** for our publishing program. We also acknowledge the financial support of the **Government of Canada** through the **Book Publishing Industry Development Program** and **The Association for the Export of Canadian Books**, and the **Government of Ontario** through the **Ontario Book Publishers Tax Credit** program, and the **Ontario Media Development Corporation**.

Care has been taken to trace the ownership of copyright material used in this book. The author and the publisher welcome any information enabling them to rectify any references or credits in subsequent editions.

J. Kirk Howard, President

Printed and bound in Canada.
www.dundurn.com

Dundurn Press	Gazelle Book Services Limited	Dundurn Press
3 Church Street, Suite 500	White Cross Mills	2250 Military Road
Toronto, Ontario, Canada	High Town, Lancaster, England	Tonawanda, NY
M5E 1M2	LA1 4XS	U.S.A. 14150

Dedication and Acknowledgements

The authors dedicate this work with much gratitude to all their friends at Armadacon in Plymouth, England, with many thanks for all the fun and entertainment that Armadacon provides, and in recognition of the great work they do for charity.

We also wish to give special thanks to Michele Jackson of Plymouth for permission to use her pirate photographs, and we give our grateful acknowledgements to the participants in the Lulworth Castle pirate re-enactment weekend.

Table of Contents

Note by Tom Danheiser
Producer of *Coast to Coast A.M.*

L ionel Fanthorpe: The Greatest Storyteller Ever Born. There's a reason we give him this title ... *because he simply is!*

As a producer, I can recall several moments in my working relationship with Lionel, but one of my favourites was when we actually met in
person. Lionel is as unique as can be with his velvety smooth voice and
style of storytelling that makes your mind take off to a world of mystical
enjoyment. This I can assure you of, as I have booked him many times on
our national radio show, *Coast to Coast A.M.* He has consistently taken
our radio audience on fantastic journeys of the mind with his wondrous
way of presenting a story. He is definitely a *Coast to Coast A.M.* favourite.

No matter if you are learning about the legend of the Wereshark, the
practices of Voodoo and Santeria, the Barbados Coffins, the mysteries of
time travel, or the infamous Spring Heeled Jack, Lionel will deliver to
you a story in his own original style that will take you to new levels and
enhance your theatre of the mind.

Now it's time to read about undiscovered treasures from a man that
is a treasure himself.

It is a pleasure for me to be able to say that Lionel and Patricia
Fanthorpe are more than professional colleagues ... they are my friends!

I enjoyed the book, and now it's your turn!

Tom Danheiser
Coast to Coast A.M.

*(The authors are very grateful to their producer friend Tom Danheiser, whose
outstanding* Coast to Coast A.M. *radio programs they greatly admire and
enjoy, for his generous comments on our latest book.)*

Foreword by Canon Stanley H. Mogford, M.A.

During my years as a young priest it was my good fortune, from time to time, to visit a very old lady who much entertained me with stories of her childhood years in America. She remembered being with her parents as part of a covered wagon train belting it across vast distances hoping to stake a claim on some small part of a rumoured goldfield. Sad to say, though, judging by the modest home in which she lived, her parents never struck it rich. Some on that rush for gold may have been luckier, but most must have searched in vain, as I fear must have happened to my old friend. Only a few ever find a fortune by looking for it, just as only a few ever come up on the football pools or win the lottery. Thousands long for fame or fortune, but only a very few find either.

But don't despair, all you treasure hunters. It can happen; it does happen; we have seen it happen.

Sometimes it's simply a matter of sheer luck, a chance in a million. One piece of evidence will prove it. The ancient Egyptian civilization had its own language, not based on a shared alphabet, as most are, but using depictions, hieroglyphics. For centuries much of their writing was available to be read, but no one knew how to do it. It was, in a sense, a code that no one could break. Until one lucky day in 1799, when Captain Boussard, a young French soldier, unearthed a large stone on which writing could be seen in three languages, one of which was Greek, widely used and known. It turned out to be an identical message in all three languages, one of which was Egyptian hieroglyphics. The known deciphered the unknown. In due course the secrets of hieroglyphics were known for all to read. Such a find was a fluke. I doubt if it made the young officer any money, but the treasure he found, the so-called Rosetta Stone, named after the place he found it, is now in the British Museum for all to see — one of the world's great treasures.

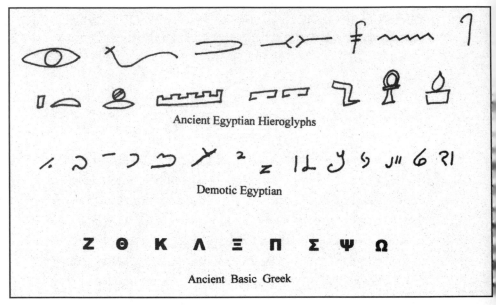

Scripts from the Rosetta Stone.

Sometimes luck has nothing to do with it. Treasure is found, but only after years of frustrated searching and disappointments. Boussard of Rosetta may not be a well-known name, but Howard Carter is. Lord Caernarvon and Howard Carter spent sixteen years and vast sums of Lord Caernarvon's money searching laboriously, first in Thebes and later in the Valley of the Kings, sometimes despairing of success ever rewarding their efforts. The frustration and despair lifted when in 1922, after all those wasted years, Carter found the first and only intact royal burial chamber. The secrets and wealth of the young Pharaoh Tutankhamen, buried in splendour, surrounded by golden images, were uncovered for all to see. That treasure was found not by chance (though, no doubt, chance played a part in it) but by sheer dogged determined scarching.

Sometimes treasure hunting is a combination of both good luck and sustained effort. One long sought after treasure, it seems, is destined to defeat both. In one of their fascinating earlier books, the Fanthorpes introduced us to the so-called Money Pit of Nova Scotia, which they refer to again here in Chapter 14, where they survey a number of Canadian treasure mysteries. Luck played a part in the beginning. Some young men with time on their hands rowed out to a small deserted island off the coast and found what looked like a pit into which something, obviously heavy, had been lowered. Remains of a block and tackle could still be seen suspended from an overhanging branch of a nearby tree. They returned with tools to dig down, but always the tide at a certain depth defeated them. Others have followed year after year with ever more powerful equipment, but as far as is known, no one has been able to get to its secret. Indeed, so much searching by so many over the years has been exerted to defeat the ingenious defences of the pit that even the entrance to it is said to be difficult to define.

Most of us, if we are honest, would like to be rich. Most of us would like to be famous. Even if, as the philosophers say, neither guarantees happiness, we are willing to risk it. In this book, chapter after chapter, the Fanthorpes tell us where fame and fortune are to be found. There are treasures everywhere, it seems, simply waiting for someone to find them. After what must have been long periods of painful research, the Fanthorpes tell us where to look. They identify for the intrepid among us the caves, the graveyards, the ruined castles and abandoned manor houses, the bottoms of wells, the riverbeds, and the ancient trees where the ingenuity of men under pressure could devise somewhere to hide the riches and valuables they held dear to them. Country after country, all have their secrets, and they are going to hang on to them unless someone determined and adventurous comes across them, either by design or luck. This book is a signpost to all such discoveries.

Over twenty or more years now, I have come to know the Fanthorpes well. We have become part of each other's lives, and I have the unique distinction of having read all of their books before anyone else — and in those years there have been at least thirty of them! Knowing them as I do, I have to tell you that in all honesty I have never seen either of them with compass or map or metal detector. They have in truth visited many countries, but if there is treasure in them they seem content to leave it for others to find. If anyone, on reading this book, is adventurous enough and determined enough (and it won't be me) to set out on a treasure hunt they go with the Fanthorpes' blessing, and they will be delighted beyond measure if someone, somewhere, finds a fortune.

They wish all who search the joy of discovery. It has been abundantly proved that much is still out there only waiting to be found. The Fanthorpes have all the treasures they need — the love of research, the joy of writing. If someone gains by what they have so painstakingly described for us, they will feel abundantly rewarded.

Canon Stanley H. Mogford, M.A., 2009

(As always, the authors are deeply indebted to their highly esteemed friend Canon Mogford for his great kindness in providing this foreword. He is rightly regarded as one of the finest scholars in Wales, and it is always a privilege to have his help and support.)

Introduction

The runaway success of every kind of lottery is a sure sign of the ubiquitous human hope of suddenly finding a fortune.

Coming across an undiscovered treasure is one facet of that same longing. No matter how happy and contented any of us may be, the thought of vast amounts of wealth still appeals — acquiring that kind of fortune enables the happiest man or woman to do even more of what he or she enjoys most. Buying a lottery ticket is a great deal simpler and easier than finding undiscovered treasure, and statistically the probabilities of finding treasure are about the same as those for winning a national lottery.

Some treasure stories are simple and straightforward: pirates bury their ill-gotten gains, marking the site by its relation to trees, boulders, or a bend in a small river. Other treasures are concealed deep in caves and labyrinths as complex as Knossos. Certain treasures accumulated during a great leader's lifetime may be buried with him in the hope that he will enjoy them again in the world to come. Gold, silver, and gems can be placed below the bed of a dammed river, which will flow over the spot once more when the dam is destroyed. Other wealth might be concealed at the bottom of a deep well. Secret panels in old houses may lead to hidden treasure. Something as simple and ordinary as a domestic garden can serve as a hiding place — John Chapman, the peddler of Swaffham, found gold beneath an apple tree behind his cottage.

What are the motives for hiding treasure? Wars and revolutions, political unrest, and invasions prompt people to hide their treasures before escaping from whatever is threatening them. All too often, the hazard they feared overtakes them, and their treasure lies in its hiding place for centuries.

Other fascinating aspects of treasure hunting are its association with ancient maps, charts, codes, and secret ciphers, and its legendary links with curses and frightening paranormal guardians.

Treasure hunting has dimensions of excitement, danger, and problem solving that are not to be found when simply buying a lottery ticket! We wish all our treasure-hunting friends the very best of luck!

Chapter One
What Is Treasure? What Forms Can It Take?

Treasure has been variously defined as that which has high value (often found in the form of precious metals and gems) or that which has been concealed in order to protect it, something eagerly sought-after because of the benefits it can bestow on the finder. Traditionally, treasure is frequently associated with pirates or with gangs of robbers (like Ali Baba's famous forty thieves in the Arabian Nights stories). Pirates and bandits frequently felt threatened by one another and concealed their ill-gotten gains accordingly — often dying before they could retrieve them. Much of what they buried centuries ago still waits to be recovered.

During the Dark Ages that followed the fall of the Western Roman Empire, the continual threat from barbarian raids and incursions made it necessary for retreating refugees to conceal treasure as they fled. Many of them never returned, and the precious things they buried still lie hidden after fifteen centuries.

In Britain, one of the most interesting treasure hunting quests concerns the location of Queen Boadicea's treasure — and the treasures concealed by her retreating Iceni — after their defeat by the Romans in AD 61. Henry VIII's rapacious attacks on the monasteries during the sixteenth century often led to similar concealments. The monks would escape with their

Boadicea Queen of the Iceni Tribe of East Anglia.

sacred treasures, leaving them with devout and trustworthy friends who loyally hid them away from Henry's avaricious marauders. During the many politico-religious disturbances of Henry's time, some of those who had concealed monastic treasures died before revealing the hiding places. Throughout occupied Europe during the First and Second World Wars, treasure was hidden in the hope of recovering it in better days. For many Nazi victims, death came first. The Nazis themselves frequently tried to hide the treasures they had stolen as the triumphant Allies moved in on their last strongholds — and many of them died before recovering the proceeds of their crimes.

In more recent times, wealth in various forms has been concealed to avoid taxes — especially death duties. Ironically, those who knew where it was hidden often died before recovering it or passing on the secret of its location to their heirs.

Some semi-legendary religious artifacts, especially those believed to possess supernatural powers, were concealed because they were considered too powerful — or too sacred — to be used. This mysterious treasure category includes the Grail (or Cornucopia), the Lance of Longinus, the Ark of the Covenant, the Seal of King Solomon, the Emerald Tablets of Hermes Trismegistus, the Seeing Stones (known as Urim and Thummim), Aladdin's Lamp, the Wishing Ring, and many more.

Over and above the general reasons for hiding treasure with the intention of recovering it later, there are motives associated with beliefs about the afterlife. The Etruscans of northern Italy, who flourished before the rise of the Roman Empire, often buried their dead in very attractive and

King Henry VIII who dissolved the monasteries.

elaborate tombs, burying their valuables along with them. These treasures were intended for the deceased to use in the next world; they were not left to be recovered in this world.

When Sir Leonard Wolley, an archaeologist, excavated the tomb of Mes-kalam-dug at Tell el Muqayyar in Ur of the Chaldees, he found that the warrior-prince, laid to rest there five thousand years ago, was surrounded by gold, silver, and jewels.

The Incas of Peru believed that their dead rulers went from this world to Hanac-paca (the paradise of the sun) and took their treasures with them. On the other side of the world, Chinese emperors of the Chou and Ch'in dynasties were being buried with gold, silver, and jade treasures nearly three thousand years ago. Scythian warrior-kings — whose magnificent horsemanship gave rise to the legend of the centaurs in Greek mythology — were buried with their favourite wife, servants, horses, and above all their jewels and ornaments. Herodotus (484–425 BC), the ancient Greek historian, who apparently studied these Scythian burial customs with keen interest, affirmed that golden vessels were buried with the dead rulers.

In the famous tomb at Chertomlyk in the Ukraine, dating from the fourth century BC, four hundred ornamental golden strips were discovered. These depicted scenes from Greek mythology as well as an assortment of animals and legendary monsters. The Sarmatians who occupied Eastern Europe and southern Russia in the third century BC have left tombs crammed with golden ornaments, amethyst, and garnet.

Mycenaean and Minoan Crete left many tomb treasures, not only on Crete itself but also throughout what had once been the ancient Minoan Empire that flourished five thousand years ago. The famous golden Vaphio Cups from Amyclae in southern Greece carry designs relating to the celebrated bull-dancing activities of Knossos and are typical of the precious works of art that the Minoan civilization created.

For every tomb that grave robbers or archaeologists have already discovered and excavated there are scores that still lie hidden and unsuspected. For every tomb treasure that has found its way into a museum there are dozens that still wait to be found.

The Cretan Labyrinth.

Treasure from British Museum.

The secret clues to many treasures — things like the map showing the way to the Lost Dutchman Mine in the Superstition Mountains near Phoenix, Arizona — become treasures themselves. Knowing the secret combination or holding the safe key is as valuable as actually opening the safe and gaining access to its contents.

Writing at the end of the sixteenth century, Sir Francis Bacon declared, "*Ipsa scientia potestas est*" ("knowledge is power"). His wisdom is equally valid today. Knowledge is another form of treasure — international military and political espionage are only too well known, and when successful their results can be beyond price. Industrial espionage can also retrieve knowledge with a huge commercial value. Computer hacking may be regarded as another version of the quest for secret and highly valuable knowledge. The illegal program that will enable a criminal to obtain the necessary knowledge for identity theft or for stealing from someone's credit card information or Internet bank account is treasure in the form of knowledge as far as the criminal is concerned.

Bringing these ideas together leads to the conclusion that whether treasure is in the form of money, precious metals and gems, mysterious magical artifacts, maps and ciphers, or pure knowledge, discovering it offers the finder a route to power.

There are additional motives, however, that send treasure hunters on their long and arduous quests. Readers of detective stories will understand the satisfaction that comes from unmasking the murderer before Holmes or Poirot reveal the answer in the final chapter. Crossword enthusiasts will puzzle over a cryptic clue for hours before experiencing the intense pleasure of solving it. Sudoku experts have similar feelings when an elusive number finally completes a puzzle for them. Human beings respond eagerly to a challenge: the more difficult the better. Solving treasure clues, interpreting ancient maps and charts, deciphering an elaborate code — all of these motivate the treasure hunter.

Ingenious code setters like the fabulously wealthy Templars arranged letters on chessboards to provide obscure clues. Clues to the controversial treasure of Rennes-le-Château near Carcassonne in southwestern France may be concealed in confusing manuscripts where Greek and Latin are cunningly intermingled. The brilliant Dr. Robert Hieronimus,

Coded Manuscript from Rennes-le-Château.

author of *America's Secret Destiny*, discovered that Spencer Lewis had found a Rosicrucian code among Thomas Jefferson's papers. What did Jefferson know? And what secret had he committed to that strange old code? Were they merely covert political items, or were they clues to some ancient Rosicrucian treasure?

The mysterious *codex magica* is traditionally associated with the secret society known as the Illuminati, and may well be used to convey secret messages about hidden Illuminati treasure — often in the form of secret knowledge rather than wealth.

As if careful concealment and enigmatic codes and ciphers were not enough to prevent treasure from being rediscovered, many treasures are associated with semi-legendary demon guardians. The Church of St. Mary Magdalene in Rennes-le-Château, for example, contains a life-sized statue of the formidable demon Asmodeus, who is a traditional paranormal guardian of hidden treasure. In the Richtersveld in South Africa is a deep and dangerous cave that is rumoured to be filled with diamonds. Sometimes referred to as the Bottomless Pit and sometimes as the Wonder Hole, the cavern is guarded (according to legend) by a gigantic snake known as Grootslang, said to be over twelve metres long.

Griffins (or gryphons) are among the most ancient and formidable guardians of hidden treasure. A cross between an eagle and a lion, the mythical griffin was of enormous size and built its nest from pure gold. They were first described in ancient Egypt more than five thousand years ago, and some researchers believe their folklore goes back even further. They were believed to guard the gold mines of Scythia and India, and ancient mythology also makes them guardians of the tree of life. Griffins were also set up to guard Greek and Roman tombs, especially those in which treasure had been buried. Analyzing the legends can guide the contemporary treasure hunter in the direction of griffin images as pointers to hidden stores of wealth. The direction in which the wings or claws are set may be of particular significance.

Guardians of a simpler but more deadly kind were sometimes placed in Egyptian tombs to kill the unwary grave robber. Booby traps could include falling stones or doorways that sealed the grave robber inside the tomb to die of thirst. The notorious armada chests were also booby-trapped with either a spring-loaded blade or a loaded gun. The rightful owner would know how to disarm the device before opening the chest; the thief would not.

Where can today's treasure hunters look for the various types of treasure? Labyrinthine cave systems often appealed to those who hid treasure. Natural alcoves deep within the caves can easily be covered with loose stones once the treasures have been placed there, and only the hider will know exactly where the treasure is.

Under water is another favourite spot: the bottom of a well, an old mill pool, a deep pond in a meadow, by the shore of a lake, or in a harbour. The very deep Callow Pit in Norfolk is said to conceal a treasure chest that was almost recovered by two workmen — a thatcher and the village carpenter — in medieval times, but it fell back into the pit and they were unable to retrieve it again. According to the colourful local legend, the Spirit of the Pit (another example of a treasure guardian) pulled it from them, leaving them only the handle that broke away from the chest.

On many occasions, the treasure container was simply buried in the ground, but the spot was usually marked by a tree, a large boulder, a

Signpost to Southwood where Callow Pit is situated.

Callow Pit.

Ruined Church at Southwood.

Ancient gravestone with skull and crossbones near Southwood Church.

sundial, or a statue. More complicated locations could be marked by the point at which the top of a certain shadow (such as the shadow of a church tower) fell at midday on a particular day, often the summer solstice. Sometimes the spot was marked by the intersection of two lines, like the coordinates on a graph with x and y axes. Twenty paces north of the black rock shaped like a horse's head, thirty paces east of the palm tree: dig where the lines cross. At other times there would be a curious zigzag path: twelve paces north of the cave mouth, turn east and take ten more paces, then go six paces south. In the case of traditional pirate treasure, it was not uncommon to find the skeletal remains of a buccaneer lying on top of the treasure chest.

Secret chambers in the hollow walls of old manor houses and castles were also favourite hiding places for treasure, as were secret compartments behind oak panelling or under the floors of wine cellars. Gems of great value were sometimes hidden in hollowed-out books in great old libraries where thousands of volumes were stored. From the outside, the book looked perfectly normal and natural — especially if it was one of a set of encyclopedias.

As with all effective detective work, the successful treasure hunter needs to empathize with the hider, to say, "If I had been looking for a good, safe hiding place, what would I have done?" The more accurately we can answer that question, the more successful our search will be.

Chapter Two
Who Hid Their Treasure — and Why?

One group of people who hid treasure did so when times were uncertain and hazardous, hoping to retrieve it later. Death in battle, or being taken prisoner and later sold as a slave in some distant land, often prevented their return. In those situations their treasures could remain undiscovered for millennia.

A second group often buried valuables — including hapless concubines and servants, horses, weapons, gold, silver, and gems — with dead rulers for use in the next world. The motive here was to ensure that the pharaoh, emperor, king, prince, or warlord would have access to everything in the world of the dead that he had enjoyed in the world of the living.

It seems likely that Bérenger Saunière, the remarkable priest of Rennes-le-Château, was typical of a third group, whose motive for concealing a large amount of treasure was to draw on it a little at a time as they needed it. If Saunière had, in fact, located an ancient Merovingian or Visigothic treasure in a secret tomb below his ancient church of St. Mary Magdalene in Rennes, he may well have decided to leave the bulk of it there in its cunningly hidden sepulchre (along with the body of Dagobert II) while simply taking and using what he needed from time to time. Such a concealed subterranean tomb might not have been quite as secure as Fort Knox, perhaps, but it would still have constituted a safe storage facility. Saunière might even have discovered a secret tunnel leading from under the notorious Tomb of Arques near Rennes to a Visigothic burial chamber concealed below the bed of the River Sals. The mysterious Tomb of Arques is close enough to the river for this to be the case — and although its top was destroyed a few years ago, the interior (which appears to be far older than the twentieth-century upper portion) will still be as it was.

Saunière's Church of Saint Mary Magdalene in Rennes-le-Château.

In the days long before the kind of safety that Fort Knox and similar strongholds can now provide, another motive for hiding treasure demonstrated by a fourth group was simply security. If a palace, castle, or manor house was raided and looted by thieves, the treasure concealed elsewhere would still be safe. Hiding treasure in various locations away from the main house or castle when it was in danger of attack was the historic equivalent of the actions of a wise financier today who does not trust all his deposits to one bank. The failure of any one financial organization does not then deprive the depositor of all his or her assets.

Another perspective on treasure relates to sources of wealth, such as gold and silver mines. Knowing precisely where and how the precious metals could be obtained was in itself a form of treasure. An intriguing example of this refers to King Solomon (circa 1000–930 BC). The First Book of Kings 9:26–28 records: "And King Solomon made a navy of ships in Ezion-Geber, which is beside Eloth on the shore of the Red Sea, in the land of Edom. And Hiram sent in the navy his servants, shipmen that had knowledge of the sea, with the servants of Solomon. And they

Zimbabwe.

came to Ophir and fetched from thence gold, four hundred and twenty talents, and brought it to King Solomon."

Many theories have been put forward about the location of mysterious, gold-rich Ophir. Tomé Lopes, who sailed with Vasco da Gama on his voyage to India in 1502, was convinced that ancient Sofala on the west coast of Africa (incorporating parts of modern Mozambique and Zimbabwe) had been Solomon's Ophir. Some historical traditions maintain that the Sofala region was once ruled by a great and powerful queen. This led some researchers to suggest that it had once been Sheba, whose queen visited Solomon. Nineteenth-century scholars, including Max Müller (1823–1900), came up with the idea that Ophir was modern Abhira, where the Indus River reaches the sea in Pakistan. Other scholars place Ophir on the African shore of the Red Sea, or in Yemen in the southwest of Arabia. Josephus, also known by his Roman name of Titus Flavius Josephus, was a historian during most of the first century AD. He concluded that Solomon's Ophir was situated in the region of the Indian River Cophen. Álvaro de Mendaña de Neira (1542–1595) was a Spanish navigator who is credited with naming the Solomon

Islands after the famous Israeli emperor because he thought they were Ophir. Some theories go even farther afield and suggest that Ophir was in northern Australia, Peru, or Brazil.

Such archaeological evidence as is available, outside the biblical accounts, points to a close friendship between Hiram I, who ruled in the Phoenician city of Tyre from approximately 970 to 935 BC, and Solomon. The two rulers sent their shared navy on voyages that sometimes lasted as long as three years — and the skilful Phoenician sailors could take their ships a very long way in that time. There is evidence that Phoenician sailors were employed by the Egyptians not long after Solomon's reign and that they voyaged all the way around Africa. They left via the Red Sea and came back via modern Gibraltar, known to them as the Pillars of Hercules. Because of the distances that these intrepid Phoenician navigators were able to cover, mysterious Ophir could have been almost anywhere. Locating it would be very rewarding for any twenty-first-century treasure hunter.

Another group of undiscovered treasures are those that were lost by accident. The best-known example of this group is probably the misadventure of King John shortly before his death in 1216. Having lost the Battle of Bouvines, John was forced to accept very unfavourable peace terms from France. The English barons and other nobles turned against him, which led to his unwilling acceptance of the terms of the Magna Carta at Runnymede in 1215.

(An interesting treasure sidelight indirectly involving King John is that on his way to sign the Magna Carta, he stopped for a night at what is now the Ostrich Inn, originally the Hospice Inn, founded in 1106 in Colnbridge, Berkshire. A century later, a murderous landlord named Jarman and his wife killed and robbed those who stayed at the inn. They were eventually caught and hanged, but not before they had hidden many of their ill-gotten gains. Jarman was caught in Windsor Forest. Is that where he had gone to hide some of the money that had been stolen from the scores of wealthy travellers whom he and his wife had murdered?)

When King John broke the terms of the Magna Carta, the barons rose against him and invited Prince Louis of France to help them — in return for which he was promised the English throne.

Retreating from the French, John himself wisely went around the dangerous marshy ground near the wide bay of the North Sea. The Wash, as the area is known, lay just to the north of Norfolk — a stronghold of the barons. Norfolk was largely populated by the fierce, bold, and war-like descendants of the formidable Viking raiders who had visited East Anglia three centuries earlier. Their belligerent offspring would have been much more than a match for John's dispirited army. Unfortunately for John, however, his baggage train had taken another route and foolishly attempted to cross part of the Wash: predictably, it was overwhelmed by the incoming tide. The English crown jewels were in that baggage train, and many of them still lie under the sea.

This grave loss of the national treasure affected John traumatically, both mentally and physically. He died at Newark Castle on October 18, 1216, either from poison or dysentery. Ironically, the barons promptly ditched Prince Louis of France and switched their allegiance to John's nine-year-old son, who became King Henry III.

On other occasions, treasure was hidden because it was believed to be cursed. Paradoxically, in many of these cases, the owner could not bear to part with it. He did not wish to sell it, give it away, or dispose of it by some other method — yet he dared not keep it close, wear it, or display it because of the perilous evil that he felt associated with it. Given those conflicting motivations, the only remaining alternative was to conceal it somewhere: a remote mountain cave, an underground chamber, a deep well or pit, an ancestral tomb, or simply a freshly dug hole in the ground.

So the twenty-first-century treasure hunter who seeks to understand the reasons why treasure was hidden needs to look in those different directions. Knowing *why* it was hidden is the first

The allegedly cursed Hope Diamond.

Field Marshal Erwin Rommel.

step towards relocating it. Was it a secret location, some hidden gold mines like those at legendary Ophir? Had it been concealed in dangerous times in the hope of later retrieval? Was it buried with the once-powerful dead in the hope that they could use it in the next world? Was it carefully concealed for safety and drawn on just a little at a time? Was it divided for safety and hidden in different places as a precaution against losing everything to a triumphant enemy? Was it hidden because its curse was feared? Or was there no motive at all for hiding it — had it just *gone* as the result of some devastating accident like the misfortune that overtook King John's crown jewels?

Sometimes, more than one clear motive can be traced when circumstances have intervened in unexpected ways. Field Marshal Erwin Rommel's lost treasure can be slotted into this category. Rommel, known as the Desert Fox because of his daring and cunning military tactics, was in charge of Hitler's forces in North Africa during the Second World War. During the period when he was most successful, Rommel knew that foreign currencies such as German deutschmarks were not particularly acceptable in North Africa. Instead he used gold, silver, and diamonds, which were universally welcomed in wartime. Being able to buy what he needed when he needed it was one of the factors that enabled Rommel to carry out Hitler's wishes and advance rapidly across North Africa.

Faced at last by the powerful British and Allied troops defending Suez, Rommel was forced to retreat first to Tunisia and then to Sicily. With Allied forces threatening to attack in Europe, Rommel was recalled to defend Nazi-occupied France. His problem was what to do with the large quantities of gold, silver, and diamonds that he still had as wartime currency for North Africa.

As Italy had surrendered to the Allies, it would not have been sensible for Rommel to try to bury his treasure on Italian soil, even if he could have reached an Italian destination safely. There is evidence that he chose to send the treasure via submarine to Corsica and buried it there. In April 1943, a German U-boat reached the east coast of Corsica, and its crew buried Rommel's treasure somewhere on the island under cover of darkness. The question is *where*. Soon afterwards an American bomber encountered the U-boat and sank it with all

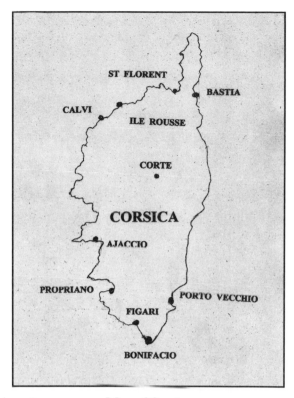

Map of Corsica.

hands. Yet some mysterious knowledge of the whereabouts of Rommel's lost treasure seems to have survived. There is a sinister account of a scuba diver — apparently getting too close to the treasure — who was found dead with one of his own speargun's harpoons through him. On another occasion, a man claiming to be an ex-Nazi with knowledge of the location of the treasure maintained that it had been taken from Corsica to Bastia. Before pointing out its exact whereabouts there, however, he vanished mysteriously.

Terry Hodgkinson, a dauntless and determined treasure researcher, has pursued the missing Nazi treasure for many years, and has finally decided that it lies in the sea just a kilometre or so from the Corsican port of Bastia. His work adds further interesting dimensions to the theories about Nazi treasure. Hodgkinson is of the opinion that the treasure lies under the sea off the Corsican coast, not on the island itself. In his view this submerged treasure is *not* the currency that Rommel is supposed to have sent to Corsica on the doomed German U-boat, but more than four hundred kilograms of Tunisian gold stolen from Jewish victims of the Nazis by the ruthlessly evil SS Colonel Walter Rauff. He constructed a fleet of mobile gas vans with which to exterminate Jewish prisoners after Rommel had beaten the allied forces at Tobruk. Rauff's murderous atrocities ended when the Allies defeated Rommel at El Alamein. According to this theory, the retreating Nazis sank the stolen Jewish treasure off the coast of Corsica, not on the island itself. These two accounts are complementary rather than contradictory, so there may well be *two* Corsican treasures linked with the Second World War waiting to be recovered: one on the land, the other under the sea.

Corsica seems to attract legends of treasure continuously, and one of the strangest to emerge from the twentieth century goes back to the 1960s. The Strait of Bonifacio separates Sardinia and Corsica and provide countless possible hiding places for treasure. There is a persistent story concerning two ex-Foreign Legionnaires who hid a mysterious treasure there in 1963 and then faded into obscurity as if they had never existed. What kind of treasure did they have? Where did they get it from? And where exactly in the Strait of Bonifacio did they conceal it?

Another fascinating Corsican treasure is linked with the revolutionary statesman Pasquale Paoli (1725–1807). After a few successful years as leader of Corsica, during which he was a genuine republican democrat, Paoli was granted a pension in England, where he spent a deservedly happy old age. However, before being defeated by his enemies and having to leave his beloved Corsica, Paoli may have buried a treasure chest on an island across from the north coast of Sardinia. Isola Rossa (meaning "red island") takes its name from the pink granite of which it is composed. Or did Paoli bury his treasure at Sardinia's Spiaggia Lunga ("the long beach"), very popular with tourists today? Or is it hidden somewhere under the equally popular Cala Tinnari beach?

Just as they featured prominently in the Corsican treasure mysteries, the Nazis feature again in a mystery centred on what became of the famous Amber Room — a treasure that was stolen from Russia during the Second World War. This beautiful artifact was made of amber panels backed by gold, and was created by highly skilled German and Russian craftsmen in the early years of the eighteenth century. King Friedrich Wilhelm of Prussia had it made as a gift for his ally, Tsar Peter the Great, in 1716. What became of it — and many other priceless treasures — after the Germans retreated from Russia is still anybody's guess. An artificial pit more than eighteen metres deep is reported to have been found in the little town of Deutschneudorf on the Czech-German border as recently as 2008. There is thought to be a great quantity of gold and silver in it hidden by the retreating Nazis, and some treasure hunters who have investigated the site believe that the Amber Room may be down there as well. Investigators are approaching the site slowly and with great caution, as they suspect that the Nazis who created the deep, labyrinthine hiding place may have booby-trapped it with high explosives.

A prime motive for hiding — or even deliberately jettisoning — treasure is to prevent it from falling into enemy hands. A prime example of this was in April 1942 when the *Harrison*, an American minelayer, dumped around $5 million in Filipino coins into twenty fathoms of water in Manila Bay so that the Japanese could not get it. Over the years some four-fifths of that treasure has been recovered, but at least $1 million is still down there.

Much greater treasure, lost when a Spanish galleon went down in Yaquina Bay off the Oregon coast, is still waiting to be found. A number of golden drinking vessels from the wreck have already turned up along the coast from time to time, but a great deal more wealth still lies below the waters. The galleon apparently went down while trying to avoid the efforts of an English privateer that was pursuing it relentlessly; perhaps the Spaniards deliberately scuttled their ship rather than allow their treasure to fall into English hands.

So the modern treasure hunter is confronted by the challenge of working out *who* hid the treasure and *why* they felt it was necessary to conceal it. The right answers to those two major questions will be as useful as a map and a metal detector.

Chapter Three
Ancient Civilizations and Their Lost Treasures

History has to be constantly revised and rewritten — especially ancient history. Just when the best and most scrupulous archaeological research suggests that ancient Chinese cultures, or Sumerian civilizations, or the first peoples of the Indus Valley represent the primeval dawning of human culture, another dig in an unsuspected place reveals something older still. What these discoveries tell us is that human beings have been here millennia longer than we think. Great cultures and complex civilizations existed many thousands of years ago. Some seem to have died out and vanished completely — apparently without leaving any discernible trace of their existence. Yet who knows what an enthusiastic young archaeologist will turn up next year ... or the year after. Undiscovered treasure of great antiquity is waiting to be uncovered from scores of unsuspected ancient sites. When they do turn up, the lost treasures of those lost civilizations will have a great deal of additional value because of their extreme age and their uniqueness.

Mehrgarh is located close to the Bolan Pass, west of the Indus River, between the modern Pakistani cities of Sibi, Quetta, and Kalat. The first inhabitants of Mehrgarh herded their cattle, goats, and sheep and grew their wheat and barley there ten thousand years ago. What ancient treasures did they leave behind? What valuables were buried alongside their leaders? What precious things did they hide in time of war?

The great Harappan culture — typical of the highly intelligent and well-educated people of the ancient Indus Valley civilization — flourished in Harappa and in its neighbouring city of Mohenjo-Daro. They were a literate people with complex economic and social systems, who traded regularly with the equally great and ancient civilization at Sumer. The Harappan people were capable of creating intriguing artifacts in copper, bronze, and steatite (otherwise known as soapstone, and

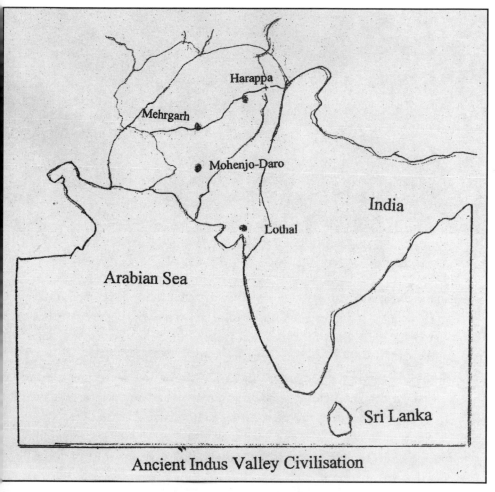

Ancient Indus Valley Civilisation

Ancient Indus Valley Civilisation.

consisting largely of hydrated magnesium silicate). The fabrics for their clothing were woven and dyed. Their wheel-made pottery was beautifully decorated with human and animal representations. They had a centralized system of uniform weights and measures. These factors, taken together, make it abundantly clear that they would have enjoyed sufficient wealth to make their area a likely source of undiscovered treasure.

The determined treasure hunter should not hesitate to examine the legends and mythologies of quasi-historical locations such as Atlantis and Lemuria. Various myths and legends refer to the vast continental

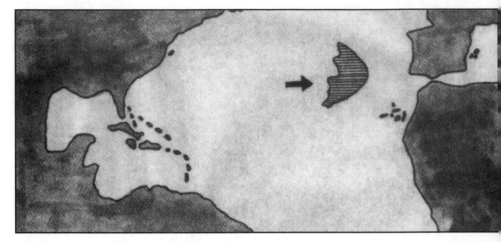

Map of Atlantis.

mass known as Mu or Lemuria. The first civilization was said to have been born there eighty thousand years ago and was believed to have lasted for more than fifty thousand years. Some esoteric theories suggest that it was destroyed by a massive earthquake involving a polar shift around twenty-five thousand years ago. Lemuria was said to have been a very wealthy and cultured civilization, one that would have left rich treasures buried after the devastating earthquake. According to these ancient traditions, when the earthquake destroyed Mu it created the deep Pacific Trench, into which a great deal of water drained — lowering the Atlantic in the process and so creating the continent of Atlantis. Numerous expert researchers, however, have placed Atlantis in very different parts of the Earth.

Wherever Atlantis was — if it ever really existed — all the Atlantean legends agree on the amazing level of technology that Atlantis enjoyed. The very talented and frequently accurate medium Edgar Cayce (1877–1945) spoke of Atlantis as having airplanes and mysterious fire crystals that were sources of energy, rather like the crystals used to power the *Enterprise* in Gene Roddenberry's brilliant *Star Trek* stories. When treasure is considered as a form of knowledge that can convey massive advantages to those who possess it and understand how to use it, the undiscovered treasures of legendary Atlantis are literally beyond price.

The modern treasure hunter would do well to begin such an Atlantean quest by searching in and around the Azores.

To understand the probable existence of ancient civilizations that may well have been rich in treasure of various kinds, it is vitally important to understand terrestrial change. Lands become seas and oceans. Great lakes dry up and become land. Fertile fields change into arid deserts. Frozen wastes become temperate, cultivated farms. Forests are felled and turn into deserts. The Gobi Desert seems to be an outstanding example of these traumatic changes. Tradition has it that

Portrait of Edgar Cayce.

the present desert — now a long way inland — once had a number of prosperous ports as its major cities. Another of the gifted Edgar Cayce's visions revealed that technological devices such as elevators would one day be discovered in a ruined city below the Gobi. Finding the remains of such ancient and apparently anachronistic technology would be treasure indeed. When the present Gobi Desert was fertile and habitable and trading prosperously from its numerous busy seaports, its occupants would have belonged to the ancient Uiger civilization. Like the Atlanteans, the Uigers were believed to have had flying machines as part of their technology. The oldest of the Sanskrit epics and the Vedas refer to "flying chariots" and aeronautical machines known as *vimanas*, which were under the control of the gods of that time.

The most ancient known Chinese culture began with the Huaxia, an ethnic group who occupied the banks of the Yellow River, on which they depended as heavily as the earliest Egyptians depended upon the Nile. The Huaxia have been credited with a very highly developed technology, including flying machines of a type similar to the vimanas and fiery chariots of other ancient cultures. Archaeological work in China in the late 1950s and early 1960s led to the discovery of aluminum belt buckles apparently made millennia ago. The ancient Chinese craftsmen who are believed to be responsible for the buckles may have discovered and used some alternative method for extracting aluminum from bauxite — but modern aluminum extraction depends upon electrolysis, and the process is a complicated one requiring great heat as well as electrical power.

A brief outline of the process used today makes those ancient Chinese belt buckles seem all the more amazing. Today, the bauxite is treated so that it becomes pure aluminum oxide, which is then dissolved in molten cryolite, another aluminum compound. Aluminum oxide has too high a melting point to be turned into a liquid suitable for electrolysis, which is why contemporary processors dissolve it in molten cryolite before electrolyzing it. Although it is common to use only six or seven volts, the current can go as high as one hundred thousand amps. The temperature stays in the region of 1,000°C throughout the process. If the Huaxia could do this millennia ago, they deserve all the respect the twenty-first century can give them! Did that level of technology really exist along the banks of the Yellow River all those thousands of years ago?

The Huaxia seem to have formed the nucleus of the later Han people of ancient China. There is some evidence of a very early connection between the Huaxia and the earliest

The Yin-Yang.

Han people with the Mayan culture of South America. Beautiful jade artifacts with particular designs such as the famous yin-yang symbol have been found in both ancient cultures.

Many stories are also associated with the ancient Osirian civilization. Traditionally, the present Mediterranean was once a wide fertile valley filled with broad lakes into which the Nile flowed before it made its way out again into the Atlantic between the Pillars of Hercules. The rich, fertile Osirian Empire was said to have occupied this pre-Mediterranean valley. Assuming that there is at least some truth in the legends of its existence, then the story that is attributed to Solon in Plato's writings concerning the war between the Atlantean Empire and ancient Greece actually refers to a war between Atlantis and the Osirians. Wars were always a major stimulus for hiding treasure, and if the war between Atlantis and the Osirians was historically factual, a great deal of treasure could well have been hidden below what is now the Mediterranean.

Baalbeck, located in the Bekaa Valley in Lebanon eighty kilometres north east of Beirut, has a history that goes back for at least five or six millennia — probably more. Early Phoenicians settled there and built a temple to their god Baal (hence the city's name). There

Statue of Baal.

was also an oracle at Baalbeck that was consulted by the Roman Emperor Trajan (53–117) during the time when Baalbeck was known by its Latin name of Heliopolis ("city of the sun"). Roman temples to Jupiter, Venus, and Bacchus were built to supersede the ancient Phoenician temples, and a fourth Roman temple in honour of Mercury was added later. Jupiter-Baal (also known as Heliopolitan Zeus) was worshipped in the largest of the temples. Venus-Aphrodite, whose temple stood close by, was identified with Astarte, Baal's nubile consort. Early Christian writers strongly disapproved of the free and open sexual practices associated with her worship.

The stones supporting the Roman temples built above earlier ruins each weighed in excess of four hundred tons, and the vast trilithon in the western wall had stones weighing a thousand tons each. From the treasure hunter's point of view, Baalbeck could be one of the most rewarding sites available anywhere in the world. Once again, the tides of war flowing over Baalbeck provided frequent stimuli for hiding treasure. A Muslim army captured the town in 637 after defeating the Byzantines at the battle of Yarmouk. The caliphs of Egypt and Damascus then fought over Baalbeck for many years. The city was sacked in 748 and again in 975 when the Byzantine Emperor John Tzimisces conquered it. The Seljuks held it in 1090, and Saladin took it in 1175.

A Templar Knight.

The fearless Templars were much in evidence in the valley near Baalbeck, and the Templars are invariably associated with hidden treasure. What did they find there, and where did they secure it later?

Ancient Ethiopia, which may well have been identical with the land of Sheba, once contained priceless treasure according to the Kebra Nagast, the book of the Glory of the Kings. The book tells how Queen Makeda of Sheba became pregnant by Solomon and gave birth to a son, Menelik, who later visited Israel and returned to Axum with the Ark of the Covenant. He became founder of the Ethiopian Solomonic Dynasty. The history contained in the Kebra Nagast is admittedly a controversial one, but there are several stubborn pieces of evidence that tend to support it, and if its central message is historically true then Axum well deserves a visit from any determined treasure hunter. Long before the well-known biblical account of the Ark of the Covenant, the ancient Egyptians had

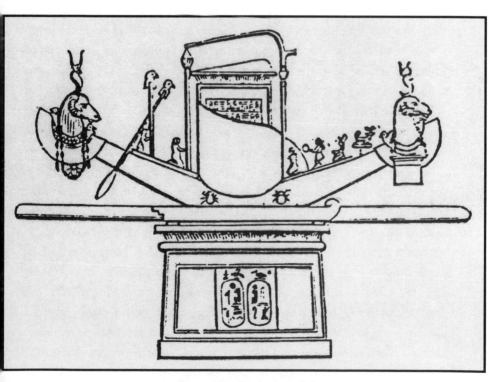

An ancient Egyptian Ark.

very similar artifacts. Some researchers link them to the evidence for electrical power having been known in ancient China and to the simple electric cells that were found near Baghdad in 1936. Dr. Wilhelm Koenig of the Iraq Museum reported at the time how an expedition from his museum had found them at Khujut Rubu'a, near Baghdad. They were several thousand years old but were unmistakably primitive electric cells.

Even greater mysteries surround the very ancient city of Tiahuanaco, situated high in the Andes. There is every indication that this was once a thriving seaport, and it is certainly surrounded by millions of marine fossils. The geology suggests that the city and its surroundings were lifted a very long way at some point in the remote past. Archaeologists hold different theories about the age of Tiahuanaco, but some experts place it nearly twenty thousand years in the past.

Just a few kilometres from the impressive ruins of the inexplicable mountain seaport is the equally strange and mysterious Lake Titicaca. Another intriguing legend suggests that when the great continent of Lemuria was sinking, Lord Aramu Meru (regarded as one of the Seven Great Masters of Wisdom) brought the sacred golden disc of the sun to Lake Titicaca to preserve it. Another tradition maintains that the Incas transferred it to Cuzco. However, when the Spaniards arrived, the sacred golden disc was taken back to Lake Titicaca and hidden below the water inside what was thought to be a mystical submarine city.

Other very strange myths and legends regard the Andes as containing mysterious hidden doorways and secret portals that lead down to vast subterranean dwelling places. In these legends there are strange quasi-human entities inhabiting deep caverns and labyrinths that are said to run for many kilometres. Similar stories of huge networks of subterranean passages are told in Tibet, Crete, Ecuador, and Bolivia. According to one old piece of Jesuit evidence, an elderly Inca scholar who was able to read the mysterious *quipu* (knotted strings) told him that below the visible surface ruins of Tiahuanaco a huge underground city lay hidden. If that story is true, what awaits the treasure hunter down there? One way or another, Tiahuanaco and Lake Titicaca offer tantalizing opportunities for locating some of the most ancient and valuable undiscovered treasures on Earth.

ROBINSON CRUSOE'S ISLAND

(Otherwise known as Mas Atierra)

Part of the Juan Fernandez Archipelago

Map of Robinson Crusoe's Island.

The ancient lost treasures of the Incas also have links with the Juan Fernández Islands, which lie a few hundred kilometres west of Chile. There are actually three islands in the Juan Fernández archipelago: Mas a Tierra (closer to the land, also known as Robinson Crusoe's Island), Mas Afuera (farther from the land), and Isla Santa Clara. Alexander Selkirk, who became the real-life inspiration for Daniel Defoe's *Robinson Crusoe*, was marooned on Mas a Tierra in November 1704 and rescued in February 1709. There is some evidence that Spanish General Ubilla y Echeverria misappropriated millions of pounds' worth of treasure — including many priceless Inca relics — and hid them on Mas a Tierra in 1714. He died in July 1715 when his fleet was smashed to pieces on the Florida reefs during a hurricane. The enigma deepens when a mysterious connection is established between British Admiral George Anson and Ubilla y Echeverria. Quite what their intrigue was is open to speculation, but it seems as if the Spanish general made Anson aware of the hiding place of the stolen Inca treasure. Perhaps it was in exchange for refuge in England after the Spanish royal family discovered what had become of their treasure. Egotism and unbridled greed for treasure seem to bring out the worst in people. Already immensely wealthy, Anson sent a navigator named Cornelius Webb to recover the Juan Fernandez Islands treasure for him, although he had little need of it. (In 1744, for example, Anson had paraded through London with more than thirty wagons filled with treasure!) Webb reached the island, located and loaded the treasure, set sail for England, and ran into a storm that damaged his ship so badly that he went back to the island and reburied the ancient Inca gold. Webb then sailed to Valparaiso to get his ship repaired. While the repairs were being carried out, he discovered that the crew were planning to mutiny, murder him, and take Anson's treasure for themselves. Captain Webb, however, was not a man to be opposed without grave risk to his opponents. When they sailed from Valparaiso, he set fire to the ship and escaped in a small lifeboat. The whole mutinous crew died in the fire. Webb then sent messages to Anson explaining what had taken place. There was also a coded reference to the location of the reburied Inca treasure. It was at about this time that Anson himself died. What became of the vitally important coded clues to the treasure? Is it just a strange coincidence that the Shepherd Monument in the grounds of Shugborough Hall in Staffordshire contains a code that has never yet been satisfactorily solved? The Anson family of Shugborough were close relatives of Admiral George Anson. Could the code carved into the mysterious Shepherd Monument refer to the location of the ancient Inca treasure on Robinson Crusoe's Island? Numerous other treasure hunters have searched for it, and some of them claim to have found part of it — the rest of it must still be out there.

The ancient Mayan civilization of Central America grew from the even older Olmec culture. These highly developed peoples had a deep knowledge of astronomy, an accurate and effective calendar system, and their own remarkable hieroglyphics. They built observatories, temples, and pyramids of high architectural quality and great durability. They were prosperous people who created a great deal of wealth, much of which remains as undiscovered treasure today. Edgar Cayce's

The mysterious Shepherd Monument at Shugborough Hall.

many intriguing psychic readings contain references to the Mayans and their advanced technology. One of the many theories is that much of their ancient wisdom is hidden on crystals, each of which is capable of storing a great deal of information. This is reminiscent of some of the legends attached to Hermes Trismegistus, alias of the ancient Egyptian god Thoth, who acted as scribe to the other members of the Egyptian pantheon. He may also have been the same powerful ancient being as the immortal Melchizedek, who is mentioned in the Bible (Hebrews 7:3) as being "without father, without mother, having neither beginning of days, nor end of life." Hermes' famous Emerald Tablets were believed to contain all the secrets of magical (or technological?) power upon which the Egyptian pantheon depended. Legend also suggests that two of the tablets fell into the hands of Abraham's sister-wife, Sarah, and eventually became the sacred stones Urim and Thummim, which were used by the high priests to ascertain the will of God. Information storage crystals like those hidden by the Mayans of Central America or by Thoth's ancient Egyptians would represent treasure of incalculable value. Searching for them in Mexico or the Nile valley could prove equally rewarding.

One of the most intriguing ancient treasure sites in Wales is the Dolaucothi gold mines at Pumsaint, Llanwrda, in Carmarthenshire. Although closely associated with the Roman occupation of Britain some two thousand years ago, there is a strong possibility that the mines pre-date the arrival of the Romans.

A human tooth — probably Neanderthal — was found in a cave in the Elwy Valley in north Wales. That tooth dates back more than two hundred thousand years. The Gower Peninsula in South Wales is rich in limestone caves, and in 1823 these yielded the body of a young man dating back thirty thousand years. A mammoth skull was also found in the vicinity. The young man's body had been dyed red and was for many years referred to as the Red Lady of Paviland. The Reverend William Buckland, who found it, thought it was from Roman times, as his religious ideas about creationism would not allow him to consider such an early date. However, when Dr. Roger Jacobi of the British Museum and Dr. Thomas Higham of Oxford University examined the remains scientifically, the correct age and sex were revealed. Other evidence at the site showed that a high degree of ritual had accompanied the young man's burial, and it was conjectured that he had been a tribal chief or leader of some description. For Wales to have had such an advanced culture thirty thousand years ago suggests that the Dolaucothi gold mines were probably in use well before the Romans arrived a mere two thousand years ago. What became of the gold from those mines?

One very interesting theory suggests that when the Roman Empire was under serious threat at the start of the fifth century AD, Romano-Welsh miners and their families took a substantial amount of gold with them and crossed the Atlantic to get away from the barbarian hordes that were then invading Roman Britain. Such a journey would have been far from impossible. The legend of St. Brendan tells how he travelled all the way to America a thousand years before Columbus, and St. Mernoc is also credited with conquering the Atlantic. If they did it, what about a party of Romano-Welsh gold miners? The second half of this theory suggests that when they reached Oak Island off the coast of Nova Scotia, they constructed the famous Money Pit in which to conceal and protect their Dolaucothi gold. This creates two avenues for the modern treasure hunter to explore: the first is in the area of the Dolaucothi mines; the second is Oak Island.

Another possible site for undiscovered treasure in Wales goes back to the early Middle Ages and the mysterious history of Sker House. An isolated stretch of the Welsh coast runs from Sker to Margam. Although the area is very secluded today, a busy and prosperous town once existed there a little to the north of Kenfig Pool. Although the medieval citizens did all they could to preserve their town, the encroaching sand was too much for them, and the town was eventually covered as if it had never existed at all. Sker House (now a Grade I listed building by English Heritage) is less than a kilometre to the south of where that buried town once stood. Its oldest parts are medieval, and the word *sker* may come from Old Norse rather than early Welsh. It would be no exaggeration to suggest that the earliest dwelling on that site was there well over a thousand years ago. The treasure legend connected with Sker House concerns the tragic loss of a sailing ship a few centuries ago. Men were seen carrying heavy burdens ashore from the wreck and heading in the direction of gaunt and bleak old Sker House. Was it treasure that they were salvaging from the wreck, and if it was, where did they hide it?

Many ancient and medieval treasures from all parts of the world are still undiscovered. Each of them presents an intriguing challenge to the determined and resourceful modern treasure hunter.

Chapter Four
Asian Treasure

A sia is the biggest continent on Earth, and the one with the biggest population. It accounts for 9 percent of the Earth's total surface area (30 percent of the land area). Its four billion people give it more than three-fifths of the world's total population. Herodotus, the great historian, seems to have been the first writer to use the word *Asia* in about 450 BC. It can be regarded as the eastern part of Eurasia, with Europe in the west. Broadly, Asia is the territory that falls to the south of the Caspian Sea, the Black Sea, and the Caucasus Mountains, while the Suez Canal and the Ural Mountains form its western edge. The vast Pacific Ocean is Asia's eastern boundary, while the Indian Ocean and the Arctic Ocean are its southern and northern borders respectively.

This huge land mass with its thriving population generated industry and commerce from earliest times, and much of its trade went by sea. Quite how far the traders went may be judged from some very old Icelandic sagas, where the first Teutons regarded the River Tanakvisl (sometimes rendered Vanakvisl), which empties into the Black Sea, as the boundary of the land they thought of as Asia. In their legends, the leading god, Odin, had his citadel of Asgard somewhere east of that river.

There is an inescapable connection between the development of large-scale seaborne commerce and lost treasure. The best-known ancient treasure from Asia (including Asia Minor) was the semi-legendary treasure of Troy. The great nineteenth-century archaeological discoveries that took place during the prolonged search for Troy would never have been made without the dynamic and unquenchable desire to find treasure that dominated Heinrich Schliemann's life and helped to form his character. Born in 1822 in Neubukow, he listened avidly to his father's versions of the Iliad and the Odyssey. When he was only seven years old, his father had also given him a copy of Ludwig Jerrer's *Illustrated History of the World*. The following year, young Heinrich vowed that one day he would excavate the ruins of Troy. His fascination with treasure was reinforced by the legend associated with a pond near his family garden. A female supernatural entity was supposed to rise from this pond at midnight holding a beautiful silver cup in her hands. Another local legend referred to a vast treasure buried beside a ruined tower on a local lord's estate. Nearby was a hill under which a wealthy knight had supposedly buried his dead infant son inside a golden cradle.

Knight in armour from Leeds Castle in Kent.

As an adult, Heinrich went to Hissarlik in Turkey and began to excavate what had been assumed to be nothing more than a simple, natural hill. It wasn't. Schliemann was right in his hunch. His men uncovered not one ruined city but *nine* — one above the other. Among those ruins he found a vast treasure, which he believed to be the treasure of Homeric Troy. The discovery of the treasure came early one morning, when he was examining the previous day's excavations just before the workmen arrived to carry on digging. To a treasure-motivated adventurer like Schliemann, the gleam of gold was unmistakable. He also knew what the lust for treasure could do to otherwise normal human beings. As a well-read treasure hunter, Schliemann may have been aware of what Captain Cornelius Webb's mutinous and murderous crew were planning in connection with Admiral Anson's treasure on Robinson Crusoe's Island. He felt that he and his exquisitely beautiful young Greek wife would be in mortal danger if the workmen saw gold among the ruins. He told her to send them away for the day with an excuse such as a birthday celebration; the ruse worked. He then told her to hold out her shawl — and he proceeded to fill it with treasure. Obsessed as Schliemann was with Troy and the tale of King Priam, he was convinced that it was some of Priam's lost treasure that he had found in the ruins. Long after Schliemann's death, research revealed that what he had found was a treasure dating back at least a millennium earlier than Priam's time. Of most significance for the treasure hunter today is not Schliemann's great discovery in 1870 — important as it was — but the very real possibility that even greater treasures lie waiting below the ruins of historic sites like the one he excavated. What Schliemann teaches every contemporary treasure hunter is to never give up. Discovering treasure is a widely shared dream. Schliemann's experiences show clearly that an adventurer with sufficient willpower and mental fortitude can turn dreams into reality. Whether it was Priam's treasure that Schliemann found or that of some earlier or later ruler, Troy's situation as a seagoing commercial power played a very significant role in amassing that treasure in the first place.

Going back to the time of the Song Dynasty, which lasted from 960 to 1270, and the Yuan Dynasty that followed it from 1271 to 1368, there is ample evidence that a great many significantly large ships were involved in Asian commerce.

The indefatigable Marco Polo (1254–1324) was a Venetian merchant adventurer who wrote in great depth about his worldwide travels. With his father and uncle, he was one of the first Europeans to travel the famous Silk Road to China and to visit Genghis Khan's grandson Kublai Khan. Marco stayed at the Imperial Court from 1275 until 1292 and wrote in detail about the ships he saw there. According to his account they carried four masts and had surprisingly modern watertight bulkheads. The biggest of them were crewed by three hundred men.

A century later during the Ming Dynasty, which lasted from 1368 until 1644, a vast treasure fleet of more than three hundred vessels was built. From 1405 onwards this huge fleet, which had been built in Nanjing, traded all over the Chinese and Indian oceans.

Where there is wealth there are quarrels over who controls it, and bitter disputes arose between the court and the seafaring merchant adventurers. It became a capital offence to go to sea in a ship with more than one mast!

Evidence of just how far these amazing old Chinese ships were able to travel at their zenith (before the court forbade their lucrative overseas trade) comes from a small African island named Pate, close to the Kenyan coast. Visitors to the island are told how several of the present residents are descended from Chinese sailors who were shipwrecked there centuries ago. These islanders have an Asian appearance rather than a purely African one, and they treasure priceless Chinese porcelain heirlooms, which must have been retrieved from the wreck when the ship was dashed on to the reefs near Pate. There are many interesting ruins on the island, which is only accessible at high tide because of the mangrove swamps that surround it. Because of its history, it may well contain many other fascinating treasures in addition to artifacts and valuables that the Chinese sailors rescued when their ship was destroyed on the reefs.

The ship that met its end near Pate was almost certainly one of the many big Chinese trading vessels that went as far as Sri Lanka (then called Ceylon), East Africa, and Arabia. Such records as exist suggest that there were close to thirty thousand men manning the fleet, which included water tankers, supply ships, and even transporters for the Chinese cavalry's horses. The biggest of the ships was said to be well over a hundred metres long and over thirty metres wide. The remains of an enormous rudder, almost ten metres across, suggests that the ship it once guided could have been 120 to 150 metres long.

Their cargoes are of great interest to contemporary treasure hunters: they carried vast quantities of silk, lacquerware, rare and beautiful Chinese porcelain, and many other valuables including gold, silver, and gems. From ports in the Indian Ocean, the Chinese merchant adventurers would obtain pearls, medicinal spices, ivory, and other rare treasures that were in great demand from their customers back home in China.

The Republic of the Philippines consists of more than seven thousand islands in the western Pacific, in the general region of southeast Asia. There are approximately ninety million inhabitants, and Manila is the capital city. The Philippine archipelago has sea boundaries with China, Malaysia, Indonesia, Palau, and Vietnam. The Philippines were already inhabited by industrious citizens who traded with China, India, and Japan when the great Portuguese navigator Ferdinand Magellan arrived there in 1521, only to be killed at the Battle of Mactan.

The Philippines still attract many treasure hunters searching for what has come to be known as the lost treasure of Yamashita. There are traditions of underground labyrinths with dangerous, booby-trapped treasure chambers — some that release poison gas and others that are rigged with high explosive. Mysterious symbols and pictographs are cut into the rock. The story behind the Philippines treasure is that when the occupying Japanese forces knew that they were losing the war, vast amounts of gold, silver, and jewels were stored in the Philippines. This wealth had been looted from all over Asia during the period of Japanese supremacy.

The Japanese governor of the Philippines during part of the Second World War was General Tomoyuki Yamashita. Having succeeded against British and Allied forces in Malaya and Singapore, the "Malayan Tiger," as Yamashita was nicknamed, looted a dozen countries in the south and east of Asia and carried his ill-gotten gains to the Philippines. When the war ended and the resistance fighters in the Philippines were able to even the score, Yamashita was duly hanged from a tree on Mount Makiling.

Waterfalls are convenient markers for hidden treasure, and enigmatic stones with Japanese characters engraved into them were found in the water at the foot of the Dampalit falls. Whatever it was that Yamashita really took from the Japanese-occupied territories in Asia and possibly transferred to the Philippines, much of it may still be there. A treasure hunter with a thorough knowledge of the Japanese language and an understanding of esoteric Japanese signs, codes, ciphers, and symbols will be the one to unravel the enigma of Yamashita's treasure.

Another mysterious Asian treasure is associated with a notorious nineteenth-century pirate named Cheung Po Tsai. Cheung began life as the son of a poor fisherman, but he was kidnapped by Cheng Yat, a successful pirate who terrorized the Chinese coast during the late eighteenth century. Something in Cheung's personality appealed to Captain Cheng Yat; he and his wife, Ching Shih, adopted him as their son. Cheng Yat was involved in a fatal accident during a severe storm, and his wife, referred to respectfully as Widow Ching, assumed control of his pirate fleet. Truth is often stranger than fiction: she and Cheung fell in love and married, and she was happy to hand over control of her pirate fleet to her charismatic young husband.

Cheung was successful for many years, but eventually succumbed to the superior sea power of the Qing Dynasty in 1810. Far from executing or imprisoning him, in one of history's greater ironies Cheung was given the rank of captain in the Qing navy — and the specific task of hunting down pirates.

But what became of the vast treasures he had accumulated during his reign as a pirate chief? As all experienced treasure hunters know, there is very rarely smoke without fire. Rumours, myths, and legends appertaining to treasure caches are always worth careful investigation and analysis. Powerful and durable traditions associate Cheung's treasure with the little island of Cheung Chau (which is actually named after the pirate) near Hong Kong. There is a small cave at the western end of the island; access to it is not easy, but it is just possible to crawl inside. Experienced speleologists know that caves and the passageways connecting them can be very deceptive: a narrow pothole can open up and lead to a spacious wonderland, a gleaming natural palace filled with stalactites and stalagmites, yet a cavern with a wide entrance that promises subterranean magic and excitement may simply peter out within a few metres. The Cheung Chau island cave may have only a small entrance and yet lead unexpectedly to bigger chambers packed with treasure. It is not beyond the wit of a man like Cheung Po Tsai to conceal his vast wealth inside a large cave and then block the entrance, leaving only what is *apparently* a small cave. A treasure hunter equipped with the best modern metal detectors could do worse than pay a visit to Cheung Chau and inspect the pirate's cave there.

One ruse that treasure hiders often employed was to leave a small cache near the surface in the hope that anyone finding it would think that that was all there was and look no further. Such was the case with John Chapman, the famous peddler of Swaffham in Norfolk, England. The first ceramic container of gold coins he found was inscribed in Latin "*sub est maioribus*," which translates roughly as "below me there is a greater." Fortunately for Chapman, who had placed the container conspicuously in his cottage window, some students from Cambridge visiting the town translated it for him. He was very careful to say that he couldn't recall where the pot had come from, explaining it as something he had simply found during his extensive travels as a peddler.

Archaeological excavations in Istanbul (once Constantinople) have retrieved ponderous limestone building units from nine metres below the present ground level. There are significantly large Byzantine tunnels below the area known as Yenikapi. What archaeologists uncovered was the site of the original fifteen-hundred-year-old harbour of Constantinople. This was the vast commercial maritime complex through which cargoes of wine, olive oil, grain, herbs, and spices came in and out of the fabulously wealthy Eastern Roman Empire. As well as these commodities, the Roman merchant ships would have carried substantial quantities of gold and silver coins to facilitate their trading. Archaeologists have also discovered the wrecks of half a dozen very old boats there, apparently all sunk by the same storm. What did they once contain, and how widely was it scattered when the storm destroyed them? The ancient harbour below Yenikapi may hold many undiscovered treasures dating back to the era of Constantinople's greatest prosperity.

A further consideration for treasure hunters is the fall of Constantinople in 1204 as part of the Fourth Crusade, and its final, terminal fall on May 29, 1453, at the hands of Mehmed II. The city then became part of the Ottoman Empire. There were treasures in Byzantium of incalculable value. The prosperous old city had amassed wealth for well over a thousand years. The threat of war stimulates the concealment of treasure. What did the Byzantines do with their treasures once it became all too obvious that Mehmed II's superior forces were going to conquer Constantinople? The triumphant Ottoman troops did not get it all. Some has been recovered over the centuries — but some has not. Istanbul and its environs are still potentially very fertile ground for a determined treasure hunter today.

It is not surprising that wartorn Afghanistan has its store of priceless valuables, and these have not all been accounted for by any means. In 2006 an amazing collection of Afghan treasure, which had miraculously escaped destruction from the Taliban during their period in power, was exhibited in Paris. These priceless artifacts had been hidden out of harm's way deep below the President's Palace in Kabul. If one set of treasures could survive in this way, so could others. Despite the many political, military, and social dangers in Afghanistan, a courageous treasure hunter could still hope to recover some of the other precious items that may well be hidden among those rugged mountains.

One outstanding example of such hidden wealth is the Oxus treasure, much of which is now in the Victoria and Albert Museum and the British Museum in London. Some of it, however, may still be buried in the original location, waiting to be discovered. The details of that original location are a closely guarded secret, but there is reliable evidence that travelling merchants dug it up from the banks of the River Oxus, as it was once known. Referred to today as Amu Darya, the twenty-four-hundred-kilometre river is the longest in central Asia. Also referred to as the Jayhoun, the Oxus may have been the Gihon that flowed from the biblical Garden of Eden as described in Genesis 2:13, which reads, "The name of the second river is the Gihon; it winds through the entire land of Cush." Originating in the Pamir Mountains, the basin of the Amu Darya includes Uzbekistan, Afghanistan, Tajikistan, and Turkmenistan.

The Oxus treasure had a series of traumatic adventures after the merchants uncovered it. They were apprehended and robbed by bandits on the road between Kabul and Peshawar. Captain F.C. Burton, who was then the British Political Officer in Afghanistan, rode to their rescue and made short work of the bandits who had taken the Oxus treasure from the merchants. Having rewarded Captain Burton appropriately, the grateful merchants went on to Rawalpindi, where they sold the rest of the treasure in various bazaars. This gave the British museums an opportunity to acquire several pieces. Finding the exact site on the banks of the Amu Darya could help a modern treasure hunter to recover more of the original Oxus hoard.

Among the many other priceless artifacts recovered in Afghanistan was the Bactrian treasure, which had been concealed below Tillia tepe (meaning "hill of gold") in Sheberghan in the province of Jowzjan in the north of Afghanistan. The Bactrian artifacts include decorated, bejewelled belts; necklaces, crowns, and medallions; and coins. They had lain undisturbed in the burial mounds at Tillia tepe for millennia. Bactrian wealth and culture were linked to some extent with the trade that prospered along the Silk Road. Some archaeologists and historians believe that Bactria was the area from which a significant number of Indo-European peoples moved into Iran and northwestern India about five thousand years ago. The prophet Zarathustra (more commonly known as Zoroaster) was believed to have been born in Bactria. In later times Bactria probably formed part of the Median Empire, which later fell to Cyrus the Great of Persia. Emperor Alexander of Macedon had considerable difficulty trying to subdue the Bactrian people, although Bactria was technically part of his vast empire. After Alexander's death, Bactria became part of the Seleucid Empire. Further wars involved the Egyptian Pharaoh Ptolemy II. The many wars that involved Bactria point to the likelihood of Bactrian wealth being hidden carefully away during times of hostility and uncertainty. This adds to the likelihood that the Bactrian area could yield many as yet undiscovered ancient treasures to match the famous Bactrian gold.

Siberia is not often associated with mysterious undiscovered treasures, yet the treasures of Kyzyl, capital of the Siberian province of Tuva,

Map of Bactria.

richly deserve to be included in any account of ancient hidden wealth. Almost three thousand years ago, fierce Scythian nomads travelled all over the Asian steppes from the Black Sea coasts to the borders of China. The area where the Tuva treasure was found during a dig that lasted from 1998 until 2002 has long been referred to by the local people as the Valley of the Kings — just like the widely known Valley of the Kings in Egypt. It got its name from the numerous ancient Scythian burial mounds near Kyzyl. The first treasure to be found there in relatively recent times was discovered by Russian archaeologists working on behalf of Tsar Peter the Great (1672–1725). The most recent discoveries were found in a Kyzyl burial mound referred to as Arzhan II. Despite some ineffective attempts by early grave robbers, the actual burial chamber itself was undisturbed. It contained the twenty-five-hundred-year-old remains of a man and a woman — almost certainly Scythian royalty. Their golden ornaments and decorations weighed close to twenty-three kilograms and consisted of beads, earrings, and pendants. In the tomb with the royal corpses, beautifully crafted items made of turquoise, amber, and iron were also found. From an archaeological and historical point of view — over and above the monetary value of the Tuva treasure — the discoveries in Arzhan II revolutionized previous ideas about the cultural and technical levels of the ancient nomadic Scythian people. They were evidently highly skilled and employed an advanced technology. Once that is taken fully into account, it suggests that the Siberian Valley of the Kings could well be of great interest to the modern treasure hunter. The downside of any exploration in the area is its potential danger: at least two tragic deaths are associated with it. The Dragon Sea, off the coast of Vietnam, is well named. Meteorologists know it to be notorious for devastating storms and typhoons. It was in this turbulent and hazardous stretch of water that the *Hoi An* went down six hundred years ago packed with priceless Vietnamese porcelain. Frank Pope's exciting account of the attempt to retrieve that sunken porcelain treasure can be found in his book *Dragon Sea* (2007). Then, on January 3, 1752, the good ship *Geldermalsen* — forty-five metres long and more than twelve metres wide — crashed disastrously on to a reef not far from Singapore on her long voyage from Canton to Holland. Her cargo included gold and a great quantity of fine porcelain. Captain Michael Hatcher discovered the wreck of the *Geldermalsen* during the 1980s and retrieved many of the valuables she had carried; these all did well at the auction at Christies of Amsterdam in 1986. What is of major interest to contemporary treasure hunters is precisely what the *Geldermalsen* was carrying and how many other vessels like her brought similar treasures from Asia to Europe in the mid-eighteenth century.

These same South China Seas are the scene of many tragic wrecks, whose valuable cargoes still lie on the seabed. For every one that has been partially salvaged a dozen are still waiting to be explored. Submarine archaeologists have recently encountered five such wrecks very close to Dongshan County in southeast China's Fujian province. The contents of these wrecks suggested that at least one of them — possibly more — had been operating internationally during the Qing Dynasty (also known as the Manchu Dynasty) that lasted from the mid-seventeenth century until the start of the twentieth. The area is a particularly dangerous one for shipping, which makes it a rich site for would-be treasure hunters. Ships that were wrecked there in past centuries were known to have included gold, silver, porcelain, silk, iron, and copper among the valuables in their cargoes. Their voyages frequently took them to Champa near Vietnam, to Java, to Sumatra, and to Sri Lanka. Even India and the Middle East were not unknown to them.

It is not the oceans alone that offer tempting prizes to treasure hunters. The Grand Canal of China links Hangzhou with Beijing and covers a length of well over sixteen hundred kilometres. It dates back twenty-five hundred years, but is still in use in the twenty-first century. Needless to say, it represents a veritable paradise for archaeologists and treasure hunters. It is thought to be the longest ancient canal anywhere on Earth, and as such has as potent a claim to fame as the Great Wall of China. Although its oldest sections go back to approximately 500 BC, it was only combined into one vast waterway during the Sui Dynasty, which lasted from 581 until 618 — well over a thousand years after the first sections of the canal were built. Unfortunately, like the Nile in Africa, the Yellow River in China is subject to continual flooding, and this threatens the Grand Canal. As well as these periodic natural floods, it was part of early Chinese military tactics to break the banks of the Yellow River deliberately with flood water in order to halt the advance of enemy armies. Valuable items are dropped, inundated with mud and water, and lost for centuries when flooding occurs.

The better informed treasure hunters are, the more likely they will be to meet with success. Archaeologists and other experts in ancient history — particularly the history of commerce — generally agree that the barter system preceded the introduction of money as a convenient medium of exchange. One of the earliest accounts of metallic money

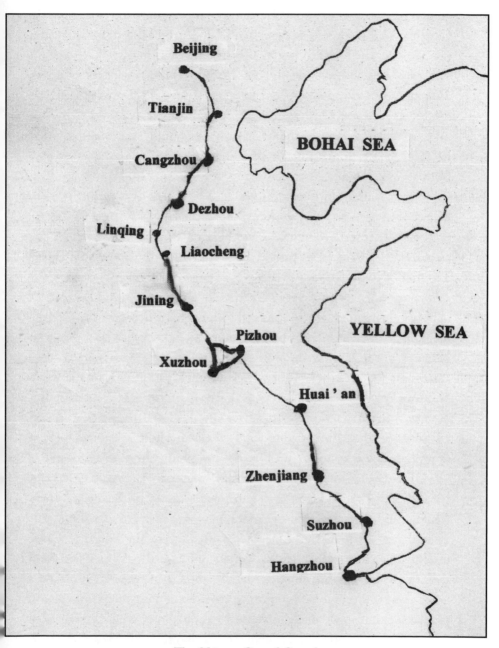

The Chinese Grand Canal.

being used in India can be found in the Vedas. Ancient religious documents from all over the world frequently contain hints and clues that will point the well-informed treasure hunter in the right direction. The Vedas (named after the Sanskrit word *véda*, meaning "wisdom" or "knowledge") originated in ancient India and are the oldest known Sanskrit writings. They are also the most ancient sacred writings of Hinduism and are revered as *revealed* texts, meaning those that were not created by human beings. Another word for them is *shruti*, which indicates something that has been heard, something that has been dictated to a human listener from a higher source. There are many very special Vedic mantras, which are always recited during Hindu religious services and are believed to help devout users to achieve eternal life.

Several esoteric hints and clues relating to possible ancient Asian treasure may be found by careful investigation of the sacred Vedic texts. The first of these is the Rigveda, which consists mainly of sacred songs that an experienced priest who is meticulously trained in this skill recites in a specific manner. The second is the Yajurveda. This consists of special religious formulas, and is in the care of the Adhvaryu, the priest who officiates at the service. The words in the third text — the Samaveda — are chanted by another priest who is trained in that part of the work. The fourth and most important text from the treasure hunter's point of view is the Atharvaveda. This gives details of apotropaic charms and talismans — those intended to ward off evil and to prevent bad luck — as well as religious stories, prophecies, and predictions.

Of particular interest to the treasure hunter are the ancient descriptions of money made from precious metals found in the Vedas. There were a number of important ceremonies and sacrifices such as the ashvamedhayaga, which was concerned with horses. The king for whose benefit the ashvamedhayaga was conducted had to pay the priests and their learned assistants in gold. Metallic money in these circumstances had a powerful religious significance that can be understood, at least in part, as a parallel to the exclusive use of a religiously acceptable form of money in the Temple at Jerusalem. This is described in Matthew 21:12, "Jesus entered the temple area and drove out all who were buying and selling there. He overturned the tables of the money changers and the benches of those selling doves." The money changers were making exorbitant profits from the many visiting pilgrims who had to exchange their normal, secular coins (which had forbidden graven images on them) for Temple money, which did not. Exodus 20:4 reads, "Thou shalt not make unto thee any graven image, or any likeness of any thing that is in heaven above, or that is in the earth beneath, or that is in the water under the earth."

However, the very first metallic currency equivalent of the type referred to in the Vedas may well have been a nishka. The earliest of these were probably small, simple nuggets, little pieces of precious metal without any regular shape. They were often worn as pendants or as parts of a necklace. Gradually, over the years, a rectangular or cuboid form was adopted, and this eventually gave way to circular coinage.

It has been argued by some anthropologists and archaeologists that the introduction of money, especially in the form of gold and silver coins, might have played some part in the development of greed both within societies and within individuals because of the extra power and influence that money (as distinct from barterable goods and services) could provide.

Conversely, there are a great many non-monetary treasures — particularly religious ones — that have been hidden when there have been traumatic regime changes. As a tragic example, there is the case of the Khmer Rouge in Cambodia. They controlled the country from the mid-1970s for a period of four or five years, and millions of lives were lost during that reign of terror. The Khmer Rouge attacked religion with particular ferocity and set out to destroy what they regarded as harmful religious objects of all kinds. More than a quarter of a century after the Khmer Rouge were defeated, workers in the Kampong Thom province were clearing an ancient ruined pagoda that had become heavily overgrown — so much so that it had almost vanished. More than thirty statues of the Buddha were found there, and the majority of them were made of gold. The site includes the Temple of Po Pich, which is just over a hundred kilometres north of Phnom Penh, Cambodia's capital city. Despite the relatively recent problems caused by the Khmer Rouge, which might well have motivated the religious community in Po

Pich to conceal their precious religious artifacts, expert opinion suggests that the statues were buried many centuries ago. Guatama Buddha, the founder of Buddhism, lived during the fifth century BC in what is Nepal today. It is certainly possible that the statues found in the Kampong Thom area in 2002 could have been hidden for safety more than two millennia before that.

The perceptive and thoughtful treasure hunter does well to look carefully at religious history, and at the cultural changes that affect it. When those changes are confrontational, religious treasures are likely to be buried by the faithful.

Another example of priceless Asian religious treasure is to be found at Ho Phra Keo ("the emerald Buddha's altar"). This sacred site is to be found to the south of Setthathirath Road in the city of Vientiane in Laos. According to a classic Laotian history, known as the *Phra Lak Phra Lam*, Prince Thattaradtha founded Vientiane when his younger brother was given the throne that was rightfully his. According to legend, a gigantic, seven-headed serpent deity, referred to as a *naga*, advised Thattaradtha to found another city to the east. This he did, and it eventually became Vientiane. There were many disputes and battles between the different peoples of Thattaradtha's day, and the politically unsettled conditions of the region would prompt many religious leaders to conceal their priceless sacred treasures.

The temple was originally built as a centre of worship for the royal family as well as a sacred repository for the famous emerald Buddha. In the early nineteenth century Vientiane was plundered and set on fire by an occupying army, and Ho Phra Keo was destroyed. Over a century later, in 1936, it was restored. Experienced treasure hunters will theorize that the area around it may well yield some of the as yet undiscovered treasures that would almost certainly have been hidden in the vicinity when the tides of war were raging around the temple.

Other important general points for treasure hunters to bear in mind are the haphazard ways and roundabout routes by which vitally important information about hitherto undiscovered treasure can reach them. A Euro-American team of professional archaeologists, art conservators, historians, and architects were working with Nepalese colleagues in the remote mountain kingdom of Mustang high in the Himalayas, about two hundred kilometres northwest of Kathmandu. They were carrying out delicate restoration work on wall paintings in a Tibetan monastery that dated back to the fifteenth century.

While engaged in their work, they got into conversation with a local villager who admired what they were doing and volunteered the information that as a boy he recalled seeing some paintings inside a cave. The scholars went with him to the cave and found that his memory had served him well: the walls were covered with pictures of deer, tigers, leopards, monkeys, and other animals. The presence of such cave paintings alone is not necessarily an indication that treasure may be concealed in the vicinity, but a people with the level of culture needed to create such fine art works may well have accumulated treasure and concealed it not far from their paintings. Some researchers theorize that the paintings may contain vital clues to the location of the treasure. Ancient Tibetan manuscripts were also found in nearby caves, and scholars speculate that the whole district might once have been a religious university similar to the ancient Buddhist study centre at Nalanda, in Bihar, India. It was an important location for Buddhist scholars from the fifth century until the twelfth. Such centres of learning tend to attract wealth as well as wisdom, and are useful stopping places along the treasure hunter's itinerary.

Chapter Five
European Treasure

One of the oldest treasure mysteries in Britain centres around an enigmatic figure from the remote past known to historians as the Amesbury Archer and the King of Stonehenge. In May 2002, archaeologists uncovered a grave dating back to 2300 BC, the early Bronze Age. It was only five kilometres from Stonehenge. More than a hundred interesting objects were in the burial site along with the dead archer, a man in his early forties who had lost a kneecap in an accident at some earlier time of his life and who was also suffering from a jaw abscess when he died. The objects buried with him included strands of gold similar to tresses of hair dating from 2500 BC. There were also copper knives from France or Spain, pottery, archer's wrist guards, and flint arrowheads: things that his people felt that their archer would need in the next world. Anatomical tests indicated that the archer had come originally from the Alpine district of France, Germany, or Austria, and other evidence suggested that he was part of the advanced Beaker culture that had spread from Europe to Britain. In another grave close by lay the remains of a much younger man, with very similar DNA. Archaeologists have theorized that he was the archer's son. Strands of gold were found with him as well. The area around Amesbury and Stonehenge may well contain similar graves containing ancient treasure similar to that found with the archer and his young companion.

At about the same period, some four thousand years ago, the Minoan Empire made Crete one of the most impressive places on Earth. But Crete itself was only the centre from which Minoan culture and commerce spread widely. After some five centuries of success, the Minoan culture succumbed to a devastating volcanic eruption on the island of Thera. Clouds of choking ash and massively destructive tidal waves brought havoc to the Minoans.

Stonehenge.

The famous golden Minoan treasures referred to as the Vaphio Cups were found in a fifteenth-century BC tomb in Vaphio near Sparta. These beautifully crafted artifacts are made from two golden sheets, one of which is plain while the other is covered with repoussé pictures of the bull dancing ceremonies associated with Crete. Repoussé work creates a relief design when the artist presses or hammers the back of the sheet that is to be decorated. (The word *repoussé* is derived from a French term meaning "to push back.")

When the tombs at Vaphio were explored by visiting archaeologists in 1888, it was clear that tomb raiders had been there in the remote past but had been forced to leave in a hurry, as various small items of treasure such as rings and seals were found scattered on the floor. Digging deeper nearby, the archaeologists found another tomb that had not been desecrated. The human remains within it were accompanied by precious objects made of gold, silver, alabaster, and bronze — as well as the superb Vaphio Cups. The technique of digging deeper when it could be seen that the first few tombs had been disturbed and robbed led to the discovery of rare treasure. This is an important principle that will not be lost on thoughtful contemporary treasure hunters.

The Vaphio area may still have plenty of undiscovered treasure buried deeply within it.

The Celts as an ethnic group seem to have originated in what is now Germany and Austria well over three thousand years ago. They were a technically and intellectually advanced people who expanded their influence in all directions. One of the most interesting of the Celtic groups was known as the Volcae Tectosages, who were mentioned by Julius Caesar: "The Volcae Tectosages seized the wealthiest and most fertile parts of Germany ... the area near the Hercynian forest." They were settled to the north of the Pyrenees in the southwest of France at the western end of the territory then known as Narbonensis, just to the east of Aquitania.

Of particular interest to the treasure hunter is the Tectosages' association with the mysterious mountaintop village of Rennes-le-Château, famous for its enigmatic priest, Father Bérenger Saunière. When the authors were among the pioneer on-site researchers into the Rennes treasure mystery in the 1970s, they interviewed Monsieur Henri Fatin, the sculptor, who lives in Château Hautpoul — the château that gives Rennes-le-Château its name. He has made an in-depth study of the village's local history and was a mine of information concerning the Tectosages, whose name means "the wise builders."

A study of ancient Celtic culture led to three types of discovery by contemporary archaeologists and treasure hunters: valuable objects were buried in Celtic graves and tombs; votive offerings were given to their gods; and hoards of gold, silver, and gems were buried by them.

When Bérenger Saunière, the priest of St. Mary Magdalene's Church in Rennes over a century ago, became amazingly and inexplicably rich, his wealth may have been based on the discovery of treasure left in the vicinity by the Tectosages. Numerous other fascinating theories have been put forward to account for his sudden financial good fortune, but Tectosages treasure remains as good a hypothesis as any.

Vix in France was once a Celtic hilltop fort close to the town of Dijon. During the sixth century BC, a Celtic queen or princess was laid to rest there along with her jewels, gold, ornaments, personal adornments, and a beautiful statuette. A huge bronze drinking vessel and various ceramic items were also found with her in the tumulus. Archaeologists decided that some of these exquisite artifacts had been created by Greek craftsmen. Vix stood on the direct trade route connecting Massilia (now modern Marseilles) with the north coast of France, which had swift and easy access by sea to the tin mines of Cornwall in the United Kingdom. Tin was an essential ingredient of bronze and as such was in very high demand during this era. The district around Vix could well repay a visit from a contemporary treasure hunter, as could the area around Rillaton barrow in Cornwall. Tin merchants travelling regularly through Vix on their way to Cornwall could well have known of the Rillaton barrow, which is in the parish of Linkinhorne on Bodmin Moor. Dating from around 1700 BC, its contents included a bronze dagger, glass objects, beads, pottery, and other interesting items including the Rillaton cup, a beautiful artifact made from gold in the style of the ceramic beakers characteristic of the period. The Rillaton cup is very similar to Mycenaean workmanship from the eastern Mediterranean.

Further evidence of the Bronze Age prosperity of Cornwall is provided by the golden treasure unearthed at Morvah, which incorporates Chypraze and Rosemergy. Morvah is east of St. Just, southwest of Zennor and northwest of Penzance. In the late nineteenth century, while searching for building materials there, workmen unearthed a hoard of golden ornaments in the form of bracelets. These were almost certainly taken to Morvah in exchange for Cornish tin. That area would be of great interest to modern treasure hunters, as would the neighbouring region of Towednack, which lies to the east of Zennor and is only about three kilometres from St. Ives. In December 1931, many valuable gold ornaments were found there, including neck rings and arm rings. Badger's Lane in Towednack leads from Lady Downs to the road connecting the village with Amalveor, and is bounded by a very ancient stone wall built in the traditional Cornish style. While this old stone wall was being refurbished, the gold came to light. Experts on Bronze Age culture describe the gold in the ornaments as being of very fine quality, and of a consistency that is compatible with Irish gold.

Moving from Cornwall up the west coast as far as Bryn yr Ellyllon in Mold in north Wales takes the treasure hunter to the site known as

Goblins' Hill, where in 1833 a priceless gold cape was found in a four-thousand-year-old Bronze Age grave along with ancient human bones. The cape weighs a kilogram and is so finely detailed that it looks like cloth rather than metal. Archaeologists believe that the cape may have been worn for religious purposes. What else may still lie concealed in mysterious Goblins' Hill? Bryn yr Ellyllon is undoubtedly another area that would be of great interest to treasure hunters today.

Another Celtic treasure mystery comes from Panagyurishte. This took the form of solid gold drinking vessels with a total weight in excess of five kilograms. In 1949, workmen were digging for clay at Panagyurishte between Plovdiv and Sofia in Bulgaria when they uncovered the immensely valuable gold vessels. This area had once been part of Thrace, lying to the north of Macedonia and the Aegean Sea. The Celts swept through the country in around 350 BC, and it seems highly probable that while the clouds of war were gathering, some wealthy Thracian converted his assets into these easily portable golden drinking vessels and left in search of somewhere safer. The war may have started sooner than he expected, leading him to bury his treasure quickly near Panagyurishte with every intention of returning for it at some less hazardous time. Did he fall at the hands of the victorious Celts? Or did he reach safety and wisely decide that life was more important than gold, reluctantly abandoning his beautiful artifacts? What else lies buried in or near Panagyurishte? More than one wealthy Thracian must have fled that way to avoid the triumphant Celts.

Alexander the Great, also known as Alexander III of Macedon (356–323 BC), was born in Pella in northern Greece in what was then the kingdom of Macedonia, but his rise to world conquest was no overnight miracle. Talented as he was, Alexander had the advantage of a great Macedonian heritage. His father, Philip II, had already unified many of the city states situated on the Greek mainland, and Macedonian military organization and social culture were second to none at that time. The rivers of Thrace and Macedonia were rich in alluvial gold, which made significant contributions to the wealth of the area.

Some biblical scholars suggest that the gospel writer Luke, who came from Antioch in Turkey, had Greek ancestry, which was possibly

Macedonian. Luke was also generally acknowledged to have been a physician, and this would fit in well with the advanced stage that medicine had reached in Greece at that time.

Excavations at Pella in 2008 have uncovered the graves of Macedonian warriors and noble ladies dating from 600 to 300 BC. The bodies were frequently found covered in gold leaf; the men had swords and daggers with them as well as their helmets and armour, while the ladies' bodies were adorned with gold and jewels. Similar discoveries were made at Vratsa when tombs dating from the fourth century BC were opened. Golden ceremonial armour was found on a male body, and a golden laurel wreath and earrings were found on a woman buried in the same grave. These finds clearly indicate a rich and advanced culture in the Pella area and in the region of Vratsa — places that are of great interest to twenty-first-century treasure hunters.

Boadicea (sometimes referred to as Boudicca), who died in AD 61, was queen of the Iceni, a fierce East Anglian British tribe. King Prasutagus, her husband, had ruled the Iceni as an independent Roman ally. When he died, the Romans treated Boadicea contemptuously: she was flogged, her daughters were raped, and the Iceni kingdom was annexed to Rome. Boadicea led a terrifyingly successful revolt against the occupying Romans, killing an estimated one hundred thousand people in the Romanized cities of Colchester, London, and St. Albans.

Suetonius, the Roman governor, finally defeated Boadicea and her allies at the Battle of Watling Street, but the warrior-queen's death remains a mystery. Some historians suggest that she committed suicide rather than fall into Roman hands, but others think that she died fighting fearlessly in the heat of the final battle. In either case, the location of her treasure remains one of history's great secrets. There is said to have been a substantial Iceni treasure, which the fiercely proud tribe was determined to conceal from Roman hands at all costs. According to one version, it was buried alongside Boadicea by members of her loyal bodyguard. They used a far older Bronze Age round barrow on Hampstead Heath in London and hid the queen's body along with her treasure beside the original occupant of the barrow. Another tradition places her grave and the secret location of her Iceni treasure under what is now platform 10 at King's Cross Station in London. A different version of the story suggests that she and her daughters took poison after losing their great final battle against the Romans near the village of Mancetter, to the north of present-day Coventry. They are said to be buried together with the royal Iceni treasure somewhere near the village. Yet another version places the burial site and the treasure near Coggleshall in Essex. The existence of a substantial Iceni treasure is extremely probable, and it may well have been buried with Boadicea. The treasure hunter has a choice of the sites described above. There are several instances of buried Iceni treasure that support this theory: a small cache of it was found at Honingham in Norfolk, and more was unearthed at Benhall in Suffolk, including the stone head of the hated Roman Emperor Claudius, which an Iceni warrior had smashed from the emperor's statue in Colchester.

One of the most intriguing undiscovered treasure mysteries in Europe concerns Attila the Hun. There are various accounts of the circumstances surrounding his death in 453, but one of the most probable versions is that while celebrating his wedding night with his newest bride (the young, beautiful, and sexually enthusiastic Ildico) Attila burst a blood vessel and died in her arms. It is one of the ironies of history that such a formidable war leader who had survived so many fights should die ecstatically in bed rather than on the battlefield!

His body was enclosed in three concentric coffins: iron, silver, and gold. In some versions, the outer coffin was said to be iron encased in lead, in other accounts it was lead rather than iron. His men then dammed a section of the great River Tisza, dug up its bed, and buried Attila and his treasure underneath it. The riverbed was then restored, concealing his tomb completely before the dam was broken and the Tisza resumed its course. The White Tisza originates in the Ukraine, and changes its name to the Black Tisza when it flows along the Romanian border before passing through Hungary and touching the Slovakian border. It finally enters the Danube. Tracking down Attila's final resting place somewhere below its bed would demand a long and exacting search.

Two centuries after Attila's death, in the Suffolk village of Sutton Hoo in the United Kingdom, a twenty-seven-metre-long ship belonging to a Saxon warrior-king was buried — although the king's body was not in it. The treasures on board the buried ship were worthy of a wealthy warrior-king. There were nearly forty gold coins dating from the first quarter of the seventh century AD in an ornate belt purse that could be secured to the wearer with three elaborate gold and garnet buckles. The funeral ship also contained a set of Byzantine silver bowls and a sceptre surmounted by a stag. There were also fragments from the king's great shield, which was later reconstructed. A number of theories have been put forward to account for the missing royal body — and its identity. Some historians have wondered whether the soil was so acidic that nothing of the royal corpse remained at all. Although the soil had proved too much for the timbers of the old vessel, it seems unlikely that a human body would have decomposed so completely that nothing of it would have been detectable. Had the warrior-king died in some distant battle, on a field so far away that it was impossible to bring him home for honourable burial? There is also the religious theory to take into account. What if this particular pagan warrior-king had been converted to Christianity, as many Anglo-Saxons had around this period? Would his body have been buried elsewhere with appropriate Christian funeral rites, while his loyal pagan followers performed one of their time-honoured ship burials for him at Sutton Hoo to ensure that whichever faith was correct, their loved and admired leader would have what he needed in the next life? A further theory suggests that the occupant of the ship burial, or the warrior-king whom it was intended to honour in absentia, was Redwald. A difficulty here is that he is known to have died in 625, but one of the coins in the purse was dated 638. Anna, king of the East Angles, had a Christian burial when he died in 654, but some theorists have suggested that he organized the Sutton Hoo burial to honour his heroic brother Egric, his predecessor, who died in battle in 634. Another theory offers the name of Aethelhere, who succeeded to the throne after Anna and his son died in battle. Aethelhere died in battle at the River Winwaed in 655, and his body is thought to have been lost in the flood water. The safest theory, and one commonly accepted, is that the Sutton Hoo ship burial was intended to honour one of the Anglo-Saxon kings who were based at Rendlesham, approximately eight kilometres from Sutton Hoo. From a contemporary treasure hunter's point of view, it is the whole custom of Anglo-Saxon ship burials that is significant. Part of that practice was to place treasure within the vessel. The area around Rendlesham and the adjoining coastline may well repay thorough and careful inspection.

Niederzier, a municipality in Germany, is an interesting site for the treasure hunter to explore. It is located in the district of Düren, which is part of North Rhine-Westphalia. Niederzier is only ten kilometres north of Düren, and lies to the same distance southeast of Jülich. Archaeologists working in Niederzier discovered a pit that was part of a late Iron Age settlement. It contained two golden neck rings, a bracelet, three rings made from sheet gold, and a number of gold coins. Several other ancient deposits examined in the locality contained similar precious objects.

Jülich is also a town that is likely to repay the treasure hunter's time and effort. The world-renowned scientific research centre there employs well over four thousand staff members who are collectively engaged in engineering, physics, biology, chemistry, and medicine. Their work is directed towards information technology, the environment, energy, and health. In this ultramodern scientific setting, Jülich is also internationally famous for its shortwave transmissions. Situated on the broad banks of the River Rur, Jülich lies just to the north of Inden and a little to the south of Linnich. In addition to its current scientific importance, Jülich has a long, proud history, having been known as Juliacum in the days of the Roman Empire. When Roman power faded, Jülich became the property of the Franks. In 1239 and again in 1278, Jülich lost important battles against the aggressive Archbishop of Cologne, and there was a disastrous fire in the town in 1547 which did Jülich as much damage as the Great Fire of 1666 did in London. The Jülich fire of 1547 gave the citizens an opportunity to rebuild their city in an ideal way using the beautiful Renaissance style under the guidance of Alessandro Pasqualini. The outstanding French military engineer Sébastien le Prestre de Vauban evaluated Jülich as excellent. The city was part of the French Empire from 1794 until 1814, and the name was changed to Juliers. It later became Prussian.

Jülich featured prominently in the Second World War, when despite the wholesale destruction of the city in an Allied bombing raid it was still able to put up massive resistance to the Allies in 1945. Because it went through so many wars and changes of ownership from Roman times until the twentieth century, Jülich's wealthy citizens would have had every reason for concealing gold and precious metals. The devastating bomb damage and subsequent rebuilding after the Second World War might well have covered many earlier treasures that still have to be rediscovered. Its nearness to Niederzier, where so much valuable old Iron Age treasure was recovered, also makes Jülich a likely treasure site, and its aptly named Witchtower, or *Hexenturm* in German, is an indicator of the eerie mysteries that were associated with the city in medieval times. The treasure of the famous Red Maidens of Diewin (the modern city of Magdeburg, Germany) was lost at some period during the eighth century and has never been discovered. The leader of the warriors known

Witchtower or Hexenturm *at Jülich.*

as the Red Maidens was Wlasta, who had served as captain of the all-female guard of Queen Libussa, the founder of Prague. When Queen Libussa died, however, Wlasta and her soldiers refused to serve the king. They captured Mount Widowle and defended their fortress there for some years before moving to Diewin (a name meaning "castle of the maidens"). From here they overran the lands around them and imposed taxes on the local citizens, producing a great deal of wealth for them.

In 746 the King of Bohemia led a vastly superior force against some of Wlasta's troops who were back in the Widowle area, where he took them by surprise and killed over a hundred of her fearless warriors. Wlasta herself, and her remaining troops, were in their castle of Diewin when news of the disaster reached them. They buried their substantial treasure of gold, silver, and gems somewhere in or near Diewin and then rode out fearlessly on what they knew would be their last, suicidal battle. None of them surrendered. None of them turned back. None of them survived. The secret of their treasure's location died with the last of them. It has lain in its undiscovered hiding place for nearly thirteen centuries.

In medieval Britain, it may be deduced that a considerable amount of ancient grave robbing took place because it was then the custom for a priest to recite a special prayer over any valuable object retrieved from an old pagan burial site. In broad outline the prayer asked for God's power to cleanse the heathen object so that it could be safely "used by the faithful throughout both time and eternity." To the medieval British mind, the tumuli left by earlier peoples had connotations of golden treasure, and this led to frequent desecrations. Inevitably, the monarchy intervened and a law was passed to the effect that anything that was dug up belonged to the sovereign. Royal licences were issued accordingly to those who were favoured with permission to dig. One such licensee was Sir Robert Beaupel, who worked on a number of barrows in his home area of Devon in 1324.

Licensed grave robbers like Sir Robert seem to have been in the minority, however. No fear of the king nor of the supernatural powers of the pagan dead interred in the tumuli discouraged the "hill-diggers," as they were called in medieval times. An interesting example comes from the British parish of Dean, which is divided into Upper and Lower

Dean and stands on the borders of three English counties: Bedfordshire, Huntingdonshire, and Northamptonshire. Upper Dean stands beside a small tributary of the River Ivel. Lower Dean, a kilometre to the north, is on the banks of the River Til. Such well-watered and fertile sites would have been favoured by the earliest prehistoric British settlers. Dean also has two historic windmills. In December 1312 there was a treasure trove inquiry in Dean concerning money "found under the ground" and carried away illegally by Alexander de Wotton, who was released from jail in 1315.

Dean will be of considerable interest to twenty-first-century treasure hunters not only because of these early fourteenth-century exploits but also because as recently as June 1875 a coroner's treasure trove inquest was held as part of nineteenth-century British law. The treasure involved approximately thirty copper coins, half a dozen silver coins, and ten or twelve pieces of gold that were found when an old farmhouse was demolished. Dates on the coins ranged from 1685 to 1734.

Other ruins, those of Old Basing House in Old Basing near Basingstoke in Hampshire, England, may well cover the hiding place of the treasure said to have been buried there by John Paulet, the fifth marquis of Winchester. The house and the village of Old Basing have a very long history, taking their name from a Saxon war leader named Basa who settled there centuries ago with his tribe, known as the Basingas.

At nearby Lychpit lie the bodies of those who died in a gruesome battle between Alfred (849–899) and the Danes, which was fought before Alfred became king. Alfred is also associated with hidden treasure known as Alfred's Jewel. This beautiful and very valuable artifact was found at Athelney in Somerset towards the close of the seventeenth century. It is the decorated top of an aestal, a pointer that scholars used when reading in Anglo-Saxon times. One side of Alfred's Jewel shows a personification of sight: the abstract quality is represented as the image of a keen-sighted person. On the other side is a pattern showing foliage, which is based on a European Carolingian design. All around the edge is the inscription "Alfred ordered me to be created." The aestal was almost certainly a gift from the king to one of the churches in Wessex or to one of his bishops. As well as once pointing to words to assist a scholarly reader, the aestal now points unerringly to Athelney as a very interesting location for the modern treasure hunter.

Returning to the treasure sites at Old Basing, there was a Norman castle there before the Tudor mansion was built. The Paulet family were staunchly loyal to Charles I, and despite their gallant defence, the fortified mansion was eventually lost to a Roundhead attack in 1645. As in so many other military situations where stubborn — but realistic — defenders know that the end will come eventually, there is a strong possibility that the Marquis of Winchester hid his valuables in or near Old Basing House before they could fall into the hands of the Parliamentarians. There is every likelihood that some at least of his treasure still waits to be discovered there below the ruins.

Cumbria in the United Kingdom is another interesting location for treasure hunters. This area to the north of the famous Lake District is close to Hadrian's Wall, which ensures that many Roman discoveries have been made in the region. An interesting example of treasure connected with Hadrian's Wall and the Roman occupation of Britain is known as Draco's Bowl. In a valley beside the River Manifold in Staffordshire, not many kilometres from Stoke-on-Trent, Kevin Blackburn discovered Draco's Bowl with his metal detector. Scarcely half a metre below the surface, the small bronze bowl was beautifully decorated and bore a Roman inscription. It had apparently been made at the request of a Roman soldier of Greek origin named Draco, who had served on Hadrian's Wall before retiring to Staffordshire and taking his souvenir bowl with him. The historical interest of the little bronze bowl gave it its enormous value of £100,000, although it was not made of precious metal and contained no gems.

There are undoubtedly many more similar items waiting to be retrieved. The Vikings were also active in this area not far from Hadrian's Wall, and treasure that was originally theirs was discovered at Cumwhitton. The cremated remains of half a dozen Vikings, both male and female, were found there complete with their swords, spears, fire-starting kit, and jewellery. A similar Viking cemetery was unearthed at Ingleby to the east of Cumwhitton, and these two sites are thought to be the oldest such Viking burial grounds in the United Kingdom.

Other Viking treasures were found well over a hundred kilometres away at Barney in Norfolk in East Anglia. In 1815 a Viking shield, some valuable coins, and a golden torque were found there.

Fifty kilometres from Cumwhitton and Ingleby in the churchyard of St. James at Great Ormside another interesting find was made during the nineteenth century. This took the form of a silver and bronze vessel known as the Ormside Bowl, which is now on view in York Museum. The village of Great Ormside was named after a Viking warrior called Orm who settled there with his people. The Viking presence in these locations is a valuable clue to the existence of treasure that still waits to be discovered. One of the most significant Viking treasures yet discovered is known as the Harrogate Hoard; it was found in a field near the town of Harrogate in North Yorkshire, England, by a father and son metal detector team, David and Andrew Whelan. There were more than six hundred coins and other gold and silver items dating back to the tenth century, some of which had come from France, Germany, Ireland, and Samarkand, which is now part of Uzbekistan. Other items had originated in North Africa, Russia, Afghanistan, and Scandinavia. These widespread sources of the Viking hoard provide evidence of how far those old sea-raiders had travelled, raided, and traded during their zenith. The careful burial of the hoard inside protective lead casing would seem to suggest that it had been hidden there by some wealthy Viking commander at the time when the Viking kingdom of Northumbria had been under attack from the Anglo-Saxons. Athelstan (895–939) had then held sway over a unified English kingdom, but Northumbria became Viking territory again after his death, and remained so until the assassination of Eric Bloodaxe, Viking King of York, in 954. The area around Harrogate would therefore seem to be of considerable interest to contemporary treasure hunters.

Mountfield in Sussex in the United Kingdom is a small village between Robertsbridge and Battle. Its earlier names over the centuries have included Moundifeld and Mundfield. It is old enough to be mentioned in the Domesday Book, where there is said to be enough land in the manor to occupy eight ploughs (six of which were operated by serfs and two by the manor house staff). William Butcher, a local farmer, turned up a number of yellow metal items when he was ploughing his fields in 1863. He assumed they were only brass or copper and sold them as scrap to a local ironmonger, who recognized them as gold but kept quiet about their source because of the nineteenth-century treasure trove laws. He melted them down discreetly and disposed of them as bullion. Only two very small pieces survived, and these eventually found their way to the British Museum. If William's field held golden treasure of that magnitude in the nineteenth century, what still remains to be turned up by a modern treasure hunter using the right equipment?

St. Cuthbert (634–687) was an Anglo-Saxon monk and bishop who lived and worked in the kingdom of Northumbria. When he died at Lindisfarne he was buried there with his ceremonial cross and various religious treasures, including the sacred vessels from the altar. When the Danes raided Lindisfarne a century after Cuthbert's death, his devoted monks made their escape — taking his body and its accompanying sacred treasures with them. For more than three centuries, the timeless adage relating treasure to war and civil unrest held good. Time after time the monks fled with St. Cuthbert's body and valuables. In 1104, however, a permanent resting place was found for Cuthbert and the religious treasures in Durham's cathedral abbey. For close to four hundred years they rested there, until Henry VIII's minions arrived in 1537 to disturb them yet again. One set of evidence suggested that Henry's men had removed everything of value and desecrated Cuthbert's tomb. A different tradition credited the faithful and courageous monks with moving Cuthbert yet again to some unknown place of safety beyond the reach of Henry's accomplices. This second theory was verified in 1827 when work below the cathedral unearthed a carefully protected concealed grave containing three coffins one inside the other. The innermost casket contained the head of St. Oswald (604–642) as well as St. Cuthbert's remains, a small silver altar, and his ceremonial cross made from garnet and gold along with other religious treasures.

St. Cuthbert's story provides a typical example of the lengths that devout worshippers would go to in order to preserve their holy relics and religious treasures. When early British Christians were being harassed, as they often were by Vikings, Danes, and other marauders, it is highly likely that some religious relics and their accompanying treasures would have been hastily concealed in shallow earth, in caves, or under lakes and rivers. The thoughtful treasure hunter who takes the trouble to trace the likely paths of such early religious refugees may well discover those lost relics.

Of all the possible sites of mysterious undiscovered treasure in Europe, Rome has a strong right to first place. Rome can justifiably claim to be one of the world's oldest cities, and as such is built over labyrinths of ancient sewers, tunnels, vaults, and catacombs.

Recent excavations in connection with Rome's underground railway system have revealed many possible sources of undiscovered treasure. A relatively short distance below modern ground level, the diggers found the remains of Renaissance buildings that had been demolished barely 150 years ago. Going deeper than the Renaissance ruins, they found a length of the medieval Via Flamina, a centuries-old road that had once been an important route across the city. Going deeper still revealed a characteristic eighth-century herringbone-patterned pavement. A sixth-century copper processing plant was unearthed beneath the Piazza Venezia. The workers there from fifteen hundred years ago had used small ovens to process the copper ores and alloys, and the archaeologists discovered copper ingots on the site. It is possible that the copper factory worked with other, rarer metals — perhaps even some gold and silver were processed there. The region near the plant would be a promising site for twenty-first-century treasure hunters.

Other discoveries that intrigued the archaeologists were numerous sixteenth-century remains, including a Renaissance palace. The diggers also unearthed an ancient Roman tavern and a kitchen from the Middle Ages that still held its original cooking utensils. These digs have shown clearly that there is still a great deal of untouched ancient material below the modern city, and much of it may be extremely valuable.

Another item of great interest to the treasure hunter is the recent discovery of the original beach near Sandwich in Kent, England, on which the Roman invaders landed in AD 43. Because of changes in the coastline over the past two thousand years, the exact site of the beach on which they landed had become lost. Archaeologists rediscovered it in 2008, nearly three kilometres from what is now the coast. Such sites are naturally of great interest to treasure hunters. Almost anything could have been abandoned, or buried in a shallow hiding place, when the British who were then in that part of Kent fled from the massive invading army of Rome. A few centuries later, at Mildenhall in Suffolk, it was the Romans who left important treasure behind when they in turn fled from sea raiders, Picts, and other marauders. There were also serious dynastic and religious conflicts rocking the Roman Empire at this time. One of the protagonists was Flavius Claudius Julianus (331–363) who was known disparagingly as Julian the Apostate because of his ill-fated attempts to bring back the old Roman pagan gods. He was the last non-Christian Roman emperor.

This hazardous combination of civil war and increasing numbers of raids on Roman Britain almost certainly prompted the original owner of the Mildenhall treasure to hide it where he thought it would be safe: and so it was for more than sixteen centuries. Then, in 1943, during the darkest days of the Second World War, Gordon Butcher found it while he was ploughing. He informed his employer, Sydney Ford, and the two of them dug out more than thirty ancient objects. The treasure at that stage did not look valuable. Ford thought that the metal was only lead or pewter; in fact, it was ancient Roman silver that had become darkened with age in the soil.

When its real nature was recognized, Ford and Butcher were given a reward of £2,000 and the treasure was transferred to the British Museum in London, where it is still on display. At the time when the Mildenhall wealth must have been originally hidden, a Roman villa had stood near the place where Butcher's plough uncovered the treasure in 1943. It may also have been significant that two very old roads — the Icknield Way and the Peddars Way — connected East Anglia with the rest of Roman Britain. Rivers through East Anglia led to the sea, and across that sea lay the mainland of Europe and eventually Rome itself. There is a theory that the treasure may once have belonged to the Roman General Lupicinus, who had apparently been sent to Britain by Emperor Julian the Apostate to try to suppress the raiders. Failure in this area led to his recall to Rome, where he fell out of favour. Had he buried the Mildenhall treasure before he left Britain in the hope that he would be able to return for it in better times? The Mildenhall area is another very promising location for contemporary treasure hunters.

Cirencester in Gloucestershire, England, is within 160 kilometres of London and is situated on the banks of the River Churn, which is a tributary of the Thames. Cirencester is the largest town in the beautiful, scenic Cotswold Hills, and was known as Corinium in Roman times. Its fame and importance in those days were such that even Ptolemy (Claudius Ptolemaeus, 83–168), the famous Greco-Roman geographer, astronomer, and mathematician, made reference to it in 150. Before its emergence as one of the most important towns in Roman Britain, Cirencester and the area around it was home for Bronze Age people who flourished from approximately 2200 until 800 BC. It was a remarkable hoard of their treasure that Stephen Taylor discovered while using his metal detector on a farm near Cirencester in 2004. The hoard consisted of almost sixty separate pieces including golden rings and bracelets, as well as bronze artifacts. The area around Cirencester is likely to yield many more historical objects and items of treasure because of its Roman and Bronze Age heritage.

It isn't always necessary to find a complete hoard of treasure like the items found at Cirencester. Sometimes one object can be worth a fortune by itself, as in the case of a single gold coin bearing the image and inscription of King Coenwulf of Mercia (circa 760–821). In 2001, the coin, known as a *mancus* and weighing only one-fifth of an ounce, was found beside the River Ivel in Bedfordshire. It was later sold for over £350,000.

On other occasions, it is an ancient artifact rather than a coin, precious stones, or articles made from gold and silver that has great historic value. In 2003, when extensions and improvements were being carried out on the A1 motorway not far from the Ferrybridge power station in West Yorkshire, a chariot burial was unearthed. Whoever the dead man might have been, he had clearly enjoyed massive power and influence twenty-five hundred years ago. The work entailed in burying his chariot had been considerable, and a feast to honour the dead leader had left behind it the bones of several hundred cattle. It seems highly improbable that such a feast and so laborious a burial would not have left treasure as well in the vicinity. This is another area that would be of great interest to modern treasure hunters.

In 1992, Eric Lawes discovered what has since become famous as the Hoxne Hoard, named after the Suffolk village in England where it was found. There were in excess of fifteen thousand silver and gold coins, along with jewellery (bracelets, necklaces, and rings), silver cutlery, pepper pots, spoons, and ladles. The dates on the coins made it possible for archaeologists to establish that the hoard had been concealed around 410. Whoever had hidden the treasure there in the first place had originally secreted it in a large wooden chest plus a few smaller containers with delicately made silver padlocks — artifacts that attested to the high level of technology available to Romano-Britons fifteen hundred years ago. Someone or some group had buried their treasure very carefully, as though intending to return for it at some safer time. But this was the period when Roman power was declining in Britain, and the fate of those who buried the Hoxne treasure may have been a grim one.

Romulus and Remus with the wolf.

Another fascinating discovery — this time in Rome itself — was made when work was being done to restore some of the monuments on the Palatine Hill. Layer upon layer in this area goes back as far as simple dwellings dating from the eighth century BC. During this restoration work, a cavity fifteen metres deep was found that led down to a decorated, vaulted cave showing the *lupercale* (associated with the legend that Rome's traditional founders, Romulus and Remus, had been raised by a she-wolf). Other discoveries included some wooden storage chests containing regalia thought to have belonged to the Emperor Maxentius (278–312), who had been decisively defeated by Constantine at the Battle of Milvian Bridge in 312. Maxentius died while trying to swim the Tiber following his defeat. The regalia consisted of lances, javelins, bases for Roman standards, and chalcedony spheres. These are of particular interest to the contemporary treasure hunter because chalcedony occurs in many different forms of semi-precious stones: agate, carnelian, chrysoprase, and heliotrope. Chalcedony in its various forms was widely used in the Mediterranean area in ancient times. It was found within the ancient Minoan Empire, and from the palace at Knossos chalcedony seals more than four thousand years old have been recovered. A characteristic of chalcedony is that hot wax does not adhere to it, which makes it an ideal material for seals. Skilled craftsmen working along the central Asian trade routes also used chalcedony for ring bezels and beads. An awareness of this widespread use of chalcedony from these very early times is helpful for the treasure hunter when identifying precious objects that have been uncovered. Apart from the chalcedony spheres uncovered among Maxentius's regalia, there was a beautifully made sceptre in the shape of a flower, inside of which was a greenish blue sphere. This symbolism may have been intended to represent the empire under the emperor's protection. Although the idea that the Earth was a globe was not part of Roman geography, the symbol of a sphere as all-encompassing could have represented the empire in the sense of its being all-inclusive. Archaeologists who have examined the regalia are of the opinion that it was carefully concealed by loyal followers of Maxentius after his defeat, so that he would not be forgotten.

As well as being renowned for their military might, the Romans were great hedonists. Pleasure was central to the lives of those who were fortunate enough to be able to afford it, and the pleasure city of Pompeii bears witness to that trait in the classical Roman character. Herculaneum, its sister city, was destroyed along with Pompeii when Mount Vesuvius erupted for two terrifying days in August of AD 79. Pumice and volcanic ash from those two traumatic days completely buried the city for the best part of seventeen centuries. This volcanic tragedy was, however, by no means the first to overwhelm the city. Radiocarbon

The ruins of the pleasure city of Pompeii.

dating of debris from the city's earliest times suggests that Pompeii was founded in the eighth century BC, and its original inhabitants were the Oscan people of central Italy. Greek and Phoenician sailors had also been there in its earliest days, and it passed through Etruscan hands as well during its long history. The Samnites had been there as conquerors at one time, but the Roman pavements seem to date from the fourth century BC, when the power of Rome was first asserted in the area. The prosperity that once flourished in Pompeii can be judged from the inscription "*Salve, lucru,*" which translates from the Latin as "Money, welcome." This was apparently connected with two Pompeian business partners named Sirico and Nummianus.

The wealth of the city was also expressed in its buildings and luxurious facilities: an amphitheatre, a swimming pool, an aqueduct, and public baths. There was also a *lupanar*, or brothel, with accommodation for over twenty clients at a time. Further indications of the wealth that existed before the volcanic disaster destroyed the city were found near the harbour, where numerous skeletons were discovered adorned with jewelled rings, bracelets, gold necklaces, and earrings. Abundant quantities of gold and silver coins were also found there. From the modern treasure hunter's point of view, the areas around Herculaneum and Pompeii could prove extremely rewarding. The numerous wars and conquests throughout Pompeii's history would stimulate hiding treasure; the frequent volcanic disturbances and damage to the city over the centuries would suggest that many valuable items such as gems, gold, and silver were likely to have been covered by the successive disasters.

Just as Roman power and affluence were characterized in the pleasure cities of Herculaneum and Pompeii, so too was it prominent in Toledo, Spain, where they established a large settlement. Wherever Rome went wealth and money went too, and Toledo was no exception. With the Visigothic ascendancy that came later, Toledo became capital of their empire because of the pronounced strategic advantages that came from its awesome rock foundation. Those strategic advantages were essential to the city throughout the many grim battles that were fought there.

In 712, Toledo became part of the Muslim Empire: more wealth and eastern knowledge flowed into the city. During a time of peace and stability, Toledo was regarded as a city of three cultures: Muslims, Jews, and Christians lived tranquilly together in a society that showed mutual respect and tolerance. The deplorable tragedy of the Spanish Inquisition eventually dismantled that enviable tripartite understanding. The period of peace, however, was a time of great prosperity, when wealth was accumulated — and when religious trouble eventually ruined that equilibrium, treasure was undoubtedly hidden by those being persecuted. The wealth of Toledo during the thirteenth, fourteenth, and fifteenth centuries expressed itself in the building of the vast cathedral, a Gothic architectural masterpiece that was finally completed in 1493, just one year after Columbus made his epic voyage to America. It was also demonstrated by building the huge fortress of Alcazar. There can be little doubt that much of the wealth of Toledo, accumulated over many centuries, was changed into gold, silver, and gems, and that many of these treasures still lie buried there waiting to be unearthed by skilful modern treasure hunters.

From the warmth of Toledo in Spain, a few hundred kilometres will take the determined treasure hunter to explore Leeds Castle near

Leeds Castle in Kent.

Maidstone, Kent, in southeastern England. Leeds Castle is old enough to be listed in the Domesday Book, and it began its long history as a Norman stronghold in the eleventh century. One vital defensive feature of the castle is that it is built on an island on what has since become a picturesque lake (which, in times of trouble, provided an additional defence for the castle's garrison). One of the most interesting features of Leeds Castle is the deep storage cellar dating from Norman times. It also had the advantage from the garrison's point of view of providing access to the water outside: an escape route in emergency, and a means of launching an unexpected sally against a besieging enemy. If fugitives were using the cellars as an escape route, what would be more natural than for treasure to be concealed there pending their return in better times? Several attempts to find extensions to the known cellars have been made without success, but archaeologists believe that further

Barrels in the cellars of Leeds Castle.

cellars once existed. Does a secret access route from the known cellars still lead to one or more of these hidden subterranean chambers? Or were there alcoves there once, later covered over and hidden behind the ponderous barrels?

Leeds Castle was a favourite resort of the devious and cunning Henry VIII (1491–1547), who might well have decided that a secret store of easily portable wealth would be an advantage and that Leeds Castle would be an ideal location for it. It was also a tradition for Leeds Castle to become the property of the queen of England in her own right. Edward I and his queen, Eleanor (daughter of King Ferdinand III of Castile), used the castle as a base for resting and hunting. Eleanor died in 1290, and Edward married Margaret (sister of King Phillip III of France). The royal couple spent their honeymoon in Leeds Castle, and Margaret lived on there after Edward's death in 1307 until she herself died in 1318. There were major problems at Leeds Castle during the time of Edward II (1284–1327). He was married to Isabella, daughter of Philip IV of France, the monarch who was notorious for his treacherous attack on the courageous and noble Templars in 1307. Without telling Isabella, Edward II gave Leeds Castle to Bartholomew, the first Lord Badlesmere, who held the rank of Steward of the Household. In 1321, Isabella arrived at the castle in search of accommodation. To her amazement and great anger, Badlesmere's men fired at her escort, killing some of them. The notoriously weak and ineffective Edward II acted with uncharacteristic power and decisiveness on this occasion. He stormed Leeds Castle despite all its defences and beheaded Badlesmere. Although Edward II was deposed and seemingly murdered in 1327, Isabella kept Leeds Castle until her death in 1358. Richard II (1367–1400) kept up the tradition by granting Leeds castle to his queen, Anne of Bohemia, in 1382. She retained it until her death in 1394.

This practice of granting Leeds Castle to the English queen may have created situations in which the queen, or some wealthy member of her household, felt it advisable to conceal private treasure there. The castle still contains a number of very interesting treasure chests dating from these early periods. The question arises as to whether others are still hidden in secret rooms or buried in the extensive grounds around the lake.

Treasure chest in Leeds Castle.

Another magnificent castle dating from Norman times is situated at Rockingham, not far from Market Harborough in Leicestershire, England. The original Norman motte and bailey structure was erected between 1068 and 1071 on an ideal hilltop site that commanded an extensive view. Throughout the twelfth century, various kings came to Rockingham, and Richard the Lionheart (1157–1199) entertained the Scottish monarch here. Rockingham was a particular favourite with King John (1167–1216), who enjoyed hunting in that area. There are numerous local traditions that King John's treasure was buried at Rockingham, rather than being lost in the waters of the Wash in East Anglia. There is an account to the effect that a lady who lived at Rockingham in relatively recent times was psychic and dreamed that John's spirit had visited her and pointed out the location of his missing treasure. Accordingly, she arranged to have that location excavated. A few coins and ancient artifacts, including arrowheads, were unearthed there — but there was no sign of John's semi-legendary lost jewels. An ancient iron treasure chest with multiple locks is still preserved in the castle, and is traditionally linked with King John. There was a major siege at Rockingham in 1219, when Henry III was forced to recapture his castle from a rebellious Constable. Numerous

The location of the treasure as pointed out in the psychic dream.

The treasure chest at Rockingham associated with King John.

major repairs were required after this siege, and these were continued by his son Edward I (1239–1307), who had special extensions built for his queen, Eleanor of Castile. Edward III (1312–1377) undertook further repairs and modifications. The last king to use Rockingham was Henry V (1386–1422). It was in such a state of disrepair by the closing years of the fifteenth century, however, that Henry VII (1457–1509) had a hunting lodge built nearby rather than use the castle itself. In the mid-sixteenth century, Rockingham was leased to Edward Watson, who began the lengthy and exacting work of transforming the derelict castle into an attractive Tudor home. It took from 1553 until 1584 to complete the work. In 1619, Edward's grandson, Sir Lewis Watson, bought the castle from King James I (1566–1625) and carried out more renovations and improvements. It was heartbreaking when all the good work that had taken place since 1553 was largely destroyed by the civil war between the Royalists and the Parliamentarians. In 1643 Lord Grey of Groby led a successful Parliamentary attack, captured

Rockingham Castle, and held it stubbornly against all the Royalist counterattacks that followed.

The castle and grounds as they stand today are most interesting and attractive, and the friendly helpfulness of the guides and other staff make a visit to Rockingham an ideal day out — as well as a wonderful source of historical information for the treasure hunter.

For example, there may well be more than a grain or two of truth in the psychic episode concerning King John's treasure being concealed at Rockingham, and there are other antique treasure chests and storage boxes to be seen in the castle — each of which could tell a remarkable story. Of major interest to the treasure hunter is what became of the *contents* of those treasure chests?

Moving from Britain to Portugal, the serious treasure seeker needs to spend time in Sintra, which richly deserves its world heritage status. Experts have described the palatial castles there as not only the pride of Portugal but of Europe as a whole. Memories of the great events of history seem to shelter peacefully behind every garden wall there. As well as this deep sense of being within a hand's breadth of the past, there is also an atmosphere of romance and adventure in Sintra. It certainly inspired Hans Christian Anderson, and Byron described Sintra as his Eden. The two vast white chimneys of the Palacio Nacional make it an unmistakable landmark, and it functioned as a royal palace until the start of the twentieth century. The building was originally constructed for Moorish sultans, but its later additions were architecturally Gothic and Manueline. This latter style is sometimes called Late Gothic, and it reflects the discoveries made by fearless navigators including Vasco da Gama and Pedro Álvares Cabral.

Seaborne trade brings wealth, and the wealth that the Portuguese merchants created from the very profitable spice trade with India and Africa was frequently turned into treasure in the form of precious metals and gems. Their riches were also spent on beautiful churches and monasteries in the Manueline style. Francisco de Varnhagen first used the name *Manueline* in the mid-nineteenth century when he described the Jerónimos monastery. He chose the word in honour of King Manuel I (1469–1521), who reigned from 1495 until his death, during which time the style was developed. The Manueline style went far beyond architecture alone. Its designs were strongly influenced by buildings and artifacts that the dauntless Portuguese navigators had seen in India and other distant places. Of greatest interest to the modern treasure hunter is the way in which this Manueline design featured on works of art that were made from precious metals.

Also of considerable interest to treasure hunters is the Room of Swans in the great Palacio Nacional. The octagonal ceiling in this chamber is decorated with paintings of these beautiful birds. Another fascinating room from the modern code-breaking treasure hunter's point of view is the Room of the Magpies, which takes its name from the many paintings of those birds that it contains. There are two legends associated with magpies: the first is that they chatter and gossip irrepressibly and irresponsibly; the second is their love of treasure. They are said to pick up bright objects — especially gold and silver coins and sparkling gems — and vanish with them. The precise position of a swan or magpie in a large picture (the arrangement of its wings, head, and feet) can indicate one particular letter of a cipher, just as the position of the signaller's flags indicates a letter in semaphore. If the swans are indicative of water — thus giving secret directions relating to rivers, lakes, seas, and oceans — so the magpies can, perhaps, reveal what type of treasure is hidden and where it is buried. The popular explanation concerning the magpies — a story that may well have originated in order to divert attention from their possible use as a clue to the location of treasure — is that King João I had been seen kissing one of the courtiers and this had triggered a tide of scandalous palace gossip. The magpies thus represented the gossiping, bird-brained courtiers.

Another building that will attract the attention of serious modern treasure hunters with an interest in semiology is the Palacio da Pena. It was erected in the nineteenth century under the orders of Ferdinand de Saxe-Coburg-Gotha, the German husband of Queen Maria II (1819–1853). The designs are full of romanticism, whimsy, and fantasy. There are strange pink and yellow towers, drawbridges, sculptures, and domes that make the visitor think of imaginary kingdoms in Arthurian legends. The interior remains much as it was during the royal occupancy of

Queen Amélia (1865–1951). There was a great deal of unrest and political disturbance in Portugal during the later years of her reign, and it is possible that she would have deemed it prudent to hide portable treasure in the form of precious metals and gems. The Palacio da Pena could possibly reveal a great deal of information that would be of much interest to the contemporary treasure hunter.

Another Portuguese location that is of special interest to the modern treasure researcher is the Quinta da Regaleira. This intriguing building enjoys world heritage status. It is hidden amidst dense forest and has a weird atmosphere. Its peculiar turrets and general architectural unexpectedness give it a strange air of mystery. There are curious subterranean grottoes here, and two mysterious wells. One of these is almost sixty metres deep and is equipped with corkscrew-like stone steps. Many parts of Quinta da Regaleira are filled with secret Masonic and Templar signs and symbols. These markings make it a particularly interesting site for treasure hunters — especially those with a basic knowledge of their interpretation.

There is substantial evidence for the theory that the noble and courageous Templars escaping from France after the treachery of the odious Philip IV on Friday, October 13, 1307, found refuge and help in Scotland and the Orkneys — and Scotland is not without its share of the Templar legacy today. Rosslyn Chapel near Edinburgh has a very controversial history, but a number of serious and objective academic researchers, including Tim Wallace Murphy, Christopher Knight, and Robert Lomas, have concluded that some genuine mysteries are to be found there.

There are remarkable similarities between the design of Rosslyn and the design of Herod's Temple in Jerusalem, the temple that was there in the first century during the time of Christ. This raises the whole intriguing question of what the Templars were *really* doing in Jerusalem. Did they find other clues to Solomon's wealth?

Recent archaeological research work south of the Dead Sea in Khirbat en-Nahas (which translates from Arabic as "copper ruins") has shown that ancient copper mines in southern Jordan were being worked during King Solomon's reign. In his day the area was known as

Rosslyn Chapel near Edinburgh.

Carving of Templar Knight in Rosslyn.

Thirteenth Century Templar Tomb in Rosslyn.

the kingdom of Edom. Was that copper ore one source of Solomon's vast wealth in addition to whatever came out of his legendary gold mines?

The First Crusade had led to the capture of Jerusalem in 1099, and in 1119 Hugues de Payens and Godfrey de Saint-Omer set about establishing the group that was destined to become the Knights Templar. Baldwin II, who was then king of Jerusalem, allocated them space for the new order on Temple Mount in the Al Aqsa Mosque, which was traditionally believed to stand above the mysterious ruins of Solomon's Temple and whatever ancient treasure secrets might lie below it.

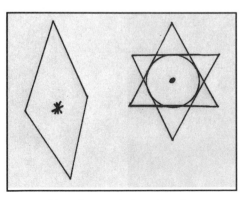

Templar symbols at Rosslyn.

With fewer than a dozen knights in these earliest days, it seems improbable that the Templars were really there to protect the vulnerable pilgrims who were heading for Jerusalem. There were many dangerous bandits in the area, and undoubtedly the fearless and combat-proficient Templars made short work of those whom they encountered molesting defenceless pilgrims — but there seem to have been other motives for the order's existence in the vicinity of Solomon's Temple. Nineteenth-century investigations indicated that there were deep excavations below what had once been the Templar headquarters in Jerusalem, and this has suggested to many researchers that the original Templars had access to secret information concerning the location of buried treasure.

One of the most probable explanations may involve what were known as the Rex Deus families. These were a group of wealthy and knowledgeable Jewish leaders who secretly buried priceless relics and precious artifacts in the area near the temple before escaping from Palestine during the first century AD. One hypothesis is that having reached Europe safely, some of these Rex Deus families intermarried with European aristocracy and royalty. The closely guarded secrets of the exact locations of the buried treasure were passed down these noble European families in the strictest confidence.

Was King Baldwin II himself in on the secret? It is said that after Baldwin's death in 1131, the Templars sent several boxes of treasure to Rosslyn Castle, and that these were eventually transferred to Rosslyn Chapel. What was in those boxes, and where are they now? The Rosslyn area is of great interest to modern treasure hunters.

A number of traditional treasure hunting legends refer to monstrous guardians of hidden hoards, and this certainly seems to be the case with another Scottish treasure mystery: the Jacobite gold hidden in or near Loch Arkaig. The loch is about 46 metres above sea level, 19 kilometres long, and 90 metres deep. Sightings describe the Loch Arkaig monster as being very similar to the more widely known Loch Ness monster: a creature with a long neck, a large body, and flippers. Cryptozoologists have suggested that both belong to the same species and that there may even be deep underwater tunnels connecting the two lochs.

Prince Charles Edward Stuart, known as Bonnie Prince Charlie, arrived in Scotland in 1745 to claim the thrones of England, Ireland, and Scotland. Financially, he was generously supported by Spain to the tune of four hundred thousand gold livres a month to finance his Jacobite army. These coins were also known as Louis d'ors. When seven boxes of Spanish gold arrived in Scotland for the prince's use in 1746, he had already been heavily defeated at the tragic and gruesome battle of Culloden. Most of the gold coins were hidden near Loch Arkaig, and amid various disputes among the surviving Jacobites, several gold coins were distributed while the rest remained hidden. According to some records, a few French coins were found buried in the woods not far from Loch Arkaig, but the rest of that substantial hoard is unaccounted for. The woods around the loch are, therefore, of great interest to contemporary treasure hunters.

Well to the south of Scotland lies Cuerdale, by the banks of the River Ribble near Preston in Lancashire, England. On May 15, 1840, workmen were carrying out repair work on an embankment beside the Ribble when they discovered a lead box containing thousands of precious items. The treasure went first to Queen Victoria and then to the British Museum. A fascinating sidelight on the Cuerdale Hoard was the ancient tradition (details of which were included in Joseph Kenyon's Report to the Royal Numismatic Society in 1841) that anyone who stood on the south bank of the Ribble at Walton le Dale and looked towards Ribchester would be "in sight of the greatest treasure in England." Kenyon added that no one knew how old that tradition was, nor what form the treasure might take. Subsequent detailed examination of the hoard by experts revealed that it had almost certainly been concealed early in the tenth century, and was very probably Viking in origin. Two basic facts of value to contemporary treasure hunters can be associated with the Cuerdale Hoard. The first is that it is very much in the serious treasure hunter's interest to pay careful attention to myths, rumours, and legends when these refer to treasure. Folklorists will agree that tales handed down by word of mouth from generation to generation may survive for many centuries: *someone* eleven hundred years ago knew about the Cuerdale Hoard and roughly where it was located. The second is that the banks of the Ribble in the Cuerdale area may well repay further careful investigation.

Just as there are legends of treasure being guarded by dragons, giant serpents, or strange water-beasts, so there are legends of treasure being associated with witches, wizards, and warlocks. Such legends lead the treasure hunter to examine Chanctonbury Ring in Sussex, and the region around it. Various magical insignia have been found there along with telltale traces of black candle wax. The notorious magician Aleister Crowley (1875–1947) and one of his colleagues, Victor Neuberg, are thought to have performed rituals at Chanctonbury. The ring is also reputedly haunted by an old man with a long white beard and a woman on horseback. An ancient magical coven is believed to meet there regularly, and there is a strange absence of birds in the trees near the ring. In 1866 a number of valuable Anglo-Saxon coins were discovered at Chancton Farm, not far from the ring. When the plough turned up the treasure, it was more or less over the site of Gurth's Barn — although no sign of the ancient barn remained. According to local tradition it was in this very

EXAMPLES OF VIKING RUNES CARVED ON STONE

Viking Runes carved on stone.

area that the old man's ghost was seen. Taking the ghost stories and the magical associations together as useful hints, a modern treasure hunter would do well to pay attention to the area around Chanctonbury Ring.

Another world-famous treasure site with paranormal legends and tales of lost treasure attached to it is to be found at Glastonbury in Somerset, England. Of particular interest to the modern treasure hunter is the tradition that when Henry VIII attacked the monasteries from 1536 to 1541, the monks hid precious items in a secret tunnel connecting the hill known as Glastonbury Tor to Glastonbury Abbey. This tradition is supported by the secret journey of several fearless young monks from Glastonbury at the time of the Dissolution. They had with them an ancient cup — which some enthusiasts believed was the Holy Grail — and to prevent it from falling into Henry's hands they gave it into the keeping of the noble and devout Powell family of Wales, where it became known as the Nanteos Cup. Numerous well-documented healings were associated with it for more than four centuries, and it was featured on co-author Lionel's very popular unsolved mysteries series *Fortean TV* on the UK's Channel 4. If the monks of Glastonbury had been prepared to protect their ancient holy cup, they would also have been prepared to hide other treasures away from Henry's greedy and ruthless minions.

Glastonbury Tor is a centre of great interest for modern treasure hunters. The Tor has what many archaeologists and historians describe as an ancient labyrinth running around it mysteriously from the base all the way up to the ruined St. Michael's Tower at the summit. This dedication to St. Michael is also significant, as it was usually given to churches built over ancient pagan shrines to indicate that the archangel Michael had conquered the old religion. An alternative explanation for the terraces around the Tor is that they were cut there in ancient times for agricultural purposes — but this seems less likely than that they were used for Stone Age rituals of some kind. Glastonbury then holds out three major possibilities for the modern treasure hunter: its enigmatic labyrinth could indicate the repository of something very old and correspondingly valuable; there may be first-century treasures hidden there in accordance with the legends concerning Joseph of Arimathea; or

Glastonbury Tor.

*Co-author Lionel Fanthorpe at the top of the Tor beside
St Michael's Tower.*

the sixteenth-century monks may have successfully concealed priceless things from Henry VIII's marauders.

Just as the Loch Arkaig, Cuerdale, and Chanctonbury treasures were associated with stories of ghosts and monsters, so Glastonbury is associated with very old faerie traditions. It has to be borne in mind that the ancient beliefs in faeries concerned mysterious paranormal beings who were far removed from the Tinker Bell types found in modern children's stories. The faeries associated with Glastonbury Tor and its enigmatic labyrinth inspired fear and awe rather than amusement and entertainment. It may also be worth considering that when smuggling was at its zenith in the eighteenth century, smugglers encouraged local people to believe that the caves and tombs where they hid their contraband goods were haunted or were the dens of monsters. Such beliefs deterred the locals from prying into places where the smugglers did not welcome visitors. Tales of sinister faeries in the Glastonbury labyrinth might perhaps have served a parallel purpose.

Glastonbury also has connections with the King Arthur stories. It is believed to be the same place as Avalon, where the seriously wounded king was taken after his battle against Mordred. In 1190, the monks claimed to have recovered the mortal remains of Arthur and Guinevere in their old cemetery at Glastonbury.

One treasure legend connected with Arthur and the Knights of the Round Table is focused on Merlin, Arthur's court magician. Known in Welsh as Myrddin, Merlin is said to have come from Carmarthen in South Wales. The hill called Bryn Myrddin is only about five kilometres from Carmarthen along the Tywi Valley. Not far from the hill is Merlin's Wood, and close to the wood is Merlin's Stone, where it is rumoured that his vast treasure is still concealed under the earth. Once again, the tradition of mysterious guardians persists. The stone itself, called Cerrig Fyrddin, is one of these traditional guardians, and legend says that it will fall and crush any raider who seeks to take the treasure buried near it. The actual words of the ancient curse refer to "a raven drinking a man's blood" in the vicinity of the stone, should anyone dare to touch the old magician's treasure.

Just as there is often a connection between treasure legends and mysterious supernatural guardians, so there is frequently a nexus between lost treasure and tragedy. The case of the missing treasure of Ann Cargill (1760–1784) is a particularly poignant one. Ann, a beautiful actress and opera singer, was the daughter of a London coal merchant named Brown. She eloped at fifteen and had a series of romantic affairs, the last of which was with Captain John Haldane, who was with the East India Company in 1783. On her way home from India she was aboard a ship called the *Nancy*, which went down off the Scilly Isles in a terrible storm. Ann's drowned body was washed ashore on the tiny, uninhabited island of Rosevear with her beloved baby son still clutched inseparably to her. Before her identity was established, Ann was buried on Rosevear, but once it became known that she was the famous opera star, she was exhumed and reburied at Old Town Church on St. Mary's. Her treasure — a vast sum in gold and gems — went down aboard the *Nancy*. Dauntless and persistent divers Todd Stevens and Ed Cummings discovered some of the remains of the *Nancy* on the seabed not far from the Scilly Isles, but Ann's lost treasure is down there still.

A century after Ann's tragic death, the men who were constructing the Bishop Rock lighthouse were living on Rosevear. Many of them reported hearing a beautiful woman's voice singing a lullaby, as though Ann's spirit was still haunting the island, caring for her baby son and guarding her lost treasure.

Chapter Six
More European Treasure

P oland offers many opportunities to the resourceful contemporary treasure hunter. As far back as the tenth century AD, hoards of silver were accumulated around Szczecin, Wolin, and Kamien. Many of them contained exclusively Arabian coins, which historians believe had made their way to Poland via Sweden. From the second half of the tenth century, the area around the Oder River came under Polish control, and attacks were made from there on the profitable long-distance trade from the Baltic. When merchants using these routes realized what was happening, they concealed their treasure; much of it must still lie there undiscovered.

Around this period, Gniezno became an important power centre. Understandably, the comparative security that it offered attracted masses of silver that had been collected by the local warrior aristocracy. As the tides of power swept first one way and then another in those turbulent times, much of that precious silver was hidden in various ways.

Among the many other problems troubling the area at that period was piracy, and treasure hunting buccaneers from Prussia and Scandinavia were much in evidence. The last of the Arabian silver in the district can be dated to the close of the tenth century, when it was replaced by coinage from the west. Hoards have been found from the early eleventh century containing Danish coins from Haithabu, as well as coins from Ireland and England. The English money likely originated as *Danegeld* (the taxes that the Danes imposed on the peoples whom they raided). Expert numismatists have suggested that the Polish coins minted by Boleslas the Brave (967–1025) were based on the design of a coin minted by Ethelred II of Britain (968–1016). In the course of moving the money from one location to another, there are strong suspicions that some items that were reported as lost were actually hidden by the couriers who had been entrusted with them. This may have accounted for the different types of coins found in the same hoard: a dishonest courier, feathering his own nest at his master's expense, would siphon off a percentage of the coins he was guarding at any one time and add them to an earlier cache already concealed below ground or in some convenient cavern — another good reason for treasure hunters to show interest in the area today.

A great deal of German money was also being produced at this time. From the second half of the tenth century, silver was discovered in quantity in the Harz Mountains. This newly minted German coinage was frequently traded with the Western Slavs, while Saxon and Frisian coin-makers were also busy minting money at this time. Trade and coinage had reciprocal effects on each other during this era: money encouraged trade, and as trade expanded more money was needed. Furs from the more northern parts of this trading zone came by sea and land and were readily exchanged for silver coins. Knowing that money and other valuables passed regularly along these trade routes, brigands and bandits frequently raided the merchants. In order to minimize the risk of theft, merchants tended to leave as much of their wealth as they could in strongholds and citadels in Poland, Pomerania, and Elba. From time to time, when circumstances were least secure and stable, this wealth would be concealed in places where much of it may still await the attentions of contemporary treasure hunters.

One of the most mysterious treasures of Europe is the Seuso Hoard, which is the centre of a serious ongoing controversy between Lord Northampton and the authorities in Budapest. A legal ruling in the United States in the 1990s found in favour of Lord Northampton, but the Hungarian argument is that the items were found by a Hungarian workman close to Lake Balaton and then smuggled surreptitiously out of the country. The former Yugoslavia and Lebanon have also made claims concerning the rightful ownership of the mysterious Seuso Hoard. An interesting aspect of the various assertions of ownership is that one of the items has the word *Pelso* engraved into it, and Pelso is the ancient Latin name for Lake Balaton, situated in central Hungary.

Another valuable old artifact that closely resembles the items in the Seuso Hoard was undeniably found in Hungary at Polgardi in Mezőföld.

The old town of Polgardi, dating back to at least the thirteenth century (probably much earlier), has approximately six thousand citizens and is the second largest population centre on the road from mysterious old Lake Balaton to Budapest. An important Roman road ran to the north of the site of the present town. Bronze Age treasures, along with Celtic and Roman remains, have been unearthed in the vicinity of that road. The Roman artifacts include a sacrificial table from an old pagan shrine. The Seuso treasure consists of various pieces of silver that were packed inside a bronze bucket dating two centuries later than the pieces themselves. These were thought to have been made during the fourth or fifth centuries. Many archaeologists and historians believe that the Seuso treasure was buried during the seventh century to protect it from Arabian invaders.

The mystery of the discovery of the treasure and the embittered controversy that followed is deepened and made more sinister by the alleged suicide of the young labourer who it was claimed found the Seuso Hoard originally. In one account, he is said to have discovered the treasure during the 1970s and reburied it. Although he appeared to have hanged himself, when his corpse was found in the 1980s there were theories that he had been silenced to prevent the truth of the treasure's origin from coming to light. The matter has never been definitively concluded, but it serves as a stark reminder to the modern treasure hunter that such adventures can be dangerous.

The baroque German castle known as Schloss Moritzburg serves the town of Moritzburg in Saxony, and is located near Dresden. The Moritzburg treasure was located in the forest near the castle during the late 1990s. It had been hidden there for safety before the Russians occupied Dresden at the end of the Second World War. The original owners of the Moritzburg treasure — comprising hundreds of items of jewellery and silver artifacts — were the royal dynasty of Saxony. These superb items included the Basket of Flowers (made from gold, silver, and enamel) and the Cup of the Moor's Head, which was a work of art by Christoph Jamnitzer (1563–1618). Jamnitzer was a highly skilled artist and craftsman whose works are greatly sought-after. He was the grandson of Wenzel Jamnitzer (1507–1585), who was also a renowned goldsmith and etcher. Christoph Jamnitzer's most famous work was the *Neuw Grottessken Buch*, a book of patterns for strange ornaments frequently based on scenes from mythology. The characteristics of his designs enabled experts to identify his work. Many boxes of treasure were hidden in the forest near Schloss Moritzburg in 1945, but only three of them were subsequently unearthed. The others were said to have been taken during the Russian occupation, but it is highly probable that some remained concealed in the depth of the forest and may well be there to this day.

An ancient Roman military establishment at Kaiseraugust in Switzerland was being excavated with a mechanical digger in the early 1960s when a number of interesting artifacts were unearthed. No one at the time, however, realized that the retrieved items were of any value. The weather was cold, and snow had been falling for some time; it covered the objects that had been dug up. Several local people found them, picked them up, and took them home simply as curiosities and souvenirs — not as valuable pieces of treasure. Including the silver candlesticks, spoons, cups, dishes, and a small statue of Venus, there were more than 250 pieces of treasure in the Kaiseraugust hoard with a total weight of nearly forty kilograms. Some were engraved with their owners' names, such as Marcellianus and Romulus, while other pieces carried the names of the craftsmen who had made them and the places where they had been manufactured. These included Pausylypos, a craftsman from Thessalonica in modern-day Greece, and Euticius, who had once worked in Naissus in Serbia.

The Roman fortifications at Kaiseraugust were built beside the banks of the River Rhine during the reign of the Emperor Augustus, and Romans flourished there until the fourth century, when the settlement was finally abandoned because of the threats from fierce Alemannic tribes in the locality. There were further unsettling problems in the area when Magnentius struggled for control of the Roman Empire, being finally defeated in 351, an event that helped expert historians and numismatists to date the treasure. This unrest undoubtedly stimulated people in the area to conceal treasure wherever and whenever they could.

In the late 1990s, an Austrian farmer was ploughing his fields near Freistadt near the border of the Czech Republic, about 140 kilometres northwest of Vienna, when he dug up a box of treasure. Like the Gniezno treasure, which contained coins from many different places, the Freistadt hoard — which seemed to date from the thirteenth century — included coins from Bohemia, Jerusalem, and Britain. In the box, alongside the coins, were several sheets of gold of a type that goldsmiths would have been likely to use for their work. This led historians to suggest that the hoard had once been the property of a Freistadt goldsmith who had buried it for safety when danger threatened the town. Experts from a local museum described the Freistadt treasures as the biggest collection of jewellery from the late Middle Ages ever to be found in Europe. If one desperate goldsmith found it necessary to hide such a treasure seven centuries ago, the possibility of finding similar hoards in the area around Freistadt is high and has considerable appeal for the contemporary treasure hunter.

King Richard the Lionheart.

The tragic death of King Richard the Lionheart (1157–1199) was linked with a mysterious treasure. The disloyal and disobedient Viscount of Limoges was under siege by Richard's men in the castle known as Châlus-Chabrol. The Lionheart was particularly anxious to capture it because there was said to be a vast treasure hidden inside, and Richard's many wars were expensive to maintain. The siege had been going on for only three days when the king himself came to inspect Châlus-Chabrol, to see where its weaknesses lay and where an attack would be most likely to succeed. Without his armour, Richard moved in perilously close to the castle and received a crossbow bolt in the shoulder, producing a wound that took nearly a fortnight to kill him. Ironically, Richard's intestines are said to be buried in the castle chapel. What became of the fabled treasure is anyone's guess. All or part of it may well have been hidden in, under, or near Châlus-Chabrol, making it a site of great interest to contemporary treasure hunters. Today, the remains of the castle stand in the *commune* of Châlus, which is part of the *département* of Haute-Vienne in France. The castle still dominates the town, although only its circular keep remains from the twelfth century, along with some additions made in the thirteenth century and enlarged in the seventeenth. Châlus-Chabrol guarded the south of Limoges, as well as protecting the main routes between Spain and Paris in one direction and the Atlantic and Mediterranean trade routes in the other. This strategic position adds weight to the idea that there was once a very considerable treasure hidden there.

In 1845, a shepherdess named Louise Forest came upon a golden treasure hoard hidden below a Roman tile marked with a cross at Gourdon, Saône-et-Loire, in Provence, France. There were more than a hundred gold coins dating from the time of the Byzantine emperors Leo I (401–474) and Justin I (450–527). There were also a golden paten and chalice that might have been associated with the Merovingian King Clovis I (466–511), who became a Roman Catholic Christian in 496. The most modern of the coins was dated 524, so the hoard could not have been hidden earlier than that. As so frequently happened in turbulent times, the treasure of Gourdon could well have been hidden when an impending attack was feared. During the sixth century there was a monastery nearby from which the chalice and paten may have been brought for safety during a war that was being waged against the Burgundians. In 524 — which may make that date particularly significant — they were heavily defeated at the Battle of Vézeronce. The chalice is especially interesting historically because its handles represent bird designs with garnet eyes. The paten is also decorated with similar garnets. The bird designs are characteristic of Merovingian, Lombardian, and Gothic art forms, and are powerful symbols in Christian art, which again links the bird-handled golden chalice of Gourdon to Merovingian King Clovis I. The goldfinch, for example, symbolizes Christ's passion; the penetrating sight of the eagle is symbolic of God's loving watch over the world; the sparrow symbolizes God's concern for even the smallest things; while the dove stands for peace and the presence of the Holy Spirit.

Wieringen, which was once a small island formed in around 1200 as the result of heavy successive floods, is now part of the mainland of Holland. It is a place of great interest to treasure hunters because of a Viking hoard of silver discovered there in the mid-1990s. Currently, the Dutch government has suggested making it into an island again. The basic scheme is to turn the Amsteldiepkanaal into a lake, which will be known as Wieringerrandmeer if the plan goes ahead. These proposals make a visit to Wieringen a matter of some urgency for treasure hunters who want to explore the area before the coastline is changed drastically. The Viking treasure of Wieringen turned up in pastureland close to the tiny village of Westerklief and consisted of nearly two kilograms of silver ingots and coins, plus a few jewels. This original find was not an isolated one, however, as several other items of Viking treasure have turned up in Wieringen since that first discovery was made.

The familiar concept of treasure being guarded by monsters and dragons is a recurring theme in the old Icelandic treasure sagas, and many academic historians who specialize in the period have suggested that there is a positive relationship between the Icelandic folklore and myths and the actual historic living conditions of people in that place and time. Although the Icelandic treasure sagas were not written down until well into the thirteenth century, they shed a great deal of light on the way that gold was thought about during the time when the myths were created in the Viking age. Gold had a special role in Viking thought and in the Iron Age in general. It was regarded as something indestructible, something that possessed paranormal power because of its indestructibility. It was not only valuable in a financial sense: it was regarded as magical. Some of the ancient heroes of the sagas seemed to bestow life and personality on their treasured golden objects. They would name them, as though they

Examples of the type of treasure found, now on display in the British Museum.

were naming a much loved horse or falcon. One such piece announces, "I was made by Sigurd." Another inscription reads, "Torvald is my owner." A golden arm ring, which had been affectionately named Draupnir by Odin, highest of the Norse gods, was thought to be capable of giving birth to other rings like itself — as though it were a living entity. The symbolism seems to be that those who understood the nature of trade realized that gold was the seed of more gold if it was used wisely. This was well known in New Testament times when Jesus related the parable of the talents, recorded in Matthew 25:16, which reads, "Then he that had received the five talents went and traded with the same and made them other five talents."

Odin's Draupnir had been created by two dwarfs, Brokkr and his brother Eitri, and it was a general underlying principle of that mythology that these precious, magical golden objects were somehow in a state of what a biologist would call symbiosis with their owners. What was good or bad for the owner was somehow good or bad for the artifact — and vice versa. This idea persisted down a chain of inheritance: what an earlier owner had put into something like a golden armlet could be inherited. A brave warrior's armlet could give the dead warrior's courage and skill to his son. Certain objects could carry luck or good fortune: others carried the shadows of tragedy and disaster. Gold was also seen in those days as the ideal gift from a ruler to his loyal servants: the more richly a man was rewarded, the more likely was he to be loyal.

Strange as it may seem, gold that had been concealed in the ground or hidden in caverns or labyrinths also had a magical ability to bring happiness and success to the family and friends of the man who had hidden it long ago. There was a strange Norse name for this buried treasure: *jardfé* ("a fairy in the Earth").

The island of Gotland featured in many of these interesting old Icelandic Norse treasure sagas. The Gotlanders are known as the Gutar, and the island has been inhabited since time immemorial. The site at Ajvide provides evidence of very early habitation. As trade and commerce developed, so the town of Visby on Gotland became an important business centre and cultural centre: money was amassed there — and in times of war and unrest, treasure was hidden there.

Two Gotlander brothers, Edvin and Arvid Svanborg, recently came across a tenth-century Viking treasure while working on land belonging to their friend Lars Jonsson. Jonsson is a celebrated artist who works mainly on scenes from nature and specializes in ornithology. The treasure that the young brothers uncovered amounted to more than a thousand coins and some bracelets.

Their discovery was reminiscent of a huge find made by farmer Björn Engström, one of the biggest Viking hoards found anywhere in the world. On July 16, 1999, he and a friend came across what has since been called the Spillings hoard, after the name of his farm. The amazing discoveries comprised some fifteen thousand pieces weighing a total of almost ninety kilograms. In addition to the silver coins, bracelets, and other artifacts, bronze relics had also been left at the site. Experts think that the hoard was buried towards the end of the ninth century. The Spillings farm is relatively close to one of Gotland's ancient natural harbours, and it is theorized that the vast wealth buried there was connected with the trade that flourished in the area eleven hundred years ago. The dauntless Viking warriors of the time were also involved in international trade. Just how far they went is attested to by the 1954 discovery of a sixth-century statue of Buddha on the island of Helgo near Stockholm. Viking voyages often took them as far as what was then Constantinople, capital city of the Byzantine Empire. As well as lucrative trade with Byzantium, the Vikings were much sought after by the emperor as soldiers — one Viking warrior being the equivalent of a dozen ordinary fighting men.

Islands like Gotland seem to attract people with treasure to conceal, and the Isle of Man off the west coast of Britain falls into this pattern. World-famous for its motorcycle races and for the strange supernatural tale of Gef the talking mongoose, who appeared in Cashen's Gap near Dalby in 1931, the Isle of Man was also the scene of a huge treasure discovery. This was the Ballaquayle Viking hoard that was found on the outskirts of Douglas at the end of the nineteenth century. The Isle of Man holds out numerous interesting prospects for today's treasure hunters.

Geographers tend to discuss whether St. Ninian's, which is part of the Shetland Islands that lie to the northeast of Scotland, is technically an island or a peninsula. At low tide it is possible to walk there along a connecting strip of gravelly beach known as a tombolo. Because of this convenient access, St. Ninian's has a very long history. The Shetlands have been occupied by Picts, Celts, and Vikings over the millennia. The important treasure hoard at St. Ninian's was actually discovered in 1958 by Douglas Coutts, who was a schoolboy at the time and was helping some archaeologists from Aberdeen University who were conducting a dig on St. Ninian's under the leadership of Professor O'Dell.

They found the site of a very old church, still known to the locals as late as the eighteenth century but subsequently covered over with gale-blown sand. The graveyard of that old church had seemingly still been in use right up into the middle of the nineteenth century. At the time of the visit from the Aberdeen archaeologists, however, the exact location of the ancient church was completely lost. Professor O'Dell's party succeeded in locating its ruins, and on July 4, 1958, young Coutts found a sandstone slab that had been damaged at some time in the past. This was near the arch of the southern chancel. The sandstone slab was engraved with a cross, as though it marked something of importance, and when the slab was removed, the hoard was discovered just below it. Whoever had concealed it there had been in a great hurry. The box containing the precious items had been buried upside down, and the wood from which it had been made had long decayed, apart from a few splinters that identified it as larch.

One very strange object found among the valuable silver artifacts (which included ring chains, collars, bowls, spoons, thimbles, and pieces of sword scabbards) was the jawbone of a porpoise. What did that signify? Did it have some curious religious significance? Similar jawbones have been found from time to time at various sites inscribed with ancient Viking runes. The amazing discovery that young Coutts made on St. Ninian's is a clear indication that the area could prove to be very rewarding for modern treasure hunters.

Other important European treasure hoards were discovered in Zidovar, near Vršac in Serbia, and in the surrounding areas, which are consequently of great interest to modern treasure hunters. The town museum in Vršac has a unique numismatic collection going as far back as 1882. Three very significant finds of bronze coins dating from the fourth century AD amounted to more than three thousand items and were the main motivation for founding the museum in Vršac. From 1894 until 1942, Felix Milleker, the hard-working curator, kept a meticulous record of everything that reached the coin and treasure department of his museum. According to his records, important finds came from all over the area known as South Banat, which is now partly in Serbia and partly in Romania. After the end of the Second World War in 1945, the new curator, Mr. Rašajski, made a particular point of setting up a cooperative and friendly numismatic network with the Vršac citizens. This resulted in many more coins and valuable articles that had been found in the neighbouring fields being brought to the museum and added to the collection. South Banat, where the treasure was systematically found over a long period, lies between the River Danube and the River Tamiš. The earliest coins were discovered in 1861, more than twenty years before the larger discoveries that prompted the establishment of the Vršac museum. Some of the earliest pieces go as far back as the fourth century BC, and there are many Greek and Roman coins that belong to the period ending in the fifth century AD. Medieval coins from the fifth to the fifteenth centuries include Bulgarian, Hungarian, Slavonian, and Serbian money. The collection also contains specimens from the sixteenth to eighteenth centuries, a period during which Banat was part of the Turkish Empire. The Turkish coins in the collection came from this period, as did coins from Italy, Holland, Poland, Austria, and Hungary. Money from the Austro-Hungarian Empire (1867–1918) is also in evidence in the museum, as is a collection of contemporary money. The fact that so many hoards of different sizes have been found locally over many years and brought to the Vršac museum indicates clearly that this is a very promising area for contemporary treasure hunting.

Not far away from Serbia, a treasure with strong Bulgarian connections was discovered in the village of Mala Pereshchepina, thirteen kilometres from Poltava in the Ukraine. As in the case of the St. Ninian's hoard, the Pereshchepina treasure was found by a boy. In 1912, this young shepherd caught his foot on the protruding edge of a partly covered golden vessel and fell into an ancient grave: the burial place of Kuvrat, known as the "father of Bulgaria." He was an interesting and unusual character. Variously called Kubrat and Kurt as well as Kuvrat, his name in all its variations translates as "the wolf." Son of an Avar father and a Bulgar mother, Kuvrat spent much of his childhood as a hostage in Byzantium, where it seems that he learned a great deal. Once freed, he organized an alliance of Bulgars and Avars that became a formidable power known as Onoguria. Kuvrat's equally formidable son, Asparuh, founded the First Bulgarian Empire. Little wonder then that Kuvrat was buried with such riches.

What the young shepherd boy had stumbled across accidentally was carefully excavated and classified by Count Vladimir Alekseyevich Bobrinsky (1868–1927), a greatly respected historian and archaeologist. He completed his description of the finds in Kuvrat's grave in 1914. There were more than eight hundred pieces, including an exceptional *rhyton* (a ceremonial vessel, sometimes in the form of a boar's

Dish with Cretan bull's head.

head, sometimes fashioned like the head of a Cretan bull) from which ritual drinks could be taken or from which libations could be poured beside graves. Other precious objects buried with Kuvrat included his signet ring, many other rings, bracelets, earrings, gold, silver, and gems such as garnets, sapphires, amethysts, and emeralds. The gold and silver together weighed almost eighty kilograms, and included a necklace made from gold coins that had been minted in Byzantium. These dated from between the reigns of the Byzantine emperors Maurice (582–682) and Constans (641–668).

When studying Thracian treasure hoards to learn who buried them, where, and why, it is helpful to remember that Spartacus, the slave-gladiator who almost defeated the Roman Empire, was a Thracian. Few characters in history matched him, and he was typical of his people. Thracians — like Spartans — were primarily warriors, but they were also brilliant craftspeople, and their gold, silver, and jewellery were exquisite. Their delightful pottery and sculpture was on a par with their jewellery. Such a race inevitably accumulated wealth, and sometimes that wealth had to be concealed in the form of buried treasure.

Another highly significant treasure hoard, known as the Preslav treasure, was discovered in a vineyard in Castana, which is barely three kilometres northwest of the city of Veliki Preslav. Nearly two hundred bronze, silver, and gold pieces were found, including Byzantine coins. Several of the gold plates were decorated with pictures of Alexander the Great. Alexander was shown in a flying chariot drawn by griffins. Historians and archaeologists believe that the Preslav hoard was concealed for safety during the unsettled years when first Sviatoslav I of Kiev (942–972) and then Byzantine Emperor John Tzimisces (925–976) attacked and conquered Preslav. Among the Preslav hoard was an exquisite gold necklace adorned with rock crystal and amethysts, which had once been the property of Byzantine Princess Maria Irina, who married Tsar Peter (905–970) in Constantinople in 927. The necklace carries images of water birds, and these were traditional symbols of family happiness, so it seems likely that the necklace was a wedding present for the princess.

Ever since Bram Stoker wrote *Dracula* and placed the sinister count in Transylvania, the area has been associated with vampires, tombs, coffins, and the undead. Of far greater real importance to Transylvania, however, is the treasure of Nagyszentmiklós. The hoard consists of more than twenty medieval gold vessels that were found in Nagyszentmiklós when it was part of the old Habsburg Empire. It is now known as Sânnicolau Mare, in Romania.

The decorations on the Nagyszentmiklós treasure are fascinating, and give the inquiring treasure hunter a number of clues to its origins. To know where treasure was manufactured and by what paths it probably travelled can provide important clues to the location of other similar hoards. The figure of a conqueror pulling a captive along by his hair suggests to experts in art history that the designs may have come originally from central Asia, Persia, or Byzantium. Another extremely interesting item is a bowl with the head of a Cretan bull turned backwards, as though the bull is looking at the contents of the dish.

The Pietroasele treasure hoard of Buzău was also found in Romania in 1837. The villagers uncovered a late-fourth-century Ostrogothic cache consisting of twenty-two pieces. One is a striking eagle-headed *fibula* (a type of Roman brooch that was used for fastening clothing, especially cloaks). Many fibulae are decorated with precious or semi-precious stones. A typical fibula is made of four distinct parts: the hinge, the pin, the spring, and the body. They are also described as having a head and a foot. The head is where the hinge or spring is situated; the foot is where the pin closes. The Pietroasele treasure hoard also included a *patera*, a round dish used for drinking as part of religious rituals. The one in this collection of precious objects is decorated with figures of Gothic gods dressed in traditional Greek costumes. A Gothic goddess is seated in a central position, as though being worshipped by the lesser deities. The village of Pietroasele (whose name translates as "rocky") is famous for its vineyards. The Romans were there at an earlier time, and the remains of a *castra* (a Roman fortification) date from the first century AD. The ruins also include Roman *thermae* (baths) from about the same period. This combination of Roman and Gothic history provides useful clues to an area where treasure hunting is likely to prove successful.

A magnificent treasure was discovered while repairs and renovations were being carried out in Środa Śląska in Poland. The hoard included a superb woman's crown, which may have belonged to Blanche of Valois (1316–1348), wife of Emperor Charles IV (1316–1378). As well as Blanche's crown, the hoard included more than three thousand gold and silver coins, golden pendants, and a number of rings. There was also an exquisite golden clasp decorated with gemstones. Środa Śląska in Poland would be a very interesting site for a modern treasure hunter to explore. There may well be other important medieval hoards below the foundations of recent buildings.

In 1908 in Brussels, Belgium, a vast hoard of nearly 150,000 silver pennies dating from 1265 was discovered. The coins were examined by experts, who found examples minted in Ireland, England, and Scotland as well as various continental countries. Puzzled historians naturally looked for theories that would explain why such a vast hoard had been hidden in Brussels in the thirteenth century and then never taken up again by those who had hidden it. A number of academic researchers suggested that the answer might lie with Richard of Cornwall (1209–1272), the younger brother of Henry III. Richard became Holy Roman Emperor in 1257. The title was awarded by numerous European electors, and three of these were thought to have been Richard's main supporters and the most influential in his election. These three were from the Palatinate, Mainz, and Cologne. Richard is believed to have bought the votes he needed — and he was an exceptionally wealthy man. He is thought to have paid nearly 30,000 marks for their support, and the going rate then was about 150 pennies to the mark. Was the vast hidden treasure at Brussels part of the money that Richard had given to secure his election? If it was, why had it never reached its proper destination? If such a sum could have been hidden for seven hundred years in Brussels, what else awaits the contemporary treasure hunter in and around that part of Belgium?

In considering European treasure hoards, the treasure hunter's chances of success are increased by detailed knowledge of the types of coins that may turn up in Europe and their various dates. One of the first large silver coins in thirteenth-century Europe, for example, was produced by Margaret of Constantinople, Countess of Hainault and Flanders in 1269. These coins weighed 2.5 grams and were known as cavaliers because they showed a knight on horseback on one side. From 1285 onwards, the Tournai Mint produced large quantities of what were known as gros tournois on the orders of the King of France. Local princes such as John I of Brabant and John of Namur tended to imitate these with coins called grooten that were also made of silver. In England in 1279, however, Edward I tried without success to introduce a silver coin weighing 6 grams. These were known as groats, but they were not welcome as currency until the middle of the fourteenth century. An interesting piece of information from these early times comes in the form of the English Pipe Roll of 1178–9. This evidence makes it clear that twenty bezants were equivalent to forty shillings. There were twelve silver pennies to the shilling in those days, so twenty bezants were worth 480 silver pennies. The dinar was used only infrequently, although the gold tari, which was equivalent to a quarter of a dinar, was minted in Sicily for a time. Frederick II successfully launched a gold coin known as an augustale in 1231. These were manufactured in the Messina and Brindisi mints.

Expert historians and numismatists divide the history of money in medieval times into two different eras. The earlier of these two periods — from the seventh to the twelfth centuries — was the age of silver coins, including pfennigs, pennings, deniers, and pennies. With the dawn of the thirteenth century, much larger silver coins came into circulation, including groats and groschen. Gold coins were also circulating widely by then. These changes in currency and coinage reflected the increased prosperity of the merchants and their overlords.

Chapter Seven
Transatlantic Treasure

O ne of the most valuable undiscovered treasures in the Americas is the one associated with the tragic Habsburg Emperor Maximilian I of Mexico (1832–1867), born in Schönbrunn, Vienna, ostensibly as the son of Archduke Franz Karl of Austria and his wife, Princess Sophie of Bavaria. However, there were persistent rumours that Maximilian had really been the child of Napoleon II, son of the redoubtable Napoleon I, and his second wife, Marie Louise of Austria. Certainly, Maximilian did not resemble either of his brothers as far as their physical build went, and he was also exceptionally intelligent. After a brilliantly successful naval career, he married his second cousin, Princess Charlotte of Belgium, also known as Carlota.

Maximilian's tragedy started when the devious and unreliable Emperor Napoleon III of France persuaded him to accept an invitation from a number of Mexican royalists to become their emperor. Napoleon's main motive was that having Maximilian in power in Mexico would ensure that a debt of $15,000,000 owing to France would be paid. On June 24, 1864, Maximilian was duly crowned emperor. He was by nature a good and kindly man and set out to rule his new people as a loving father would care for his children. When the American Civil War ended in 1865, the United States ordered the French out of Mexico in accordance with the Monroe Doctrine. Maximilian sent Carlota back to Europe for safety, where she implored Napoleon III to do something to help her beleaguered husband. The feeble, cowardly, and treacherous emperor did nothing. Carlota became mentally ill from the stress of worrying about her beloved Maximilian.

Without European help, Maximilian was hopelessly outnumbered and fled to Queretaro with a handful of supporters who were still loyal to him. Knowing perfectly well what the outcome of his battle with Juarez, the leader of the Mexican republicans, would be, Maximilian loaded on to wagons all his treasure (consisting of American, Spanish, and Austrian gold and silver) and headed for Galveston, Texas. The plan was apparently to ship it out to Austria and into the safekeeping of Carlota. Texas in 1867 was wild and dangerous, no place to try to take treasure. Some fifteen or twenty loyal Maximilianos, as they were called (including one woman, their leader's daughter), headed for San Antonio on their way to Galveston. They crossed the Texas border successfully not far from Presidio. Then, unfortunately for them, they met a group of ex-Confederate soldiers and told them that the treasure wagons were carrying flour. The Confederates became suspicious when they noticed that the Maximilianos never left their so-called flour wagons unguarded. They soon discovered that the Mexicans were actually carrying treasure, and murdered them somewhere between Castle Gap and Horsehead Crossing on the Pecos River. There was too much treasure for the murderers to transport, so they buried it near the killing ground and then burned the wagons and the bodies of their victims. Their plan was to return for the treasure later.

The leader of the killers according to some accounts was named Bill Murdoch, and he apparently became ill as they travelled east. Leaving him behind, the others pressed on beyond Fort Concho, where they ran into an Apache war party with predictable results. After that encounter, Murdoch was the only man who knew where Maximilian's treasure was buried, and he decided to head for Missouri to see if the notorious James brothers would help him in return for a share of the treasure. On the way, he encountered a number of outlaws wanted for horse theft, and Murdoch was assumed to be one of their gang when the law caught up with them. Dying in jail in Denton, Texas, Murdoch told the doctor who attended him about Maximilian's buried treasure, and even gave him a roughly sketched map of the location. Dr. Black, as he is named in some versions of the story, had a lawyer friend named O'Connor, who tried unsuccessfully to get Murdoch released — but he died in prison. A few years later, when the area had become more law-abiding and settled, O'Connor and Black went in search of Maximilian's treasure. The landscape had apparently changed dramatically since Murdoch was there, or he had lied to them, or they had gone to the wrong place. Unable to relate any of the features from Murdoch's map to the landscape around Castle Gap, Black and O'Connor finally gave up. Not even the burned-out wagons provided a worthwhile clue, as there were too many wagon remains in that area. The district around Castle Gap must still be one of the most interesting places for contemporary treasure hunters. Maximilian's treasure would be a very worthwhile find. A much older and more mysterious treasure is generally described as El Dorado, or Eldorado. Although literally meaning "the golden man," the words became associated with an imaginary *place*, a utopia where gold could easily be obtained.

A great many tragic and unsuccessful attempts were made to locate Eldorado, and the modern treasure hunter can derive a lot of useful information from those abortive attempts. Early in the sixteenth century, a conquistador named Gonzalo Jiménez de Quesada met the Muiscas people who still live in the highlands of Colombia. From them he learned of the custom of covering a king-apparent with adhesive resin and gold dust, taking him out into the middle of Lake Guatavita on a ceremonial boat, and allowing him to plunge in. The water removed the gold dust, and having completed the ceremony the king-apparent was accepted as a full king with all the rights, powers, and privileges that went with that high office. In one version of the legend, courtiers and citizens also flung costly offerings of gold, silver, and gems into the mysterious waters of Lake Guatavita as offerings to the spirit believed to live below the waters. In other versions of the legend, it was the magical wife of the king-apparent who lived at the bottom of Guatavita, and the precious objects thrown into the lake as part of the Eldorado ceremony were intended as presents for her. Whichever version of the ancient Muiscas legends is correct, there would logically seem to be a great quantity of gold dust and precious objects on the floor of the lake, which is situated within an old volcanic crater, only a few kilometres from Bogotá. The mountains and thick vegetation surrounding it make access very difficult. De Quesada exhausted himself in his quest for Eldorado, and finally died in abject poverty in Bogotá.

Ambrosius Dalfinger was in the area from 1531 to 1533, and although he succeeded in acquiring some worthwhile treasures he was killed by hostile locals. Legend suggests that he buried a substantial proportion of what he had discovered; its exact whereabouts remain unknown. George Hohermuth and his companions were there from 1535 until 1538. Hundreds of them died, and Hohermuth himself was irretrievably wrecked by the indescribable hardships of his ill-fated expedition. Sebastian de Belalcázar actually succeeded in reaching Guatavita, but was accused of inhumane conduct and murder. He was duly arrested but died in 1539 on his way back to stand trial in Spain. Nicholas Federmann fared little better. He reached Guatavita on his second attempt, but was tried for embezzlement when he got back to Europe. Conquistador Francisco Pizarro was one of a group who followed the entire course of the mighty River Amazon, but he died in the jungle along with many of his team. Hostile locals drove Philip von Hutton back from the Guatavita area; on returning to the coast he was killed by a competitor. In 1546 Hernán de Quesada not only reached Guatavita but began to search it: there was much understandable speculation about the wrath of the lake goddess when he was killed by a thunderbolt! Pedro de Ursua made a successful trip along the Amazon but was then slaughtered by mutineers in 1561. Nearly twenty years later, Antonio Sepúlveda actually succeeded in draining part of Guatavita in his search for gold. Unable to pay all he owed, he died bankrupt. In 1801, the brilliant German bio-geographer Alexander von Humboldt made accurate scientific observations of Guatavita, which were extremely valuable for later researchers. Bankruptcy was one of the major perils that the treasure hunters faced when they attempted to drain the lake in search of the gold on its bed. It overtook José Paris in 1825, and two different treasure hunting companies in 1901 and 1913. The gold is undoubtedly there — and a lot of it — but is it spread over too wide an area and enmeshed in too much mud to make its recovery economically feasible? Whatever the hardships, dangers, and difficulties, the Lake Guatavita challenge is one that still appeals powerfully to the well-equipped and well-financed contemporary treasure hunter.

Another lost transatlantic treasure — and a particularly mysterious one — was said to have been carried aboard a ship called *El Pensamiento*, which was alleged to have made its way secretly into Leith harbour in

Scotland late in December 1803. She was believed to have been carrying hundreds of millions of pounds' worth of gold, silver, and jewels at today's values, and these were alleged to have been deposited in the Royal Bank of Scotland by the enigmatic Sir Francis Mollison (whose name was also rendered as Mollinson, to add to the mystery). According to some accounts of what the *El Pensamiento* was carrying, there were almost one hundred bags of valuables aboard her. This treasure had been put on board at Lambayeque, a region in the northwest of Peru with an intriguing ancient past involving the pre-Inca Chimú and Moche peoples, as well as the old Lambayeques. (A persistent legend in the area describes a fleet of big, sea-going rafts made from totora reeds that arrived millennia ago in what is now San José Bay. The formidable warriors who manned this fleet were led by a heroic, benign demi-god called Naylamp. A temple simply named Chot was erected to him, and a statue of him was carved from strange green stone resembling emerald. This temple still exists about six kilometres away from the present city of Lambayeque and is currently known as Huaca Chotuna. If, as was customary, treasure was buried with the great leader Naylamp, Huaca Chotuna might be of considerable interest to contemporary treasure hunters. The descendants of Naylamp and his raft borne warriors occupied the area for some time — some may be there still — and were acknowledged at their zenith to be expert goldsmiths and masters of an advanced technology.)

Antonio Pástor de Segura, a colonial officer in Lambayeque, was thought to have been involved with loading the enormous treasure that was destined to land at Leith in 1803. The *El Pensamiento* had two commanders: John Fanning from America and John Doig from Scotland (his surname is also rendered as Doigg in some accounts). There were also alleged to be connections between the *El Pensamiento*'s joint commanders and the redoubtable Captain John Paul Jones (1747–1792). If all three men were cast in the same mould, *El Pensamiento* and her cargo of treasure could not have been in safer or more skilful hands.

An interesting later development in the saga of the missing treasure of Lambayeque occurred in 1965, when the Royal Bank of Scotland was alleged to have been inundated with inquiries from descendants of

Antonia de Segura. According to this branch of the mystery, there was a will in which he had left his heirs the treasure, alleged to be secure in the vaults of the Royal Bank of Scotland. It was also alleged that powerful and influential Masonic lodges were taking an interest on behalf of de Segura's descendants, and this would be compatible with the high Masonic principles of justice and fairness.

If this part of the account is factual and historical, it appears that the bank took the inquiry sufficiently seriously to have all its oldest vaults and secure storerooms checked very carefully for the one hundred containers of the vast Lambayeque treasure that had supposedly been there since 1803. Nothing of it was found.

Historian James Gilhooley, who died recently before being able to complete his proposed book on the Lambayeque hoard and the Royal Bank of Scotland, was of the opinion that the treasure may have been diverted to France.

What is of interest to contemporary treasures is that *something* of enormous value came out of Lambayeque and was ostensibly destined for Leith in Scotland. Whatever else became of it, it failed to reach the vaults of the Royal Bank of Scotland. Where is it now? Was it diverted to France? Or is some of it at least hidden in or near Leith harbour? And what of the other amazing treasures originating in Lambayeque — how many of them are still hidden there?

The lost treasures of the Incas have fascinated archaeologists and treasure hunters alike ever since the arrival of the conquistadores in South America.

The enormous Inca Empire, with its fabulous wealth in gold, began as a tribe in the vicinity of Cuzco, where their first great leader, Manco Capac, founded the empire at the start of the thirteenth century. His dynasty absorbed the neighbouring Andean peoples until by the middle of the fifteenth century Pachacutec (whose name translates roughly as "the earthquake maker") had firmly established what was destined to become the biggest, wealthiest, and most powerful empire in America before the arrival of the Spaniards. Pizarro's invaders made the most of an Incan civil war between two royal brothers and took over most of the Inca Empire. By 1572, the Incas made their final stand against the conquistadores at their last refuge: the city of Vilcabamba. The conquistadores had the city burned to eradicate the risk of any further Incan resistance. Before the last of the defenders succumbed to the superior Spanish forces, however, it is highly probable that the Incas hid their treasures. The exact location of the incinerated city became lost until 1892, when the site was rediscovered by Manuel Torres and two companions. In 1911, Hiram Bingham III (1875–1956), an American explorer and politician, reached Machu Picchu — another very important Incan settlement — as well as Vilcabamba, located in remote forest 129 kilometres west of Cuzco at a site referred to locally as Espíritu Pampa.

It is always providential for historians when confirmatory evidence turns up from an unexpected source, and this was certainly the case when Professor Guillen found and studied sixteenth-century letters from Spaniards who had actually been at Vilcabamba at the time it fell to the conquistadores. The details of the terrain and the city itself in these amazing eyewitness accounts confirmed that Espíritu Pampa really

Machu Picchu.

was Vilcabamba. Gregory Deyermenjian's photographic work there in 1981 provided further evidence for the conclusion that Espíritu Pampa was Vilcabamba.

Built around 1460, the city of Machu Picchu is another site of tremendous interest to the modern treasure hunter. The name in the Quechua language means "ancient summit," and the peak that gives Machu Picchu its name stands almost twenty-five hundred metres above sea level. It forms part of a ridge of mountains above the valley of the Urubamba River, which is part of the headwaters of the mighty Amazon. Before Bingham got there in 1911, there is some evidence that a German explorer named Augusto Berns found it in 1867. Unlike Vilcabamba, Machu Picchu was not discovered by the conquistadores, and whatever treasures — sacred or secular — that the Incas left there may still lie undisturbed.

The ancient and mysterious city of Cuzco is also alleged to provide a major clue to lost Incan treasure. According to Erich von Daniken in *Gold of the Gods* (1974) a network of tunnels runs for hundreds of kilometres under South America. Accompanied by the discoverer of these strange and mysterious tunnels, a Hungarian explorer named Juan Moricz, von Daniken claimed to have seen vast rooms filled with inscribed metallic plaques. What secrets were inscribed on those plaques, and in what strange symbols?

In von Daniken's opinion, the inscriptions on the plaques might have referred to the most ancient history of the world, when, according to his theories, highly intelligent and technically advanced astronauts *from elsewhere* were responsible for the development of the first human beings. Admittedly, von Daniken is a highly controversial figure — attacked vigorously by both orthodox scientists and orthodox religious groups. And yet, however strange his theories may sound, there may well be more than a few grains of truth in them. Von Daniken maintains that one of the entrances to this amazing network of prehistoric tunnels can be found in Morona-Santiago, Ecuador. It is also theorized that there is an entrance in Cuzco. Stories about these weird tunnels go back to the days of the Spanish conquistadores, some of whom maintained that they existed under several of the ancient ruined cities.

Strange South American symbols related to Mayans and Aztecs.

When Pizarro captured the Inca Emperor Atahualapa, an order was given that immense quantities of gold would be accepted as a ransom for him. Before it arrived, however, the emperor was killed, and there is evidence that the gold intended as his ransom was hidden by his bitterly disappointed subjects. Load after load of it was diverted from its original destination: Caxamarco, where Atahualapa was imprisoned. Tradition suggests that it was hidden in the labyrinth of subterranean tunnels, which had one access point in Cuzco.

In some versions of the story of the missing ransom, it is said that the preserved bodies of a dozen or more Inca emperors from earlier times were included with it. Originally seated on golden thrones in the area of Cuzco known as the Temple of the Sun, each of the mummified emperors was further honoured with a great slab of gold that was placed beneath his golden throne. A quarter of a century after the ransom and the mummified emperors disappeared, a conquistador named Polo de Ondegardo found three of them. They had all been stripped of their gold and jewels, and their bodies had been smashed into fragments in the process. Of great significance to modern treasure hunters — if these versions of the Cuzco story are historically reliable — is the disappearance of the other ten bejewelled mummified emperors. They are believed by some researchers and historians to have been concealed in the tunnels below Cuzco and Saqsaywaman, an amazing fortification close to Cuzco itself. Supposedly constructed by the Incas early in the sixteenth century, Saqsaywaman is possibly far older, and was simply taken over, modified, and adapted by the Incas. Approximately six hundred metres long, the fortified walls of this stronghold contain huge blocks of stone, some of which are twelve metres long, six metres high, and two metres thick. Somehow, they were transported for a considerable distance over rough and difficult terrain. It is believed by some authorities on Cuzco and its strange history that Saqsaywaman is connected by underground tunnels to Coricancha (sometimes called the Golden Courtyard) as well as to the Temple of the Sun. It seems to have been of great religious importance to the Incas, and was dedicated to their sun god, Inti. When it was in pristine condition, its walls and floor were covered with gold, and there were many golden statues in it as well. Conquistadores who had seen it described it as beyond belief. Some historians believe that much of the gold for Atahualapa's thwarted ransom had been taken from Coricancha.

It was a pervasive Christian custom to build churches over pagan religious sites as a sign that Christianity had overcome the old pagan faith. Normally such "conquest" churches were dedicated to St. Michael, the all-conquering archangel. The church built over Coricancha, however, was dedicated to St. Domingo and was constructed using parts of the foundations of what had once been the Inca temple to their sun god. Despite several severe earthquakes, the old Inca stone foundations have held their ground because of the superb interlocking construction technique that the old craftsmen used.

Among its many other riches, the sun temple once held a gigantic golden sun disc that was attached to the altar in such a way that it threw out the reflected rays of the morning sun. Another, slightly smaller golden disc was positioned to reflect the rays of the evening sun. The mummified bodies of the dead emperors were located in places of honour within this temple.

Another strange mystery in Peru that may possibly provide a series of clues to undiscovered treasure can be seen in the Nazca Desert. This desert is an infertile plateau that runs for some eighty kilometres between Palpa and Nazca on the area known as the Pampas de Jumana. Its dry, windless climate has preserved the mysterious Nazca lines for many centuries. Dating back for more than two thousand years, strange figures cover the Nazca desert for some three hundred square kilometres. Some are clearly discernible as animals, birds, fish, and lizards. Others are geometric shapes and simple lines, some of which may have been intended to indicate the location of treasure. Most of the surface of the Nazca Desert is covered by red stones and gravel that owe their colouration to a coating of iron oxide, and the lines have been created by removing this top layer to expose the white soil beneath.

Whoever made them and for whatever reason, the figures are enormous — as much as two hundred metres wide in some cases. A number of archaeologists and historians who have studied them closely feel that the lines probably had religious purposes originally, but there are other possibilities. An observer high on one of the neighbouring hilltops will find it just possible to make out the designs, but theories have been advanced that the ancient Nazca people's technology included simple hot air balloons, and there is no doubt that the Nazca lines are at their most effective when viewed from high above. Researcher Jim Woodman put forward a well-reasoned case for hot air balloons, and actually experimented with the construction of one using only materials that would have been available to the Nazca people at that time. Other theories examine the idea that the Nazca people worshipped vital water sources from the surrounding mountains, and it has been suggested by leading archaeologist Johan Reinhard that the lines and figures relate to the gods whom the Nazca people regarded as responsible for providing them with life-giving water. In his view the lines were holy tracks leading to sacred places where the water-giving divinities could best be worshipped. Other interesting theories regard the lines as akin to sacred labyrinth paths along which worshippers walked to honour and placate their gods. Astronomer Robin Edgar has put forward a very different but equally interesting hypothesis that links the Nazca lines to solar eclipses that were visible from Peru at about the same era as the lines appear to have been made. One theory of how they were constructed suggests that wooden stakes were used to mark out important positions along the designs, and the few stakes that survived were subjected to radiocarbon dating. The results suggested origins in excess of two millennia in some cases, and this dating fits well with Edgar's solar eclipse theory.

Despite all these logical and interesting theories, the Nazca geoglyphs have never been definitively interpreted. From the treasure hunter's point of view, irrespective of which theory of the Nazca lines is correct, there is a high probability that a people who were capable of constructing those geoglyphs were also more than capable of amassing wealth and preserving it. Concealed somewhere below the Nazca desert there may be more than one hoard of precious metals and gems.

An unsolved treasure hunting mystery was reported from a cemetery in Montevideo, Uruguay, on the Atlantic coast of South America. One part of the story begins with a heroic naval officer, Commander Valdes, who went down with his ship during the Second World War. His priest friend, Father Pedro de Catala, who died in 1945, had told Commander Valdes that there was a secret treasure — a hoard of gold and gems worth millions — hidden in a secret chamber accessed by a tunnel deep below one of the Montevideo cemeteries. Before departing on his last voyage, as though he had had some premonition about not returning, the commander told his wife what the priest had said. Fortunately, she remembered his account of what Father Pedro had told him, and she in turn passed the story of the Montevideo cemetery treasure to others.

The second part comes from the Massilotti family and refers to the cemetery in question as being the Cementerio Central in Montevideo. The spot at which Clara Massilotti's team began to dig was close to the Pantheon Nationale, honouring Uruguay's heroes. The entrance to some mysterious secret tunnels was duly discovered — tunnels that dated back at least to the early years of the nineteenth century, and probably considerably before that. Her grandfather and great-grandfather had been involved in the Montevidean War of Liberation, times when the usual motives for concealing treasure would have applied. President Rivera of Uruguay (1790–1854) drove the occupying Argentinean forces out of Montevideo. When other forces attacked Montevideo, the famous Italian patriot Garibaldi helped to defend the city. British and French naval help also arrived and blockaded Martin Garcia Island in the mouth of the Uruguay River. The Montevideans won the battle and retained their proud independence.

Clara Massilotti also possessed some extremely valuable old family records that referred to the mysterious treasure. One of these included extracts from the diary of Michele Massilotti and recorded how when he was in Italy in 1846 he had acquired confidential documents regarding the ancient defence system of Montevideo and a diagram of the tunnels. These were the same tunnels about which Father Pedro had informed Commander Valdes, who had in turn told his wife about them before he was lost at sea. There had been a close bond of loyal friendship between the Massilottis and Garibaldi, as shown from these vital family records. Apparently, it had been a vast Italian treasure that the Massilotti family had taken to Montevideo in 1833 to preserve it from a war that was then threatening Italy. The mystery deepens. Where did it come from originally? From the point of view of the modern treasure hunter, the tunnels below Montevideo — known to Father Pedro and the Valdes family — would be very fertile searching ground.

Only for the most daring sub-aqua treasure hunters is the recovery of what remains of the valuable hoard that was aboard HMS *Thetis*, a forty-six gun frigate that sank in Cape Frio, Brazil, in 1830. Tragically, Captain Burgess was relying on dead reckoning instead of taking soundings, and the *Thetis* was smashed to pieces on the granite rocks of Cape Frio. Twenty-eight people died in the disaster, and a treasure hoard consisting of gold, silver, and coins was lost on the seabed under the awesome cliffs. Against all the odds, by using primitive diving bells some of the treasure was miraculously recovered, but there is still much of it waiting to be salvaged. The place at which the ship went down is now known as Thetis Cove.

Another highly dangerous underwater treasure hunt involved the dauntless diver and explorer Lieutenant Harry Rieseberg. The adventure took place off the coast of Malpelo Island, which lies almost five hundred kilometres west of Colombia at the northern end of South America.

The stormy sea at Cape Frio.

Malpelo is a barren islet with a number of treacherous rocks around it. The Tres Mosqueteros are found to the northeast, while the rocks referred to as Salomon, Saul, La Gringa, and Escuba lie to the southwest. Swarms of hammerhead sharks fill the waters around the island.

A schooner carrying treasure was ripped open when it struck submerged rocks to the southeast of Malpelo. Knowing the value of what was on board, six or seven salvage expeditions attempted to raise the submerged treasure with fatal consequences for their divers, who never returned to the surface. A man as tough and adventurous as Rieseberg regarded this danger as a challenge he could not refuse to answer. He went down to the wrecked schooner with no weapons other than his trusty shark-knife — and was attacked there by an octopus of enormous size, which had killed all the earlier divers. Rieseberg described it as being six metres across and having a central body about one and a half metres in diameter. He had already found the long-dead remains of several of the earlier divers when the huge beast went for him in the gaping, broken cabin of the wrecked schooner. Thinking that his end had come, but determined to go down fighting, Rieseberg hacked through one tentacle after another as the monster tried to crush and kill him. When he failed to return to the surface, other divers descended to find out what was happening. During the life and death battle the octopus had penetrated his suit, and he was losing air fast, but the rescuers got him to the surface just in time. The fierce defence that Rieseberg had put up against the monster with his razor-sharp shark-knife had been too much for it. The divers who had come down to rescue him reported that it was dead and that when they found Rieseberg three of its huge severed tentacles were still attached to his suit! Some of the treasure from the wrecked schooner was recovered as a result of Rieseberg's fearless battle with the monstrous octopus — but how much is still down there off the dangerous coast of Malpelo? How many other ships have suffered the same fate as the treasure schooner where he fought the octopus? Only for the bravest of the brave, perhaps, but a stirring challenge for any warrior diver cast in Rieseberg's mould.

The treasure of Catamarca begins with a ruthless threat to the city of Cordoba in Argentina from the brutal and rapacious Juan Facundo Quiroga (1788–1835), who was known as "the tiger of the plains" and who certainly deserved his nickname. He was finally assassinated in 1835.

When Cordoba was being seriously threatened and it looked as though its defenders would have no chance against the tiger of the plains, the nervous Bishop Dom Balboa decided to take all the cathedral treasure to what he wrongly assumed would be the relative safety of the Salinas Grandes. Few decisions could have been more mistaken. The treasure in the bishop's mule train included a dozen golden candelabra, gem-studded reliquaries of the saints, golden pyxes, chalices, and other precious altar furniture. There were also various jewels included among the bishop's accessories, and a huge golden crucifix that was traditionally thought to have been brought to South America by Pizarro himself. Apart from the grave basic error of planning to take such treasures to the wild and lonely Salinas Grandes, the bishop made another major mistake in trusting a strange character with the nickname of "Colorado" because of his flaming red hair to be their guide.

The bishop's mule train packed with the priceless ecclesiastical treasures had just about reached the village of Ambargasta when a messenger on a fast horse from Cordoba overtook them with the news that contrary to all expectations Quiroga's attack had been effectively repulsed, and his army of wild gauchos heavily defeated. The tiger's metaphorical teeth and claws had been well and truly removed! The most sensible course for Bishop Balboa would then have been to return immediately to the safety of Cordoba — but unbelievably he was persuaded by the crafty Colorado that the message was a lie sent by Quiroga to tempt them back to the city so that Quiroga could take the treasure. Furthermore, Colorado claimed that he knew of a secret pass through the mountains that would enable them to reach the Pacific coast. Where the bishop hoped to go with the cathedral treasures *after* reaching the Pacific coast was anybody's guess. Some historians have suggested that Balboa had become mentally ill at this point. Other theorists even wonder whether he had taken up some weird form of black magic. For whatever strange reason, Balboa pressed on westwards. Finally, his exhausted party reached the ruins of an old sun temple in the Catamarca Mountains. One gruesome account describes the later finding of a bizarre scene in which the large golden crucifix was found upright in the centre of the old sun temple with a human head on top of it, and surrounded by the cathedral's golden candelabra. Other versions maintain that Colorado was in league with the Catamarca sun worshippers and had arranged to bring Balboa and the treasure to them. According to this version, the treasures were hidden in a secret labyrinth below the ancient sun temple. One expert researcher into the Balboa tragedy maintained that this sun temple can be found at latitude 29 south and longitude 69 west. Whatever the ultimate fate of Balboa and the cathedral treasure, that area will be of great interest to contemporary treasure hunters.

From the tragedy of the ill-fated Emperor Maximilian to the insanity — or worse — of Bishop Balboa, the treasures of South America have demonstrated the dangers that accompany hoards of gold, silver, and gems. There is also a dimension of strange unsolved mysteries accompanying some of the greatest treasure hoards. What do the Nazca geoglyphs really mean? Do they point to ancient treasures hidden below the desert? And what about the vast network of underground tunnels that von Daniken claimed to have entered? The greatest assets that treasure hunters can possess are indomitable courage — like Rieseberg's when he killed the giant octopus — and unbreakable determination to overcome every obstacle.

Chapter Eight
Pacific Treasure

O ne of the most extraordinarily able and benign Pacific rulers
was King Kamehameha I, who was also justifiably known as
Kamehameha the Great. He lived from 1738 until 1819, having established the kingdom of Hawaii in 1810. When he died on May 8, 1819,
there was a great funeral cortege in his honour, and his body — accompanied by vast royal treasures — was escorted by his most trusted deputy
chieftains. The last resting place of the noble Kamehameha is a mystery.
One version of the story suggests that he was taken to the island of
Kauai, which is characterized by its high cliffs, steep ravines, and numerous caves, and that his body and his treasure are hidden together in one
of those many caves. Another tradition states that he was laid to rest in
thick forest on the main island of Hawaii itself not far from Hilo. A third
theory states that he and his treasure were thrown into the crater of the
volcano as an offering to Pele, the goddess of the volcano. All three sites
would be worth exploring. Searching the volcanic crater would be the
most hazardous and the least likely to prove rewarding, but the other two
possibilities hold out high hopes of recovering the great king's treasure.

The wreck of the American clipper *General Grant* on the Auckland
Islands south of New Zealand's South Island in 1866 created a treasure
mystery as uncanny as the unexplained loss of the personnel from the
Mary Celeste some six years later. The *General Grant* had a displacement
of well over a thousand tons and was carrying eighty-three passengers
and crew. She was also carrying more than twenty-five hundred ounces
of gold from the mines at Ballarat in Australia, as well as her main cargo
of wool. Captain Loughlin took her out of Hobson's Bay, Melbourne, on
May 4, 1866, and according to reports made by survivors when they were
eventually rescued, all went uneventfully until May 13. There was insuf-
ficient wind to give the *General Grant* any significant steerage: she was

Kauai.

at the mercy of the treacherous currents, which smashed her against one rocky promontory after another, doing major damage each time until finally she was washed into a large cave. The roof of the cave drove the masts down through the hull and sank her.

The handful of survivors lived on the island for eighteen months before being rescued. One dauntless man came back soon afterwards to try to rescue the treasure from the cave-entombed wreckage of the *General Grant*, but the pounding seas at the mouth of the huge cave prevented the salvage team from getting at the wreck. Numerous salvage attempts were made over the years with equal lack of success. Then in 1969, a modern salvage team went in with all the latest technological equipment and found absolutely nothing. There was no trace at all of the ill-fated *General Grant* in the cave where the seas had driven her over a century before. No one knows what became of the last vestiges of the wreckage and the treasure that it had once contained. Dangerous as they are, the Auckland Islands hold out rich prospects for today's treasure hunters.

The Dutch East India Company was established in 1602; it was known in the Dutch language of the time as Vereenigde Oost-Indische Compagnie (VOC). One of these VOC vessels was the *Vergulde Draeck* (*"The Gilded Dragon"*), which sailed from Texel, Holland, to what was then the East Indies, now Indonesia. As well as her passengers and crew, the *Vergulde Draeck* was carrying nearly two hundred thousand silver coins. She had got safely from Holland to the Cape of Good Hope and set sail from there to Batavia on March 13, 1656 (the modern city of Jakarta in Indonesia was known as Batavia from 1619 until 1942). Captain Pieter Albertszoon may have mistaken his bearings, but for whatever reason, on April 26, 1656, the *Vergulde Draeck* smashed into a reef near the mouth of the River Moore in Western Australia. Over seventy survivors reached the mainland, and a small boat known as a schuyt, which had been saved from the wreck, carried seven heroic volunteers on a desperate journey across the Indian Ocean to Batavia where the VOC had its Java offices. Captain Albertszoon decided that it was his duty to stay and defend the survivors on the dangerous mainland, and he placed his second officer, Abraham Leeman van Santwitz, in charge of the schuyt. Superb courage and seamanship brought him and his six companions to Batavia, and all credit belongs to the VOC for doing everything possible, as fast as possible, to rescue the party of survivors led by Captain Albertszoon. Leeman was involved in several of the search parties, and his outstanding seamanship saved other lives when the savage weather damaged more boats. Despite every effort, no sign of Captain Albertszoon and his party was ever traced.

In 1931, however, a skeleton and a few coins were discovered on a beach to the north of the River Moore. They might have belonged to a member of Captain Albertszoon's party, but there were many wrecks in that area, and nothing could be proved conclusively. In 1957, divers found what seemed to be all that was left of the *Vergulde Draeck*, but in those difficult and dangerous waters, they failed to relocate it immediately. Six years later they did find it again and succeeded in bringing up various relics and some of the coins that she had been carrying: but many more must still be down there. The dangerous western coast with its horrendous weather and deadly reefs has been responsible for many wrecks, especially ships belonging to the VOC. There are rich treasures down there still, but retrieving them is extremely hazardous.

Borneo is among the largest islands in the world: geographers rank it in third place. The island is shared by Indonesia, Brunei, and Malaysia, and is often referred to as Kalimantan by the Indonesians.

Dr. Theodor Posewitz, a mining expert who spent three years in Borneo, was fascinated by the quantity of diamonds to be found on the island. In his opinion, the area known as Landak was especially rich not only in diamonds but in gold as well. According to Posewitz, two rivers, the Sikajam and the Meran, yielded diamonds of varied colours and great value. Where such treasure exists as a natural resource, there will inevitably be those who try to take it illicitly and conceal it. There will undoubtedly be hoards of diamonds and gold buried secretly in many parts of Borneo, waiting for the right treasure hunter with up-to-date technical equipment to locate them.

The Philippines are another site where treasures are waiting to be recovered, but many of these are below the water, like the wreck of the little *patache* that went down when it struck the Calantas Reefs in 1735. Although every endeavour was made to haul up her treasure cargo, and 1.5 million pesos were recovered, a great many more were left on the reefs, where some must still be waiting to be found.

Nearly half a century before the loss of the patache on the Calantas Reefs, there was a similar reef sinking when the *Pilar* went down near the island of Guam on June 2, 1690. Her full name was *Nuestra Senora del Pilar de Saragoza y Santiago* ("*Our Lady of the Pillar of Saragossa and Saint James*"). The *Pilar* ran into the Cocos Reef just south of Guam, which was then a vitally important stop on busy trading routes across the

Pacific. For close to three centuries, Spanish treasure ships loaded with silver from Mexico, Bolivia, and Peru took the route from Acapulco, Mexico, to Manila, Philippines, and they needed to break their journeys at Guam for fresh provisions. Goods were traded in Manila and in Japan, and then the galleons returned to Acapulco. From there, the precious merchandise was carted overland to the Atlantic coast and then sailed back to Spain. The voyage was a desperately dangerous one, and dozens of the Spanish trading vessels were lost.

When the *Pilar* went down off Guam she went down fast, and only a few thousand of the million or so coins aboard her could be saved. The passengers and crew numbered close to two hundred — but not a single life was lost. Divers using the best modern equipment have been searching for her since the 1990s, but without any major success so far. The reefs off Guam present a fascinating and potentially lucrative challenge to the courageous modern underwater treasure hunter.

One of the greatest treasure recovery operations ever undertaken in the Pacific was centred on RMS *Niagara*. Launched in 1912, the property of the Union Steam Ship Company, she had been nicknamed "the *Titanic* of the Pacific," until the *Titanic* tragedy prompted her owners to change that title to "Queen of the Pacific." In June 1940 the *Niagara* was in service with the Canadian Australasian Line and running from Auckland, New Zealand, to Suva and Vancouver. A German mine-layer, the auxiliary cruiser *Orion*, had been at work off Bream Head, Whangarei; the *Niagara*, captained by William Martin, struck one of the *Orion*'s mines and sank in over a hundred metres of water. Discipline and excellent seamanship prevented any loss of life, but the *Niagara* took a treasure secret to the bottom with her: she was carrying nearly six hundred bars of gold — about eight tons — from the Bank of England to the United States to pay for war materials.

A Melbourne salvage company was called in urgently, and they went to work aboard the *Claymore* and succeeded in recovering most of the gold bars — but not before the *Claymore* herself had struck a mine and almost gone down to join the *Niagara*. More of the gold was recovered in 1953, but not all of it. Over $1 million worth is still on the ocean bed at Bream Head.

The little island of Corregidor lies in Manila Bay in the Philippines. It has a mysterious ancient history going back many millennia before the arrival of the Spaniards. The territory was fertile. Its mountains were covered with trees, providing a valuable source of timber. It was a welcome staging post for the first merchants travelling from East Asia to Oceania. In short, it was the kind of place where wealth was generated from its earliest days. The first inhabitants of the Philippines — including Corregidor — were skilled agriculturalists, toolmakers, weavers, painters, and craftsmen who could create beautiful jewellery. They were also literate, and, because theirs was an island kingdom, they were skilful boat builders. Where had these earliest inhabitants come from?

The islands must at one time have been connected to Taiwan and Borneo by land bridges because fossils of animals from elsewhere have been found there, and the archaeological site in the Cagayan Valley situated at the northern end of Luzon has yielded stone tools many thousands of years old. The *Homo erectus* hunter-gatherers of the remote past seem to have followed their prey from the mainland to the Philippines. Other adventurous travellers seem to have made the journey to the Philippines from Borneo, Malaya and Sumatra as much as thirty thousand years ago. Fearless Arabian traders reached the Philippines during the fourteenth century, and Ferdinand Magellan, the great Portuguese explorer, reached the islands in 1521. Lopez de Villalobos (1500–1544) travelled from Mexico to the Philippines in 1542 and gave the islands their name in honour of the *Infante*, who was destined to become Philip II of Spain.

This long history of international trade both before and after the arrival of the Spaniards made the Philippines in general — and Corregidor in particular — very likely hiding places for surplus wealth in the form of gold and jewels whenever hostilities threatened the islands.

Over and above such treasure hoards as were concealed on Corregidor in past centuries, which may still await recovery, there are the far more recent deposits associated with the Second World War. Among the ruins on Corregidor is a sturdy, time-defying old fortification to which the Philippine government sent the core of its national treasury in 1942 when the threat of a Japanese invasion was imminent. With the help of the United States, several tons of gold ingots were loaded on to the

Detroit and taken to America. That still left several million pounds' worth of silver coins. Because the Japanese were now so close, and there was little or no chance of getting the silver coins away before the Japanese reached the Philippines, it was decided to sink the coins in Manila Bay. Once the Japanese occupied the Philippines, they found out about the submerged silver and tried retrieving it — but with very little success. After Japan had been defeated, American treasure hunters began salvaging the silver coins, until the Philippine government stopped them. Consequently, there are still a great many silver pesos awaiting recovery on the bed of Manila Bay.

Another strange and enigmatic sunken treasure mystery from the Pacific theatre of war in 1945 concerns the *Awa Maru*. Shortly before her sinking, the *Awa Maru* was working as a Red Cross relief ship, and as such was protected from attack from Allied warships. Having delivered her Red Cross supplies, she was sailing back with more than two thousand Japanese personnel aboard her, plus a vast amount of gold, silver, and platinum — if the rumours are to be believed. On April 1, 1945, she was intercepted by the American submarine *Queenfish* and practically blasted out of the water by four lethally aimed torpedoes. The skipper of the *Queenfish* had mistaken the *Awa Maru* for an enemy destroyer and, wartime being wartime, he had not unreasonably decided to strike first. When the China Salvage Company located the wreck of the *Awa Maru* in the early 1980s, they failed to find the treasure that she was alleged to have been carrying. But it was dark when the *Queenfish* sank her, and fugitives can easily escape on a dark sea. Did any of the high-ranking Japanese officials aboard her get their treasure into a lifeboat and get clear of the sinking ship? If they did, what became of them, and what became of the treasure? It is well within the bounds of possibility that their lifeboat sank with the illicit treasure on board. Is it still there, just off the coast of China at approximately 24°N 120°E?

There are close to 170 islands in the kingdom of Tonga, but fewer than a quarter of them are inhabited. They run more or less in a line from north to south and cover a total distance of about eight hundred kilometres. Tonga is roughly two-thirds of the way from Hawaii to New Zealand. In 1806 a pirate vessel, the *Port au Prince*, was on the lookout for

Spanish treasure ships to plunder in American and South Pacific waters. The pirates dropped anchor just off the sandy shore at Faka'amumei, part of Ha'apai, which is a group of islands in the central range of the Tongan archipelago. Local history maintains a tradition that the formidable Ha'apai island warriors slaughtered the pirates who had threatened them and then looted the *Port au Prince* before setting fire to it.

During the last two centuries, several treasure hunting expeditions have looked for the incinerated wreck of the pirates' ship — but without success. There is some evidence that a treasure seeker by the name of Onodera had authority from the Tongan royal family and from the governor of Ha'apai to search for the missing pirates' treasure. There was enormous political controversy over whether Onodera actually found the treasure and whether he had then shared it secretly with the Tongan royal family. Whatever the facts may be, the central point of major interest to modern treasure hunters in Ha'apai is that the *Port au Prince* was almost certainly carrying a huge amount of pirate wealth when she came to grief in 1806.

There are also some strange treasure mysteries surrounding the little-known Phoenix Islands in mid-Pacific: strange because so little is known about the nature or origin of whatever treasure may be concealed there. The fairest thing that can be said about it is that the Phoenix treasure is highly speculative. The Phoenix Islands, legally part of the Republic of Kiribati, are not much more than a couple of coral reefs along with seven or eight atolls. They lie west of the Line Islands and east of the Gilbert Islands. The Phoenix Islands are practically uninhabited apart from a few dozen people who survive with great tenacity and courage on Kanton Island (also spelled Canton), which has the alternative names of Abariringa Island, Mary Island, and Swallow Island. It is the biggest and northernmost in the Phoenix group. At approximately 2°S 171°W, Kanton is approximately halfway between Fiji and Hawaii. The only settlement on Kanton is the tiny village of Tebaronga.

The possibility of treasure on or near the remote and lonely Phoenix Islands goes back to the early part of the nineteenth century, when whalers were in the area. It was part of the story of the pirate vessel *Port au Prince* that the pirates combined piracy with whaling and set after Spanish treasure galleons or whales with equally callous disregard. The two roles were not as distinct as might be thought. It has been suggested, therefore, that the whalers who called in at the Phoenix Islands might have wished to conceal something very valuable there: the sheer remoteness of the islands and the difficulty of finding them added to the security of anything buried there. It is a well-known and documented fact that two London whalers, the *Phoenix* and the *Mary*, reached the Phoenix Islands in 1824 — not many years after the *Port au Prince* met its just deserts at Ha'apai. Could there be a pirate treasure still hidden among the Phoenix atolls, and was either — or both — of the London whalers involved in the same illicit sidelines as the notorious *Port au Prince?*

Remote islands — like many of those dotted around the vast expanse of the Pacific Ocean — seem to appeal to those who have treasures to hide and ships with which to reach those remote islands. Huge as it is, and difficult to search as it is, the mighty Pacific provides golden opportunities for modern treasure hunters.

Chapter Nine
Secret Societies as Guardians of Treasure

I t is an inescapable truism that the most powerful and effective secret societies are those known only to their members, who naturally deny their membership and the very existence of the society itself. Secret societies whose existence is known — or claimed — serve a broader purpose: by dropping hints that they *might* belong to such a group, its members are subtly warning real or imaginary opponents, competitors, and enemies that they are not to be trifled with. By claiming to be a member of Organization X and by claiming that Organization X can and will deal ruthlessly with any threats to its members, a person who feels vulnerable in a hazardous and uncertain world can put on the equivalent of invisible armour.

There are, undeniably, real and effective secret societies, with genuine histories, established organizations, rules, procedures, and obligations. In many cases, such as the Freemasons and some modern Templar groups, these societies are entirely benign; they provide a great deal of charitable help to those in need and they provide an effective social support structure for their members. It can be argued that such semi-secret societies are more like extended families in which different relatives have different gifts and talents brought into the common pool for the benefit of all the other members. Although popularized Masonic history dates the present organization from as recently as 1717 when four groups of lodges joined together, serious research into the real history of the Masons shows that they go back many centuries. Because of their integrity and high moral principles, Freemasons were frequently entrusted with treasure in much the same way that the Knights Templar were. If the treasure hunter is interested in treasure in the form of secret knowledge and ancient wisdom, then the most likely guardians of it will be Freemasons or Templars.

The Rosicrucians are also regarded as guardians of treasure in the form of hidden wisdom and knowledge. The movement is generally credited with having started in Germany during the early years of the seventeenth century, when their foundation documents were published. These were *Confessio Fraternitatis, The Chymical Wedding of Christian Rosenkreuz,* and what has probably become the most widely known of their texts, *Fama Fraternitatis Rosae Crucis.* The documents tell how an exceptionally able alchemist named Christian Rosenkreuz travelled to the four corners of the Earth to expand his knowledge and formed a secret brotherhood of alchemists whose aim was to change the world. The documents also delve into deep and enigmatic symbolism in which a mysterious king and queen are married chemically in a castle full of miracles. The most intriguing and powerful of the Rosicrucian messages concerns the tomb of the founder, Christian Rosenkreuz, who had allegedly lain uncorrupted in a secret tomb as though in a state of suspended animation rather than death. This ties in with the legends in which Sarah (the sister-wife of Abraham the Hebrew patriarch) came across Hermes Trismegistus (alias Thoth, scribe of the Egyptian pantheon and guardian of their secrets) in a cave in a state of suspended animation.

In the oldest Rosicrucian traditions, Rosenkreuz had designed and built this secret tomb himself and had intended it to be a repository of ancient secret knowledge — just as the secrets of the Egyptian gods were written on the timeless Emerald Tablets of Hermes Trismegistus, two of which were taken by Sarah and later became the miraculous Urim and Thummim stones of Old Testament fame.

Academic historians and researchers who have made proper in-depth studies of the Rosicrucians and the Freemasons have advanced various theories on the possibility that the two organizations are guardians of vital ancient secrets, tying them in with the secrets that the Knights Templar discovered below Solomon's Temple in the eleventh and twelfth centuries. As with all secret and mysterious groups, the Rosicrucians have a great many codes and ciphers. One of the most intriguing of these is the word *vitriol,* which, of course, has chemical and alchemical connotations. In Rosicrucian code the letters are said to stand for "*Visita Interiora Terrae Rectificando Invenies Occultum Lapidem.*" This translates very broadly as "By visiting the interior of the Earth, putting things right will reveal the secret stone." Is it remotely possible that the secret stone of this code is one of the Emerald Tablets? Perhaps even the missing tablets associated with Sarah? Is that what has to be rectified? Urim and Thummim would be priceless, if they could be found. Is their whereabouts part of the innermost secrets of the Rosicrucians? Can their location be discovered by painstaking study of the Rosicrucian codes and ciphers?

Another angle on Rosicrucian treasure leads back to the mysteries and secrets of Rennes-le-Château and the enigma of Father Saunière's inexplicable wealth. Expert researchers have suggested that Christian Rosenkreuz was a member of a very old German noble family, the Germelshausens (although there is also a strange short story by Friedrich Gerstäcker concerning a village named Germelshausen that was cursed and vanished for a century at a time — rather like Brigadoon in the musical). In the Rosicrucian version, Rosenkreuz came from Castle Germelshausen in Thuringia; the family had been converted to Catharism, also referred to as Albigensianism (a version of Christianity condemned as heresy by the Catholic Church) and savagely persecuted. The Landgrave of Thuringia was Catholic and ordered the deaths of the entire Germelshausen family — except for a five-year-old son, who grew up to be Christian Rosenkreuz after being cared for and educated by a pious old Albigensian holy man from the Languedoc, not far from Rennes-le-Château.

The references to Thuringia as the site for the Germelshausen family and their castle also have mysterious connotations. The stark Hörselberg Mountain rises there like a vast stone sarcophagus, and within it is the deep cavern known as the Hörselloch. An underground river rushes through its stygian depths, and the strange sounds issuing from this noisy subterranean torrent have been variously interpreted as the screams of the damned being tortured in Hell or the cries of sexual ecstasy from the delighted guests in Venus's pleasure palace as she and her nubile maidens entertain them. In pre-Christian days, the Hörselloch was thought to be the entrance to Venus's palace of exquisite carnal pleasure. After the arrival of Christianity it was regarded instead as an anteroom of Hell.

In the Tannhauser legend, the famous, romantic, adventurous minnesinger found himself descending into the Hörselloch as the guest of Venus and her handmaidens — and staying with them until the world's end. Whatever the hidden symbolism of Germelshausen and the Hörselloch, legends of this type *can* refer obliquely to treasures concealed in the awesome depths of such caverns.

Another strange angle on the semi-legendary Christian Rosenkreuz and his Rosicrucian followers relates to the mysterious Count of St. Germain, who was supposed to possess either great longevity or eternal life. Voltaire described him as, "A man who knows everything and never dies." He was also reputedly able to create diamonds, and so acquired enormous wealth and power. Like Rosenkreuz, he had travelled the world and acquired vast amounts of mysterious knowledge from the remoter parts of Asia. More than one Rosicrucian researcher has wondered whether St. Germain and Rosenkreuz were one and the same abnormally gifted and powerful person. There are even some investigators who believe that he's still around. His secret of such great longevity — if it exists — would be infinitely more valuable than his diamonds. Was he also Hermes Trismegistus, alias Thoth? From the contemporary treasure hunter's point of view, the legend of St. Germain is well worth examining in minute detail: this man could seemingly defy time and make diamonds. What exactly were his secrets, and where are they now?

The secret society known as OTO is a very different organization from Freemasonry and Rosicrucianism. Its initials stand for Ordo Templi Orientis, which translates as "Order of the Temples of the East," and although its rituals bear some resemblance to those used by orthodox and accepted Freemasonry, it has its own unique style based on the teachings of Thelema, the brainchild of the notorious Aleister Crowley (1875–1947). Crowley devised this magical-religious system on two basic precepts: "Do what thou wilt is the whole of the law" and "Love is the law under the *will*." An entire book would need to be written to explain exactly what Crowley meant by these ambiguous and controversial statements. All that is relevant at this point in examining his OTO group as a secret society, however, is that it *possibly* had treasure to guard. It is also relevant to consider that what he meant by *will*

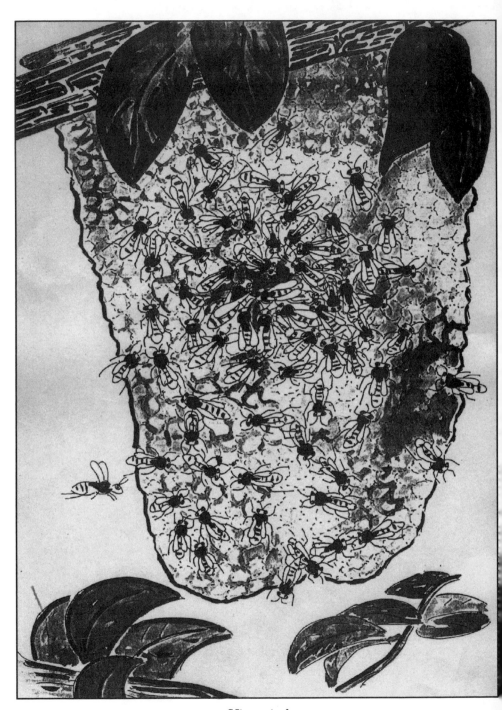

Hive mind.

was a great deal more than the will of a single, egocentric human being. Crowley's Thelema teachings could be extended to include the concept of group mind, or hive mind, and the combined power of the wills of the many. To give Crowley his due, he was brilliant, a superb chess player, a courageous mountaineer, and a gifted poet as well as a formidable theologian and philosopher. Used in a positive direction, his many talents could have done great and lasting good. Did Crowley's OTO really have any treasures to guard? There are grounds for suspecting that they did. Crowley's extensive travels and the various expensive historical, magical, and ritualistic items that he bought are clear indications that for most of his lifetime money was no problem. The details of the OTO rituals, like many of Crowley's writings, are complicated, and their symbolism is not easy to decode. However, it is certainly possible that the OTO, which still exists and has several thousand members worldwide, has the custody of certain rare old magical items that once belonged to Crowley. Perhaps it also jealously guards the secret whereabouts of other magical treasures that Crowley might have felt it wiser to conceal.

The Hermetic Order of the Golden Dawn could well be another secret society with treasures to guard. The Golden Dawn's teachings are based on their Cipher Documents, sixty folios in a code devised by the amazing Johannes Trithemius (1462–1516), whose life is well worth close scrutiny as a series of clues to where sixteenth-century treasure may have been concealed on his authority and under his directions. Originally known as Johann Heidenberg, the name *Trithemius* was derived from the town of Trittenheim on the River Mosel in Germany. While studying at Heidelberg University in 1482, he was on his way home to Trittenheim when he was driven by a violent snowstorm to ask for refuge in Sponheim, a Benedictine abbey not far from Bad Kreuznach. This changed the entire course of Johann's life: he decided to stay with the monks, who elected the brilliant young student as their abbot the following year when he was still only twenty-one years old. Under Trithemius's guidance and leadership, Sponheim became a great centre of ecclesiastical learning, and its meagre library of fewer than a hundred volumes rose to over two thousand. However, there were problems because of Trithemius's interest in magic and his extensive knowledge of it. He left

Sponheim in 1506 to accept an offer from the Bishop of Würzburg, Lorenz von Bibra (1459–1519), to become the Abbot of St. James in Würzburg, a post he held for the remainder of his life. Perhaps the most telling tribute to Trithemius is that the great physician and magician Paracelsus (1493–1541) was one of his pupils.

Trithemius's codes were hidden in six volumes named *Polygraphia Libri Sex*, meaning simply "the six books of polygraphy," which can be defined as the art of writing in ciphers and decoding them. One of these volumes held close to four hundred columns of Latin words, each of which represented one letter of the alphabet. Trithemius also wrote *Steganographia*, meaning "covered or concealed writing."

While on the subject of secret codes, symbols, and ciphers of the type that Trithemius designed and used, it is important for the treasure hunter to be aware that such codes are the hallmark of almost every secret society, and are especially relevant when the society has treasure to conceal. One of the most mysterious and intriguing coded documents — and one that has so far defied the finest cryptographers and the best computer decipherment programs — is known as the Voynich Manuscript. Some researchers and cryptographers have wondered whether the Voynich Manuscript was the work of Roger Bacon (1214–1294), often referred to in Latin as Doctor Mirabilis, who was a gifted empirical scientist and philosopher light-years ahead of his thirteenth-century contemporaries. The problem arises in that the Voynich Manuscript is generally regarded as dating no earlier than 1400, which makes it too recent to be Bacon's work. It is written in a completely unknown script and is profusely illustrated. If it is not Bacon's work, then all that can be said of it is that the author, the language, and the alphabet in which it is written are unknown. A book dealer named Wilfrid M. Voynich acquired the manuscript in 1912, and by 2005 it had found its way into the Rare Book and Manuscript Library at Yale University. The Voynich Manuscript is clearly divided into sections by the illustrations; these sections are categorized as herbal, with one plant drawn on each page; astronomical, with pictures of suns, moons, stars, and signs of the zodiac; biological, with anatomical organs and nude female figures (some wearing crowns); cosmological, with maps and what look like volcanoes; pharmaceutical, with herbs and the jars an apothecary would use; and recipes, or what seem to be culinary instructions or spells.

If the Voynich Manuscript can ever be deciphered, it may contain clues to both types of treasure: valuable knowledge and the secret location of precious metals and gems.

Runes combine an alphabet with supposed magical properties. They were known and used by early Germanic-speaking peoples as well as throughout Denmark, Sweden, and Norway. Originally, the runic alphabet was designed to be inscribed on flat pieces of wood, and its letter shapes reflect this. But there was more to runic communications than simple messages: the letters were believed to possess protective powers that would bless and guard the person carrying an object with a runic inscription. For example, a golden neck ring with a runic inscription was found in a barrow in Pietroassa in Rumania in 1837 and is referred to as the Buzău torc. It was part of a treasure hoard, and archaeologists believe that it throws useful light on the pre-Christian religion of the Goths. The runes on the ring are thought to have been intended to provide magical protection for the wearer. Runic inscriptions, when properly deciphered and understood within their historical contexts, may put the modern treasure hunter on the trail of hoards like the one found in Pietroassa. Ogham is an ancient system of writing — as early as the runes, or even earlier — used by the Celts in Ireland, Scotland, and Wales. It was basically very simple, yet at the same time extremely versatile for the user. The underlying principle was a straight line, above and below which other straight lines could be placed perpendicularly. Up to five of these could be placed through, above, or below the anchor line. This meant that the human hand could be used to signal Ogham letters by pointing upwards or downwards with the fingers. The authors' great friend George Young, now sadly deceased, was an ex-Canadian naval officer and surveyor and a world authority on the Money Pit mystery in Nova Scotia. George was also an authority on Ogham and believed that it might have an important role in deciphering some of the coded messages relating to the treasure concealed below Oak Island. He was also keenly interested in the work of the enigmatic painter Nicholas Poussin (1594–1665), whose coded paintings were connected with the "Et in

Arcadia ego" mystery that was linked to the Rennes-le-Château treasure. George's expert knowledge of Ogham and the way that it could be signalled by hand enabled him to see that several of the characters in Poussin's paintings were holding their hands in such unusual positions that they were actually spelling out messages in Ogham. Such clues hidden in the paintings shed a great deal of light on the Rennes-le-Château treasure mystery.

When Nicholas Fouquet was the superintendent of finance in France during the reign of the immensely powerful Louis XIV (1638–1715), Fouquet's younger brother met Poussin in Rome and wrote to Nicholas to the effect that Poussin had some great secret knowledge: "things which will give you through M. Poussin advantages which kings would have great difficulty in obtaining from him and which according to what he says no one in the world will ever retrieve in the centuries to come ... " That mysterious message has great significance for treasure hunters today.

The painters, Poussin included, had their own mysterious secret society, and one of their coded messages was the Latin phrase from the tomb in the Arcadian shepherd paintings, "Et in Arcadia ego." Giovanni Francesco Barbieri (1591–1666) was better known by his nickname of *Il Guercino* on account of an eye problem, despite which he was an extremely effective and productive artist. His version of the *Shepherds of Arcadia* is very different from Poussin's treatment of the theme, but his knowing use of the Latin phrase sounds as if he is using it as some kind of password or secret society membership clue.

Although he predated Guercino and Poussin by a century, another mysterious genius who would undoubtedly have been a prominent member of any secret society that existed among painters was Leonardo da Vinci (1452–1519). He too seems to have used codes and ciphers extensively; one of his favourite tricks was to write in mirror image style, but this may simply have been the result of his natural left-handedness.

This Order of the Golden Dawn was the creation of three very able men with Rosicrucian and Masonic connections: William Woodman, Wynn Westcott, and Sam Mathers. They blended alchemy and ancient Egyptian beliefs with the secret teachings of the Qabalah, hermeticism,

Guercino's version of Shepherds of Arcadia.

and theosophy. Poet William Butler Yeats and Aleister Crowley were closely associated with the Golden Dawn and would have known many of its deepest secrets. The wealth and power known to have been part of the Golden Dawn at its zenith may well have led to the secret concealment of certain valuable items, and treasure hunters with a special interest in cryptography may well find that a study of the sixty folios and the work of Trithemius can produce exceptionally important clues.

Another important secret society — possibly a branch of the Rosicrucians — is inseparably linked with the enigmatic Sir Francis Bacon and his younger brother, Anthony. Francis was born in 1561 and his death is recorded as having taken place in 1626, but there are serious doubts about this. Contradictory evidence suggests that there was a mock funeral for him in 1626 and that Bacon actually went secretly to France, where he lived under an assumed name for many more years. He was thought to have been the son of Sir Nicholas Bacon, who held the rank of Lord Keeper during the reign of Queen Elizabeth I (1558–1603),

Sir Francis Bacon's portrait.

but there are significant doubts about his parentage as well as about the date of his death.

As a young man Francis became interested in paranormal and anomalous phenomena as well as studying science and philosophy. Combining these two areas of study, Francis paid close attention to the displays of peripatetic acrobats, conjurors, and jugglers to determine whether they were simply using well-developed natural skills or whether they had genuine magical powers that could not be explained within the laws of science as he understood them. Codes and ciphers were also included in his wide range of interests. He himself devised a code using watermarks, often in the form of bunches of grapes and wine jugs.

After leaving Cambridge University, Francis became a member of Gray's Inn, where he trained in the law. He then went to France from 1576 to 1579 with Sir Amyas Paulet, Queen Elizabeth's ambassador to the French Court. A number of expert academic historians support the controversial theory that Francis was actually the illegitimate son of Queen Elizabeth herself — by Lord Robert Dudley. This hypothesis is based to some extent on the Biliteral Cipher, which Mrs. Elizabeth Wells Gallup discovered within Francis Bacon's books and Shakespeare's First Folio and about which she published a report in 1899. One of her discoveries read: "Queen Elizabeth is my true mother, and I am the lawful heir to the throne." Mrs. Gallup's work was powerfully reinforced and supported by the photographic experts at George Fabyan's world-famous Riverbank Laboratories.

Francis's apparent mother, Anne Cooke, was his father's second wife, and as such was supposedly the mother of both Francis and Anthony. However, she was Chief Lady in Waiting to Queen Elizabeth, and both she and her husband were devoted to the queen. They were also staunch Protestants at a time when the religious struggles between Protestants and Catholics in England were at their most dangerous. Elizabeth's pregnancy would have destabilized the government had it become known. What was more natural than that Anne, her loyal lady-in-waiting, should conceal it for her? That dramatic information gave Francis in turn a powerful motive for secrecy.

Another significant motive for his desire for secrecy came from a stern warning from his ostensible father, Sir Nicholas. In 1564, Nicholas had written a book — albeit under the pseudonym of John Hales — which supported the claims of the House of Suffolk to the English throne. When Elizabeth discovered the author's real name, it was not surprising that Nicholas fell heavily from royal favour, although

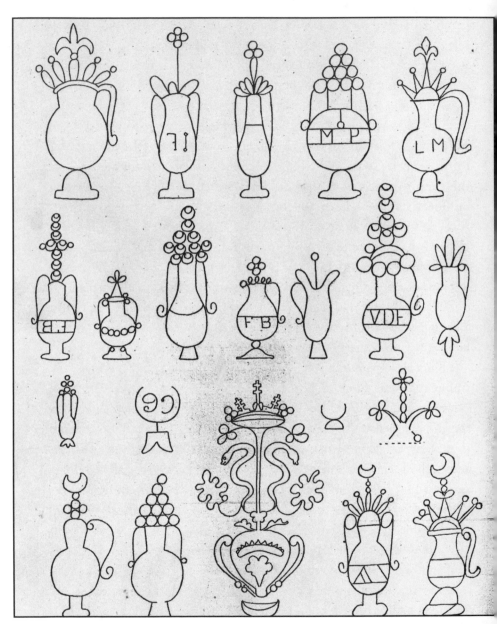

Watermarks of jugs and grapes.

he was restored in due course. Francis took careful note of his father's literary misadventures.

In so far as there was a secret service in Elizabethan times, there is a body of evidence that suggests that both Anthony and Francis were prominent members of it. Their secret society — whether connected with the Rosicrucians or not — was then a semi-official one, serving Elizabeth and her government.

What treasure did the Bacon brothers accumulate, and where did they conceal it? There are clues that suggest they had connections with Nova Scotia, and there is a possibility that the Oak Island treasure was connected not only with them but with the Ansons of Shugborough.

Francis Bacon's legal career was meteoric: he became Solicitor General in 1607, Attorney General in 1613, and Lord Chancellor in 1618. William Anson of Staffordshire was also an outstandingly effective lawyer at this time, and in 1624 he purchased Shugborough Hall. He was related to the famous and highly successful Admiral George Anson, who returned from his many voyages with vast amounts of treasure worth millions. The strange coded memorial in the grounds of Shugborough has never been effectively deciphered — and it could provide a vital clue to the Anson treasure.

In the brilliantly written and researched *America's Secret Destiny*, Dr. Robert Hieronimus has explained clearly that the Illuminati were a secret society founded in Ingolstadt in Bavaria in 1776 by Adam Weishaupt. Although banned officially, the Illuminati were a functioning group that had among its members some of the most powerful and influential German leaders. Unlike Freemasonry, membership of the Illuminati did not require belief in a supreme being, and many freethinking atheists and agnostics were in its ranks, although Adam Weishaupt himself had been educated by the Jesuits. There are very differing accounts of what became of the society. The widely held view is that it went out of existence during the eighteenth century. Some well-informed researchers, however, believe that it is still functioning very effectively in complete secrecy and that its overall aim is the establishment of a single world government along non-religious lines.

Of all secret societies, perhaps the highly controversial Priory of Sion is the best known. The authors were among the pioneer researchers at Rennes-le-Château in 1975, when Lionel was lecturing for the Extra-Mural Board of Cambridge University and conducting a course entitled "The Psychology and Sociology of Unexplained Phenomena." They have written, broadcast, and lectured on the Rennes mystery ever since, and the nature of the Priory of Sion is inseparable from the Rennes enigma. Strangely, it has now become fashionable to deride the existence of the Priory and argue that it was merely a hoax created by Pierre Plantard in 1956, as part of his elaborate scheme to lay claim to the throne of France. Those who follow this Plantard hoax hypothesis maintain that he created the whole imaginary history of the Priory from its inception as a secret society in the kingdom of Jerusalem in 1099, and its centuries old attempts to restore the Merovingian bloodline to the throne of France. Baigent, Lincoln, and Leigh supported the idea that the Priory was real history in their controversial work *The Holy Blood and the Holy Grail* (1982). Dan Brown's 2003 *The Da Vinci Code*, which was clearly and intentionally written as entertaining fiction, nevertheless claimed in the preface that the Priory of Sion was a historical reality. The Plantard hoax theory may possibly be the correct one, but there are other arguments that deserve to be carefully considered. This chapter opened with the idea that the most powerful and effective secret societies are those that are known only to their members, who naturally deny their membership and the very existence of the society itself. Just suppose for the sake of argument that the Priory of Sion *does* exist, that it *does* have a long and mysterious history, and that it *does* even now exercise very significant secret powers on a global scale.

Now examine Plantard and his apparent motives from an entirely different perspective. Agreed, he is a man in search of wealth, power, and influence. He stumbles across a real secret society — the Priory of Sion — which exercises power and influence and controls the kind of wealth that he dreams about. Plantard tries, rather unwisely, to pressure them. He threatens to expose their secrets unless they help him. They call his bluff. In retaliation he publishes what he has *really* discovered about their real and very powerful secret society — a society that is far more dangerous than he ever dreamed. How better to neutralize Plantard's unwelcome exposure of their secrets and the truth about their very existence than to tell him that he either confesses that it was all a stupid hoax or he will simply be removed?

The Plantard hoax hypothesis is not quite as watertight as it seemed. Why do so many leading academic historians and investigative media personalities promote the hoax theory so vigorously? Is it remotely possible that some of the leading hoax theory protagonists are actually members of the Priory who are doing everything in their power to undo whatever damage Plantard's disclosures may have done?

So if the Priory is real, and if it has existed for centuries, what ancient secret treasures has it acquired and concealed? There will almost inevitably be links between the Priory of Sion and the Knights Templar, and Templarism is inseparable from stories of one hidden treasure after another.

Chapter Ten

Templar Treasure in Arginy, France — and Elsewhere

On the surface, the Knights Templar were active for only a couple of centuries between their inauguration early in the twelfth century to their destruction by the odious, impecunious, and treacherous Philip IV in 1307. There is, however, a gulf the size of the Grand Canyon between the official, formal history of the Templars and the reality behind their noble and fearless order. Officially, Hugues de Payens, a French nobleman from Champagne, led eight other knights, including the dauntless Godfrey de St. Omer, to Jerusalem to protect pilgrims from brigands. Baldwin II, who was then King of Jerusalem, gave them the Al Aqsa Mosque on the southeastern side of Temple Mount as their headquarters. This site was very precious and sacred to Muslims, Jews, and Christians — all the Abrahamic faiths. It was thought to be the site of Solomon's Temple, identical with Mount Moriah, where Abraham almost sacrificed his son, Isaac, and the location of the Ark of the Covenant.

The great Caliph Abd al-Malik ibn Marwan (646–705) was one of the finest of the outstanding Arabian Muslim caliphs. His army decisively defeated the Byzantines at the Battle of Sebastopolis in 692, and in his reign Muslim currency was adopted throughout the Islamic world. He was also responsible for a number of excellent commercial and agricultural improvements, and one of his most lasting achievements was to build an Islamic shrine known as the Dome of the Rock. It protected the sacred rock from which Muslims believe that Muhammad ascended to paradise. When they conquered Jerusalem, the Crusaders turned the Al Aqsa Mosque into a Christian church, naming it the Templum Domini, which translates as "the Temple of the Lord." The round shape of this temple became the pattern for many other Templar Churches and the Templar seals.

Bypassing the official history of the Templars, it becomes clear that the nine original knights — and undoubtedly King Baldwin II himself — were well aware that something of immense value was buried below, or very close to, the Dome of the Rock. Hugues de Payens and his loyal followers were looking for sacred buried treasure.

St. Bernard of Clairvaux was a key figure in the growth and development of the Templars. Bernard was born at Fontaines, near Dijon in Burgundy. His father, Tescelin Sorrel, a Burgundian knight, was thought by some historians to have been killed in action during the First Crusade. Other evidence suggests that Tescelin not only survived but came home with secret information that he passed on to his famous and influential son. Tescelin's own ancestry is something of a mystery — but a very important one for the contemporary treasure hunter. He must have been of high rank and distinguished ancestry in order to qualify as a suitable husband for the noble lady Aleth de Montbard, who became Bernard's mother. Aleth had connections on her mother's side with the Taillifers (spellings vary), who were counts of Toulouse. They were involved with

Co-author Patricia Fanthorpe in Montségur.

the mysterious religious sect known as Cathars or Albigensians, who guarded some vitally important ancient treasure. Just before the Cathar stronghold of Montségur fell in 1244, four fearless Cathar mountaineers escaped from their besieged fortress with something that meant more to them than their lives — or the lives of the families and comrades they had left behind to die. Many of the warriors involved in the First Crusade took their spiritual guidance from Peter Bartholomew, a strange monk with mystic tendencies, who reported having dreams and visions of St. Andrew during the siege of Antioch in 1097. After the crusaders had taken the city, Peter Bartholomew told them of further mystical dreams and visions in which he had been shown the Lance of Longinus, also called the Spear of Destiny, hidden below the floor of an ancient church in the city. Raymond IV, Count of Toulouse, accompanied the monk to the church and duly recovered the magical spear, which was alleged to confer military supremacy on whoever held it. Its alleged travels and adventures before and after 1097 would fill several volumes: in ancient times it was said to have been used by Constantine, Justinian, Alaric the Visigoth, Charlemagne, and Barbarossa. In recent times, it was said to have been in the hands of Kaiser Wilhelm II and Hitler at various stages in their nefarious careers. After the Second World War, it was thought to have been sent back to the Hofburg Treasure House, although other ancient lances that claim to be the Spear of Destiny are to be seen in Etschmiadzin in Armenia and in Krakow.

How much did Tescelin, Bernard's crusader father, really know about the Holy Lance under the church floor in Antioch? Is the Spear of Destiny one of the sacred treasures that the Templars found below the Dome of the Rock? The connections between Tescelin, Bernard, the counts of Toulouse down in the Languedoc not far from Rennes-le-Château, and the missing Albigensian treasure are too close to be ignored. The clues are there, and the ingenious modern treasure hunter who can untangle and decipher them will be on the brink of a great discovery. Bernard has left one cryptic quotation ringing down the centuries: "I know with certainty so you must believe me: you will find something greater and more important in the forests than in any books. Trees and stones can teach you far more than the wisest men can teach you." Is he only making a general metaphysical comment, or is he saying something about the forests around Rennes-le-Château and the mysterious cromlech of Rennes-les-Bains that was of such concern to Father Henri Boudet, a contemporary of Bérenger Saunière and author of *La Vraie Langue Celtique et le Cromlech de Rennes-les-Bains*?

There is a strong case to be made for taking the history of the Templars far back beyond their ostensible beginnings in 1119 and seeing their visible work from then until 1307 as nothing more than a relatively short chapter in the millennia-old history of a shadowy order of benign but mysterious guardians of humanity going far back into the mists of time.

Other theories concerning the Templars, their mysterious codes, and their vast treasure are centred on activities that were thought to have taken place in the Aruba Valley a few kilometres south of Jerusalem. Thousands of Templar knights, according to this theory, occupied five or six major Templar castles not far from the ruins of Petra — and those formidable castles commanded clear views of a secret gold mine.

The ancient name for Petra appears to have been Rekem, and under that name it is mentioned in the Dead Sea Scrolls. Situated among massive rocks and well supplied with water, Petra enjoyed many advantages in the ancient world. Not surprisingly, it amassed great wealth because it had become an important centre for the caravan traders: and places that amass great wealth in that way are very likely locations in which treasure will be deposited. The ancient Nabateans who inhabited Petra at the time of its peak prosperity were technologically advanced and had developed means of controlling the periodic floods with dams, water channels, and cisterns that were every bit as advanced as the Roman water control systems. Other intriguing theories about Petra suggest that its original inhabitants were neither Arabic nor Semitic — rather, their exact origins are a matter of conjecture.

It is believed by some historians that the real core of the fabulous Templar wealth and power came from the mysterious secret gold mine near Petra. Their power was greatly increased in 1139 when Pope Innocent II issued the order that Templars could pass freely wherever they chose, need not pay taxes, and owed obedience and allegiance only to the Pope himself. The strong hand of Bernard of Clairvaux can clearly be seen behind these orders, as he had been largely responsible for establishing Innocent II in the Vatican. By the middle of the twelfth century, the Templars' international banking services meant that they were guarding substantial treasures and valuables and issuing letters of credit.

Just as valour on the battlefield and their secret gold mine near Petra had brought the Templars to their pinnacle of success, so a loan to young King Philip IV of France began their tragic downfall. Philip wanted cash for his wars against England. He asked the Templars for a loan, and they refused him. There were other complications over the next few years that made the vicious and treacherous Philip IV take sudden, precipitous action against the Templars. On Friday, October 13, 1307, his seneschals made surprise raids on as many Templar commanderies as they could identify in France. The Templars, taken by surprise and imprisoned, were tortured to obtain "confessions" to the ridiculous charges of heresy and blasphemy levelled against them by Philip's minions.

The weak Pope Clement V gave in to pressure from Philip and dissolved the noble order of Templars in 1312. This was by no means the end of the Templars, however. Many were accepted into other orders. Some remained Templars in all but name; in Portugal, the name was simply changed to the Order of Christ, which maintained all the great Templar principles. They provided financial support for the Portuguese navigators, and Prince Henry the Navigator was leader of the Order of Christ for some twenty years. Although Philip's greedy henchmen succeeded to some extent in robbing the Templars whom they had caught and arrested — just as Henry VIII's thugs robbed most of the monasteries in England two centuries later — there was a great deal of Templar treasure that was never found. Where did those resourceful Templars go who were fortunate enough to escape from Philip? Leaving many of their precious treasures buried swiftly and secretly in France before they left, a number of them were thought to have escaped to Switzerland. Swiss villagers in the early fourteenth century began achieving victories by force of arms that were entirely new and totally unexpected by the aggressors who had rashly attacked what they had mistakenly thought were soft targets. Leopold I of Austria, for example, had a rude awakening when he tried to capture the St. Gotthard Pass with more than five thousand knights. A mere fifteen hundred Swiss villagers destroyed Leopold's army. Legend tells of mysterious "white knights" who galloped in to help the villagers. Were they grateful Templars whom the villagers had helped and sheltered in their hour of need when they had fled from Philip?

The riddle of what happened to the fleet of Templar ships that were in Rochelle harbour the day before Philip's seneschals struck remains unsolved. That fleet must have had considerable treasure on board, and they vanished as if they had never been. There are suggestions that some went to Scotland and the Orkney Isles, while others sailed all the way across to Nova Scotia where they deposited their vast treasures on uninhabited Oak Island. Templars could design and build as well as they could fight: the ingenuity and technical skill required to construct the Money Pit and the labyrinth below it would have been well within their capabilities. Scotland's Rosslyn, the Orkneys, and Nova Scotia could all be concealing Templar treasure.

The association of Arginy Castle with Templar treasure goes back to the destruction of the order in 1307, when a loyal and fearless Templar, a member of the Beaujeu family, was said to have raced from Paris ahead of Philip IV's hoodlums and reached the temporary safety of Arginy Castle, where the Templar treasure was skilfully concealed — probably within the labyrinth under the castle.

Anne de Beaujeu, otherwise known as Anne of France (1461–1522), was the daughter of King Louis XI (1423–1483), who was called "The Spider King" because of the webs of intrigue that were the main characteristic of his reign — and perhaps Anne acquired some of those characteristics. In any event, having studied the traditions concerning the de Beaujeu who had fled from Paris with Templar treasure in 1307, Anne had all the underground passages below Arginy Castle searched thoroughly. When nothing of any significance came to light — unless the prudent Anne was keeping it all secret — she ordered a wall to be built sealing off the access to the labyrinth below Arginy Castle. Nothing further seems to have been done until 1914.

In that year, Duke Pierre de Rosemont, who had acquired the property, demolished the barrier wall that Anne had erected and sent men

Arginy Castle.

to explore the labyrinth. It was booby-trapped, however, like some of the tombs that Lara Croft and Indiana Jones raided in their adventure films, and this had tragic consequences for one of Rosemont's workmen, whose legs were badly injured when two massive stone spheres rolled out of an opening concealed in one of the labyrinth's walls. It says a great deal for Rosemont's courage and unselfishness that he himself took on the next stage of the investigations so that no more of his men would be killed or injured.

He discovered an aperture that led him downwards and gave access to a sinister tomb that he had been told was a vital clue to the whereabouts of the Templar treasure that de Beaujeu had hidden there in 1307. According to some chilling accounts of what happened next, Rosemont saw globes of coloured light and felt as though he was being attacked by something invisible. He is also said to have heard strange cries emanating from below him. To add to these unnerving phenomena, water began rising towards him, and Rosemont — never a man to lack courage — decided that this was one of those moments when discretion was decidedly the better part of valour. When he reached the surface again, he thought things through and decided that whatever was down there presented too great a threat to risk a second encounter — either for him or for anyone else. He closed the aperture that had given him access to the strange labyrinth below Arginy Castle.

One of the oldest and most mysterious parts of the Arginy fortifications is a tower, variously known as the Tower of the Eight Beauties, the Tower of the Eight Beatitudes, and the Tower of Alchemy. This is made doubly interesting because one of the towers on Castle Hautpoul at Rennes-le-Château is also referred to as the Tower of Alchemy. The old tower at Arginy looks circular from the outside, but proves to be octagonal once an observer gets inside it. Although now faint and difficult to read properly, there are strange — possibly alchemical — symbols still visible on its ancient walls. Or are they ciphers relating to Templar treasure rather than to alchemical formulae?

The castle of Gisors in Normandy, France, is another strong contender for the title of hiding place of Templar treasure. The mystery of Gisors centres around a man named Roger Lhomoy, who was caretaker and custodian there for many years. Amidst great controversy that has not yet been effectively resolved, Lhomoy reported that he had found a Roman chapel built of enduring stone beneath the keep. He reported it as approximately thirty metres long, ten metres wide, and five metres high. There was a stone altar there, and around the walls were statues of Jesus and the twelve apostles. Lhomoy also reported seeing twenty or so stone coffins arranged around the chapel floor together with dozens of metal treasure boxes in the nave. The controversy arises because no one else has ever been able to see what he claimed to have seen — or if they have, they have either denied it or simply kept silent about it.

The old Templar commandery at Payns, France, the original home territory of Hugues de Payens, one of the founder knights, has yielded a

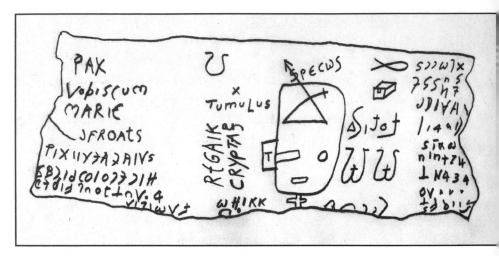

Strange coded manuscript found by Ben Hammott.

Ceramic containers from first century.

LEFT: First coin found in tomb near Rennes.
RIGHT: Second coin found in tomb near Rennes.

treasure of more than seven hundred coins dating from Templar times. They were discovered by Bernard Delacourt in 1998 during archaeological work in Payns. Do those coins provide a clue to other Templar treasure on that site?

The authors were asked to participate in the intriguing film *Bloodline* made by 1244 Films Inc. in 2008. It is an accurately detailed historical documentary centred on the discovery by Ben Hammott of a mysterious tomb near Rennes-le-Château. The authors have actually seen and handled some of the unique treasures that Ben found during his research in the Rennes area, including centuries-old coins with Templar connections and other ceramic relics from as far back as the first century AD. The findings provide powerful additional evidence that the Templars were closely involved in the mysteries and secrets centred on Rennes-le-Château. Among the articles that Ben recovered was a mysterious parchment manuscript covered with strange ciphers and symbols — typical of the Templars.

There can be little doubt that close perusal of Templar sites and their many coded messages will be of great value to contemporary treasure hunters.

Chapter Elven
Pirates and Buccaneers

P irates and buccaneers are inseparable from accounts of buried treasure. Piracy seems to be as old as seaborne trade itself. It was flourishing in Roman times to such an extent that even Julius Caesar as a young man was captured and held hostage by pirates on his way back from the siege of Miletus. True to form, he promised to make them pay for what they had done. On returning to Rome, Julius gathered an appropriate force, went in search of the pirates who had captured him, overwhelmed them, and had them all crucified. This clearly indicates that given the right motivation, Rome could easily have dealt with piracy — but the political motivation was lacking. Too many wealthy senators counted on pirates to provide them with the slaves they needed to labour on their estates.

Klaus Störtebeker (1360–1401) was the leader of a company of privateers with the rather strange title of *Vitalienbrüder*, which translates approximately from the German as "victual brothers." The name *Störtebeker* itself was a reference to his being able to drink a gallon of ale at one swallow: possibly something of an exaggeration, but he seems to have been a big, powerful man. The Vitalienbrüder whom he led had originally been employed to fight for Sweden against Denmark and to bring supplies to Stockholm, which was under siege. When the war ended, however, the Vitalienbrüder started to work independently under the name *Likedeelers* ("those who take equal shares"). The privateers had once been headquartered in Visby on the island of Gotland in the Baltic Sea, but were driven from it. They preyed on ships belonging to the Hanseatic League until Simon of Utrecht, at the head of a fleet from Hamburg, defeated them in 1401. Störtebeker offered enough gold to fashion a chain long enough to encircle the entire city of Hamburg in exchange for his freedom. His offer was declined, and he and his men were beheaded. The Likedeelers undoubtedly had vast amounts of treasure, much of which is still hidden. Theories about its location include Marianhafe, not far from the Frisian coast; Bornholm, near Denmark; and Haven, which is close to Lubeck. One or more of those sites could prove rewarding for a contemporary treasure hunter.

Much farther south, the Mediterranean pirates in those days raided the primary shipping lanes, which carried merchants' goods and gold and silver coins from the eastern parts of the empire, including Egypt and Syria, to the western provinces in Spain and North Africa. Parts of the coastline in what is now Turkey provided ideal refuges for Roman period pirates: that convoluted coastline was full of hiding places and secret ports. Not all of the treasure that those old Mediterranean pirates acquired has yet been recovered from the tortuous Turkish coastline.

The Barbary pirates, also known as the Barbary corsairs, were a mixture of pirates and privateers operating from the North African coast from the eleventh century until the nineteenth. They raided as far north as Iceland and North America, mainly in search of slaves. These raids, referred to as *razzias*, were launched against European coastal towns, and the men and women the pirates captured were sold in the slave markets of Morocco and Algeria. Over and above their slaving activities, the Barbary corsairs were always on the look out for treasure, and they targeted valuables of any kind.

Piri Reis (1465–1554), whose full name was Hadji Muhiddin Piri Ibn Hadji Mehmed, is best remembered for his famous map of the world, which showed a great many places in a degree of detail and accuracy not

Admiral Piri Reis, the man with the mysterious map.

generally thought to have been known in the sixteenth century. Piri was born in Gallipoli on the coast of Turkey and spent a long and distinguished career at sea, where he became involved in one battle after another with the Genoese, Spanish, and Venetian navies. He took part in the victorious siege of Rhodes in 1522, which drove out the Christian Knights of St. John.

After a gap of some four centuries, part of one of Piri Reis's maps came to light in the palace at Topkapi in Istanbul. In 1547 he was in command of the powerful Ottoman fleet in the Indian Ocean. Aden fell to him in 1548 and Muscat in 1552. He also captured Hormuz, gateway to the Persian Gulf, and soon afterwards occupied the island of Bahrain and the Qatar peninsula.

The most significant facts about Piri Reis from the contemporary treasure hunter's point of view are first, his accurate maps, which were far ahead of the cartography of their time, and second, the vast wealth he must have amassed from the ships he conquered and the Portuguese colonies he occupied. Were there clues in his amazing maps to the secret locations where he had buried the treasure that he had undoubtedly accumulated? Piri Reis was an Ottoman admiral rather than a pirate, but he lived and fought for decades across pirate-infested seas, and among the enemy vessels he conquered some may well have belonged to pirates rather than to the navies of Spain, Genoa, Venice, and Portugal. Aden, Hormuz, Bahrain, and Qatar would be worth investigating today in the search for Piri Reis's missing treasure.

It is also worth considering the *real* reason why Kubad Pasha, the Ottoman governor of Basra, had Piri publicly beheaded. Ostensibly, Kubad was angry with the old admiral for refusing to start a new campaign in the gulf against the Portuguese; but secretly, it may have had something to do with Piri's refusal to disclose to the avaricious governor the whereabouts of any treasure that he had taken from pirates during his long and successful naval career.

The French conquest of Algiers in 1830 put an end to the pirates' activities there, but it also meant that the defeated pirates realized that hiding their treasure was essential. The North African coastline along what was once the territory of the Barbary corsairs still offers tempting prizes to treasure hunters — but it is also fraught with above average danger.

The fourteenth and fifteenth centuries were sometimes referred to as the Golden Age of Mediterranean piracy because of the decline of European sea power and the growth during that period of Ottoman power. It was during this period that Béjaïa, also nicknamed "Bougie," became infamous as a pirate stronghold. In Carthaginian and Roman times, Béjaïa enjoyed only minor importance. A Roman veteran colony known as Saldae was established there in the time of Vespasian (AD 9–79). Later, it became the main city of the Vandals until they were overcome by the Byzantines in 533. After that it became an important city in the Hammadid Empire until the middle of the twelfth century. It was in Spanish hands at the start of the sixteenth century before falling to the Turks, who then held it until the French captured it early in the nineteenth century. Such a chequered history in a city that passed from one occupying force to another leads to the kind of anxieties that cause the wealthy to bury their treasure before the latest tides of war wash them away. Béjaïa and its surroundings are very probable sites where buried treasures might well be found today.

Captain William Kidd was born either in Dundee or Greenock in 1645 and executed on May 23, 1701. The son of a Church of Scotland minister who died while William was still a boy, Kidd moved to New York, where he became the friend of many prominent citizens. He was commisioned to sail out and attack Thomas Tew, John Ireland, and others who were described as pirates, and to attack any French ships that came within sight of him. Most of the cost of Kidd's voyage was met by a group of wealthy and powerful English lords, including the Duke of Shrewsbury and the Baron of Romney. Kidd's official letter of marque had been signed personally by King William III. Part of its conditions included that 10 percent of everything Kidd took was to go to the British Crown. The ship for his voyage was called the *Adventure Galley*. She had a displacement of nearly three hundred tons and carried thirty-four cannon. There were 150 men in her crew, all of whom Kidd had hand-picked. For fighting at sea in those days, galleys had a significant advantage over vessels that relied only on sail: a galley's oars could manoeuvre her advantageously when there was no wind.

There was a most unfortunate incident — the result of a misunderstanding — when Kidd failed to give an appropriate signal of respect to a Royal Naval vessel that he passed in the Thames. Many of his best men were taken from the *Adventure Galley* and pressed into naval service. Kidd was forced to replace the missing men in New York, and many of these replacements were former criminals, pirates, and privateers.

Bad luck struck again, as it had done in the Thames, when a third of the crew died of cholera and the brand-new *Adventure Galley* started to leak badly. They failed to find any pirates in or near Madagascar, so Kidd sailed on Bab-el-Mandeb, famous as a pirate lair — but again there were none to be seen.

Desperate to get some plunder from somewhere, Kidd foolishly attacked a Mughal convoy being escorted by Captain Barlow of the East India Company; Barlow drove Kidd off without much difficulty. The total lack of success continued. Kidd failed to attack a number of ships that might have provided the plunder he desperately needed; part of his motley and unreliable crew deserted, and most of those who remained aboard continually threatened mutiny.

Things continued to get worse for Kidd when he quarrelled with William Moore, one of the *Adventure Galley's* gunners. The quarrel came to blows, and Kidd killed Moore with an iron bucket.

When a British Royal Navy officer told Kidd that he needed to impress thirty or so of Kidd's crew, Kidd sneaked away rather than hand the men over. The Navy responded by branding Kidd a pirate.

In 1698 Kidd made what was probably his biggest mistake and seized an Armenian ship, the *Quedah Merchant*, which was loaded with gold, silver, and many other rare and valuable items. Kidd's misfortune was that she was captained by an Englishman named Wright. When he discovered this, Kidd tried to persuade his crew to restore what they had looted — but they refused. Kidd gave in to his crew's demands to keep what they had stolen.

Knowing that he was now wanted as a pirate — and in mortal peril if he was caught — Kidd hid much of his treasure somewhere on Gardiner's

Island, a small island situated in Gardiner's Bay, Suffolk County in New York, which is at the eastern end of Long Island between two peninsulas. This raises fascinating questions and clues for contemporary treasure hunters. As well as the theories connecting Kidd's hidden treasure with Gardiner's Island, there are legends associating it with the Money Pit on Oak Island in Nova Scotia or with Thimble Island or Charles Island (both of which are in Connecticut). Two fearless treasure hunters, American Cork Graham and British Richard Knight, went looking for Kidd's treasure on an island within Vietnamese territorial waters, and were promptly arrested for spying and imprisoned for over a year.

Kidd was also thought to have visited Block Island off New Shoreham, Rhode Island, and to have left some of his treasure there with Mrs. Mercy Raymond as a generous reward for her kindness and hospitality to him. Years later she and her family moved to New London in Connecticut where she was able to buy a great deal of land. Did she use all of what Kidd allegedly gave her? Did he conceal any other valuables on Block Island while he was staying there? It would be an interesting site for a contemporary treasure hunter to explore. Yet another anecdote concerns an attack by Kidd's pirates on an island in the Tokara archipelago south of Kagoshima, Japan. Attention for treasure hunters is focussed on Takarajima, which translates as "the island of treasure." The legend that associates Kidd with this island refers to numerous caves, in one of which the treasure is said to be concealed. Another suggestion is that some wreckage very recently discovered off the coast of Catalina Island in the Dominican Republic could prove to be the remains of the *Quedah Merchant*. If the submarine archaeologists can conclusively identify her, then it would seem possible that some of the treasure taken from her by Kidd and his pirates is concealed on Catalina Island. This could turn out to be of great interest to contemporary treasure hunters.

Sir Henry Morgan (1635–1688) was one of the best known and most colourful buccaneering characters of all time, and he ended his career with a knighthood and the rank of lieutenant-governor of Jamaica. Born in Llanrumney (or Llanrhymni), Wales, he was sent to Bristol and went from there as an indentured servant to Barbados. The life of indentured servants was barely one step up from slavery at that time. Morgan's chance to escape came in 1654 when Cromwell, then Lord Protector of England, sent a fleet to the West Indies. When they anchored in Barbados, many indentured servants — including Henry Morgan — escaped from their owners and joined Cromwell's fleet. Their subsequent attack on Santa Domingo was not a success, but they conquered the Spanish colony on Jamaica. Once English rule was established there, privateers were appointed as the British government's cheapest way of protecting Jamaica, and these adventurers normally gave a generous bribe to the governor when their privateering work was successful.

Morgan had command of his own ship by 1666 and raided both Puerto Rico and Porto Bello. His later adventures included the sack of Maracaibo and an almost unbelievably successful battle against great odds when he fought Admiral Don Alonso Del Campo's fleet of heavily armed galleons. Another of Morgan's great successes against all the odds was his attack on Panama. Although Charles II had to make diplomatic gestures towards the Spaniards when they protested about Morgan's raids, the English king was secretly delighted and rewarded Morgan with a knighthood and the lieutenant-governor's post in Jamaica.

The great question for contemporary treasure hunters is what became of Morgan's treasure. Was some sent back to trusted family members and friends in Llanrumney in Wales? Was some hidden in Jamaica? There was far more than Morgan could have spent in a lifetime — even with his taste for luxury. A Jamaican hiding place would seem the stronger possibility.

Another Welsh pirate in Morgan's heroic mould was Bartholomew Roberts (1682 –722), who was also known as Black Bart (or Barti Ddu in his native Welsh) and who has often been accounted one of the most successful and industrious pirates ever. Where some famous piratical characters have taken only a few ships — sometimes fewer than a dozen — Black Bart accounted for at least four hundred, possibly more. He was a Welshman from the village of Casnewydd Bach (Little Newcastle) in Pembrokeshire between Haverfordwest and Fishguard. His father, George Roberts, christened him John, but he seems to have adopted the name Bartholomew as a tribute to another famous pirate, Bartholomew Sharp. For the three years, ending with his death in battle in 1722, Black Bart preyed on ships in the sea lanes between West Africa and America.

A pirate helmsman of Black Bart's time. Photo © Michele Jackson.

Having gone to sea in 1695 when he was thirteen, his career as a pirate began when he was serving as third mate aboard the London based slaver *Princess*. They were at Anomabu in what was then known as the Gold Coast (now Ghana) when a Welsh pirate captain named Howell Davis — another Pembrokeshire man like Bart — took the ship and enrolled Bart in his crew. The two men liked and trusted each other and were able to speak confidentially in Welsh when there were any important navigational matters to discuss. Roberts was an exceptionally able navigator and was a great asset to Captain Davis. At what was then the Isle of Princes, now known as Príncipe, Davis was ambushed and killed by the Portuguese and Roberts was elected captain in his place. Under his command, the pirates took their revenge on the islanders, killing most of the men and loading their ship, the *Rover*, with all the valuables they could find: it was a substantial hoard. After many successful captures of richly loaded merchant ships, Roberts and his men were finally brought to book by the *Swallow* in 1722, and Black Bart died of grapeshot wounds to the throat. Before his enemies could board, his men fulfilled his last request to be buried at sea. His body was duly wrapped in sailcloth, weighted, and thrown over the side.

The courage that was an essential part of a pirate's career was not exclusively male. Two of the bravest and fiercest pirates, Mary Read and Anne Bonney, were women. Anne had a love affair with pirate captain Jack Rackham, became pregnant by him, went ashore to have their baby, left it in the care of friends in Cuba, and rejoined her lover for more piratical adventures. Mary Read dressed as a boy and obtained domestic work with a French family before joining first the navy and then the army. She fell in love with her future husband, a fellow soldier, and they left the army to start in business together as innkeepers at the Three Horseshoes near the Dutch town of Breda. Sadly, her husband died young; the inn did not prosper, and Mary's money soon vanished. She dressed as a man again and enlisted aboard a merchant ship that was captured by English pirates. Mary joined them and sailed with them until Jack Rackham caught up with them, and Mary joined his pirate crew, which included the equally adventurous Anne Bonney. The two girls soon realized the truth about each other and became firm friends.

Women pirates. Photo © Michele Jackson.

During her army training, Mary had become an outstanding swords-woman, and when one of Rackham's men who had become her lover was challenged to a duel by a stronger, more dangerous pirate, Mary picked a quarrel with him and killed him before he could harm her man.

When the forces of law and order finally overtook Rackham and his crew, all were sentenced to hang — including the two women. The records are uncertain about their actual fate, however, and the most likely end of the story is that their courage and resourcefulness enabled them to escape shortly before they were due to be executed together. One version of their story maintains that after their escape they were able to recover some hidden treasure from one of Rackham's many voyages and used it to live in quiet but comfortable obscurity together in Louisiana. That, of course, raises the question of what became of the rest of the treasure that they recovered after their escape from prison. Is it somewhere in Louisiana to this day? Their hideaway there would now be very difficult to trace, but a pirate historian with access to Louisiana's archives might just be lucky.

Piracy has always attracted strong and unusual characters, both male and female, and none were stronger nor more unusual than the semi-legendary Father Domingo Mugnoz and his exquisitely beautiful and sexually insatiable partner, Rosita. Their story begins in the opening decades of the nineteenth century and features the small island of Aruba, which is close to Cape San Román north of Maracaibo, Venezuela. The main geographical feature of Aruba is the Cerrito Colorado, a precipitous hill of red rock containing a number of caves.

Mugnoz was serving as an honest priest in Quito in what is now Ecuador — and would undoubtedly have served there to the end of his days had it not been for Rosita. Her beauty matched her sexual enthusiasm and responsiveness, but she had the misfortune to be married to a brutal alcoholic. Not surprisingly, she acquired a great many ardent admirers in the town, and after each adulterous liaison — being a devout Catholic — she made her confessions to Father Mugnoz, who sympathetically absolved her every time. Knowing how sympathetic Mugnoz was, and feeling that he would always protect her, Rosita ran to him one night with her enraged husband in hot pursuit brandishing a knife. Mugnoz loyally hid her in the presbytery until her villainous husband had gone. The situation reached breaking point a few days later when Rosita rushed to him once more for help. "Is he after you again?" asked Mugnoz. She shook her head: "No, father, this time he attacked me with his knife. We fought — and I killed him in self-defence!"

This was the day when the battle between the Spanish authorities and the fervent revolutionary republicans was surging through Quito. The town was in dangerous uproar. Nowhere was safe. Father Mugnoz's life changed forever at that moment. He swept the beautiful Rosita into his arms, all vows of celibacy forgotten. Determined to defend the irresistibly beautiful girl who was now his woman, the powerful, ruthless, and resolute Mugnoz fought his way savagely through the dangerous backstreets of Quito and out of the beleaguered city.

During the next few months even more radical changes came over this remarkable man who had once been a quiet, kindly, and sincere priest. Domingo Mugnoz became a dauntless pirate chief; the exquisite Rosita was his loyal and faithful comrade in arms and constant companion. They and their crew raided ship after ship, port after port, and piled up masses of treasure in their cave in the Cerrito Colorado on Aruba.

What became of them at last is unclear. According to most accounts, when the authorities finally raided their headquarters, there was no sign of the pirate lovers — nor of any treasure. The cave was empty. According to one version of their story, which seems highly probable, Rosita and Domingo died together in 1826 just thirty kilometres south of Aruba in the forest of the Paraguaná Peninsula, where they had sought refuge from their pursuers. But where is their missing treasure? Was it concealed so cunningly within a covered side cave or natural alcove inside the Cerrito Colorado that the authorities failed to find it? Did the fugitive lovers take it to the Paraguaná Peninsula with them? One location or the other must hold the vital clues to the treasures of the ruthless pirate-priest Domingo Mugnoz and his delectable mistress, Rosita.

A bolder woman pirate than the nubile Rosita was the redoubtable Irish buccaneer Grace O'Malley (1530–1603). Her seafaring father had refused to take young Grace on a trip, so she cut her hair short and dressed as a boy in an effort to convince him that she was as capable of undertaking a voyage as any man would be. This led to her nickname of Grainne Mhaol, which was shortened to Granuaile, referring to her near baldness. Her strength of character and massive determination overcame all opposition, and she was at last allowed to join her father and his squadron on a long sea voyage.

Her father had given her strict instructions in those days of piracy and buccaneering that if they were ever attacked, she was to go below and hide until the fighting was over. Pirates duly attacked them, and Grace's bold disobedience saved her father's life. Instead of going below as instructed, she climbed the rigging to get a bird's eye view of the fight. When she saw a pirate creeping up behind her father with a knife in his hand to strike him in the back, Grace gave a loud Irish battle cry and leapt fearlessly down from the rigging, bringing the murderous pirate smashing

Daredevil pirates would often leap down from the rigging as fearless Grace O'Malley did. Photo © Michele Jackson.

down under her well-aimed feet. This one action turned the whole tide of battle, and the O'Malleys drove off the remaining pirates.

Within a relatively short time Grace was in command of her own fleet and soon married into another seafaring family, the O'Flahertys. After nearly twenty years of marriage, her husband, Donal, was killed in battle. The adventurous Grace was what might best be termed a borderline pirate — depending upon which side chronicled her activities. She finally died at Rockfleet Castle, the home of her second husband, Richard Burke, in 1603, the same year that Queen Elizabeth of England died. The great question remains: what became of Grace's treasure? The most likely theory is that it is concealed in or near Rockfleet, but it may equally well have been hidden in one of Ireland's many coastal caves or secretly buried on the old O'Malley lands.

One of the most successful pirates ever known was Henry Every (alias John Avary, Ben Bridgeman, or simply Long Ben). Born in Plymouth, England, in 1653, Ben vanished into a safe and happy obscurity in 1696.

Whatever else befell him, there is no record that he was ever killed in battle or arrested for his piracy and hanged.

His early career included service with the Royal Navy, and he was thought to have been with the English fleet that attacked Algiers in 1671. There are accounts of him working as a privateer in the Caribbean and later serving as the skipper of a freighter carrying timber. In the 1690s he was taking part in the slave trade — but with a difference. Pirate or not, Every had a bizarre sense of poetic justice. Having bought a cargo of slaves and taken them aboard, he then turned on the slave traders who had provided them, overpowered them, and chained them in the hold with their former captives — all to be sold together after crossing the Atlantic.

In 1694 Every was first mate aboard a privateering vessel named *Charles II* where he was serving under Captain Gibson. As one of the leaders of a well-planned mutiny, Every put Gibson ashore and renamed the ship *Fancy*. He then sailed for the Cape of Good Hope. He successfully robbed three English merchant vessels near the Cape Verde islands, then rounded the Cape of Good Hope and sailed on to Johanna Island in the Comoro group. Here, Every displayed his considerable skill and expertise as a shipwright; he did things to the *Fancy* to lighten her and make her more streamlined. This gave her a turn of speed that few other ships could equal and enabled him to capture a French pirate ship. Every's men looted the vessel they had captured and invited its crew to join them; many of them did, bringing Every's new fighting strength up to something nearing two hundred men.

When the *Fancy* reached the Mandab Strait, Every made an alliance with four or five more pirate ships, and their fleet attacked the *Ganj-I-Sawai* together with its formidable escort vessel, the *Fateh Muhammed*. The *Fancy*'s forty-six guns, however, overawed the crew of the escort vessel, which put up only token resistance. Every's men removed treasure worth at least £50,000 by seventeenth-century reckoning. Every now went after the mighty *Ganj-I-Sawai*, which carried over sixty guns plus several hundred Indian marksmen. One of the *Ganj-I-Sawai*'s own guns exploded when it was fired at the *Fancy* and several of the gunners were killed. Every's first broadside brought down the *Ganj-I-Sawai*'s mainmast, and the *Fancy* drew alongside ready for Every's men to board their victim. Outnumbered as they were, the pirates fought fiercely and successfully — although they lost more than a score of men. The superior Indian forces might well have won, however, had it not been for their leader, Ibrahim Khan. He panicked, scuttled below decks, and hid among his concubines. Without their leader to direct the battle, the Indian troops surrendered. The total value of the gold and silver coins and gems aboard the *Ganj-I-Sawai* amounted to £600,000. Every's crew each received £1,000 and a handful of jewels. The *Fancy* sailed to Nassau, where Governor Nicholas Trott provided refuge and sanctuary for them in return for a very substantial bribe. Every then sailed for Ireland in the sloop *Isaac* — and vanished from history.

Part of the mystery may have been solved in 1967, when an inscription was discovered in a temple situated in a fishing village near Fort Colaba, some ninety kilometres south of Mumbai. It reads simply: "Henry Every — County Donegal, Ireland — Death 1699."

The great questions for contemporary treasure hunters remain unanswered. Where did Every leave his vast treasure? Was it left for safekeeping in Nassau with Governor Trott, and if so, where did Trott hide it? Did Every take most of it to Ireland with him? If he did, where did he hide it there? How much, if any, of the residual treasure accompanied him to the little fishing village in India — a very remote place for a man like Every to hide in comparative safety? All three locations are well worth the modern treasure hunter's careful attention.

The notorious Edward Teach lived from 1680 until he was killed in battle in 1718. (There are some doubts about whether his surname was Thatch rather than Teach, and there is also evidence that his family name may have been Drummond.) Better known as Blackbeard, he was in the habit of burying much of the treasure that he captured during his piratical career. It was rumoured that he would put the treasure chest in a small boat and take one companion to row him ashore: that companion never returned. The dead pirate's body was said to lie in the refilled shaft above the treasure chest that Teach had buried. Apparently Blackbeard assumed that any treasure hunters looking for his concealed wealth would be put off by discovering the body of the man he had murdered.

The wreck of one of Teach's famous vessels, *Queen Anne's Revenge*, was found near Beaufort, North Carolina, in 1996 and has since become a major tourist attraction there. It was believed to have run aground near Beaufort Inlet in 1718.

Blackbeard's nickname was derived from the huge black beard that he grew to make himself look as terrifying as possible. He would go into battle with a wide range of swords, knives, and guns as accessories, and he also wore a large tricorne hat of the type traditionally associated with highwaymen of the period. Some historians of piracy believe that he was from Bristol, England, but there is conflicting evidence that places him in Jamaica, Philadelphia, or Virginia. Having sailed on a British ship during the War of the Spanish Succession, Teach went privateering on the Spanish Main but turned to piracy when Britain withdrew from the war in 1713.

Teach met his match when he came up against a dauntless and determined British Navy lieutenant named Robert Maynard, who found Blackbeard anchored not far from Ocracoke Island on the coast of North Carolina. As the fight continued, Maynard ordered most of his men to conceal themselves in the hold and be ready to spring out fighting when he gave the order. Blackbeard fell for the ruse, saw that Maynard's deck was almost empty, and decided that the exchange of cannon fire had killed most of the British sailors. He boarded the English ship with less than a dozen pirates: it proved a fatal error. Maynard himself went for Blackbeard, and they fought a ferocious hand-to-hand battle while the British sailors leapt from the hold and despatched his hopelessly outnumbered men. When Blackbeard finally died, he was decapitated and his head was hung from the bowsprit. It eventually found its way to the English city of Bath where as a deterrent it was again put on public display.

Benjamin Hornigold was a pirate who later accepted a pardon and thereafter worked assiduously for Woodes Rogers (1679–1732), governor of the Bahamas — who had also been a privateer at one time. During Hornigold's career in piracy he had been associated with Teach, but they had parted amicably after sharing out a very considerable quantity of treasure they had together captured from a French vessel. At least part of that loot was almost certainly hidden in the Caribbean, where the two pirates had been working co-operatively for months.

During the later part of his sea-going career when he was working loyally for Rogers, Hornigold's ship was reported as having struck a reef and gone down with all hands. But is that what *really* happened to him and his crew? There are theories that they had decided to give up the dangers of high seas adventures, collect their treasure, and settle down elsewhere in peaceful anonymity. The mystery of the location of Hornigold's Caribbean treasure — and other wealth that he may have concealed — remains unsolved to this day Thomas Anstis operated as a pirate during the early eighteenth century, before being murdered in 1723. He had served under both Black Bart and Howell Davis before working independently in the Caribbean and along the eastern seaboard of the Americas. Anstis's career began when he sailed from Providence, Rhode Island, aboard the *Buck*. When a mutiny took place, he was one of the mutineers who voted for Howell Davis as their pirate captain. Black Bart later replaced Davis, and when the highly successful Bart built up a small fleet of pirate craft, Anstis was placed in command of the *Good Fortune*. Anstis and his crew broke away from Bart's fleet in 1721 and operated in the Caribbean after Bart's fleet had sailed towards Africa. During their raids on other vessels in the Caribbean they plundered the *Irwin* and brutally gang-raped and murdered one of the female passengers.

Not far from Bermuda they captured the treasure ship *Morning Star*. Anstis began building a fleet by keeping the *Morning Star* and putting one of his men, John Fenn, in charge of her. Their piracy continued until Admiral Sir John Flowers was sent out to destroy them with HMS *Adventure* and HMS *Hector*. Fenn's *Morning Star* ran aground on the Grand Caymans, and while Anstis was trying to rescue his men the formidable British warships arrived — heavily crewed with dauntless marines. Over forty of the pirates died in that engagement, but Anstis and Fenn got clear.

After a few more piratical adventures, during which Anstis added more ships to his fleet, he and Fenn and their crews moored at Tobago to careen their new ships. To their dismay, the unstoppable Admiral

Flowers arrived aboard a massive British warship, HMS *Winchelsey*, while they were working. Anstis and the pirates abandoned their ships and tried to escape, but the British marines were again too fast and too powerful for them. Almost all of the pirates were captured, but the wily Anstis got clear, regained his *Good Fortune*, and set sail yet again. But this was his last voyage. Many of the crew had been pressed into piracy when their own vessels had been captured, and now they turned on Anstis and his few loyal followers with a vengeance. Anstis was murdered as he slept, and the men who remained loyal to him were taken prisoner. The rebellious pressed men, who had regained their freedom, sailed into Curaçao and surrendered to the authorities there, who were from Holland. The mutineers were pardoned and their prisoners were hanged.

The modern treasure hunter wants to know what became of Anstis's treasure. Bermuda and Tobago are the most likely sites, and burial sites not far from the moorings are favoured. Tobago is particularly likely. The appearance of Admiral Flowers and his marines aboard the *Winchelsey* might have sent a desperately urgent treasure hiding party into the interior.

Black Sam Bellamy (1689–1717) was as great a contrast to the brutal savagery of Anstis's men — especially in their attack on the *Irwin* — as it might be possible to find among pirates. Known as the Prince of Pirates and the Robin Hood of the Sea, Bellamy was

A pirate being hanged.
Photo © Michele Jackson.

always generous and merciful to those aboard the fifty-odd vessels that he captured.

Bellamy was born in Devonshire, and went to sea as a teenager. His travels took him to Cape Cod, where he fell in love with Maria Hallet, and they began living together. When Sam's meagre seaman's pay ran out, he became a treasure hunter. With his partner, Paul Williams, he looked for gold, silver, and jewels from the many wrecks off the Florida coast. The venture was not a success, so they joined Ben Hornigold's pirate crew aboard the *Mary Anne*. When Hornigold was deposed as captain in 1716, Bellamy took over. When they captured the *Sultana*, Paul Williams took over the *Mary Anne* and Bellamy used the *Sultana*. The following year they captured the gold-laden *Whydah Gally*, which Bellamy took for his flagship — but he gave the *Sultana* to the captain and crew of the *Whydah Gally* to enable them to get safely home. Bellamy, now a very rich man, began sailing back towards Rhode Island to be with his beloved Maria again. He almost certainly intended to give up the sea, change his name, and escape with her into safe anonymity. It was not to be. A disastrous storm sank his fleet off the coast of Massachusetts: Bellamy and around 150 of his men were drowned. Only seven or eight men survived the storm, and they were arrested for piracy and hanged — except for one, who instead was sold into slavery.

The wreck of the *Whydah* was found in 1984, and many artifacts from her made their way to a museum named after Bellamy and his ship in Provincetown, Massachusetts. But the great question remains — what happened to Bellamy's treasure from the fifty-plus ships that he plundered? Did he put in to one of the many secluded coves up the eastern seaboard of America on his way to Rhode Island and bury some of it as a reserve for his future with Maria? That coast is long, and its hiding places are many — but it is well worth a visit from the modern treasure hunter. Perhaps there are even some obscure clues to be found among the many fascinating objects salvaged from the wreck of the *Whydah*.

John Callice was a Welshman from Pembrokeshire who took to piracy and acquired huge amounts of treasure from his many successful raids on merchant ships. Born in 1545, he went to London as a young man and worked in a retail business before joining the navy. This turned out to be his niche, and he acquired the skills of seamanship so fast that he had his own command in 1574. Despite his senior rank, he decided to bend the rules after he captured an Italian merchant ship: he took the cargo to Wales and sold it. This gave him a taste for piracy, and he attacked and captured several similar vessels until 1577, when he was charged with piracy and jailed in London. A plea from James VI of Scotland saved Callice from hanging, and he left Britain to avoid any further legal problems.

His exceptional seafaring skills got him a job with Sir Humphrey Gilbert's expedition to the Spanish Caribbean as pilot aboard Sir Henry Knellys's ship. Gilbert's mission was to attack Spanish vessels in the Caribbean, but Knellys and Callice decided to attack shipping in English waters instead. After many more borderline, rule-bending adventures, Callice was employed by William Fenner to go in pursuit of other pirates. He didn't. Instead he took up piracy again himself and sold the cargoes of two captured Scottish ships in Portsmouth, keeping one of the vessels for his own use and renaming it the *Golden Chalice*.

He spent the last years of his turbulent life as a Barbary Coast pirate, finally dying in battle in 1587. This raises the vital question of what became of Callice's treasure: some may well have been concealed in his home territory of Pembrokeshire with loyal and dependable Welsh friends and relatives. Some may have been hidden in Ireland, which was another of his haunts. Yet more may have been left in or near Portsmouth, or hidden in one of the pirates' havens along the notorious Barbary Coast.

Christopher Condent was born in the final years of the seventeenth century and enjoyed a longer lifespan than most pirates of his era. When the redoubtable Woodes Rogers became governor of the Bahamas, Condent and his men decided to leave the area. During a voyage across the Atlantic, one discontented crewmember threatened to set light to the powder store and blow the ship to kingdom come. Condent showed his mettle by leaping fearlessly into the hold and shooting the man dead. Shortly afterwards, they captured a merchant ship. The crew divided, and half sailed away on their new prize, while the other half elected Condent as captain. His next adventure was to capture a Dutch warship in the Cape Verde Islands and keep it as his own, renaming it the *Flying Dragon*. In his very effective new vessel, Condent sailed the length of the Brazilian coast capturing and plundering ship after ship. His lengthy pirate voyages also took him to Madagascar and around much of the African coast, the Indian Ocean, and the Red Sea. One of his greatest prizes was an Arabian merchantman that he captured in 1720 near what was then called Bombay (now Mumbai) on the western coast of India. The valuables he took from it were estimated to be worth £150,000 in those days: a fortune that would now be calculated in millions. Condent and his men shared out the loot, which came to about £2,000 each (at least £200,000 each in today's money). Condent and many of his crew then reached Bourbon Island, now known as Réunion, and bargained with the governor for pardons, which were duly granted. Several of Condent's former pirates settled peacefully on Bourbon to enjoy the ease and luxury that their wealth bought them. Condent himself married the governor's sister-in-law, moved with her to France, and became a wealthy and successful merchant there. He died peacefully at a ripe old age in 1770.

What treasure might Condent have left, and where? Unlike most pirates, who concealed their loot and died before they could recover it, Condent lived to enjoy his, and even multiplied it by virtue of his successful mercantile trading after being pardoned. On the other hand, the contemporary treasure hunter needs to consider where Condent's trail of piracy had taken him *prior* to his successful retirement from the sea at Bourbon Island and his long journey from the Indian Ocean east of Madagascar to his new, peaceful, and successful life in France. There were times in that earlier, adventurous life when Condent might have had strong motives for hiding his treasure, and the contemporary treasure hunter might well consider looking at the Bahamas, the Cape Verde Islands, the coast near Mumbai, the West African coast, and Madagascar. It's a wide field, but anything that the highly successful Condent did leave behind would be very well worth retrieving.

Chapter Twelve
Cursed Treasure and Its Strange Guardians

From earliest times, myths and legends of treasure have included powerful and dangerous guardians: dragons, gigantic serpents, and griffons. There have also been curses associated with individual items of treasure, such as the Hope Diamond. When facts are sifted out of the myths and legends, they can often provide valuable clues for contemporary treasure hunters to follow. The story of Jason and the Golden Fleece is a prime example of such myths involving treasure guardians. The fleece gives every indication of being a real, valuable object. Placed in rivers rich in minute gold fragments, a fleece might be the ideal way to collect waterborne gold dust. Hung up to dry later, so that the specks of gold could easily be combed from it, such a fleece catching the sun would appear to be solid gold and accordingly very valuable.

There are numerous versions of the Jason story, but most emphasize the important role of the enchantress Medea, who assisted him. The fleece was guarded by a gigantic serpent, so vast that its moving coils resembled black smoke swirling up from a large fire. Medea hypnotized this terrifying guardian of the precious fleece and rubbed tranquilizing ointment into its awesome head. She also sprinkled sleep-inducing elixir into its otherwise ever-vigilant eyes. At her bidding, Jason snatched the fleece down from the great oak where it hung and raced off to his ship, with Medea close behind.

According to the ancient Greek accounts of the Golden Fleece, it was located in Colchis (now Georgia) on the eastern shore of the Euxine, or Black Sea, somewhere between the modern cities of Sochi and Batumi. The Aegean Sea at the north of the Mediterranean connects through narrow straits with the Sea of Marmara, and from there past Istanbul into the Black Sea. This is the route that the historical Jason might well have taken in his quest for the Golden Fleece. The geography of the legend can be of considerable significance for the contemporary treasure hunter. What still remains to be recovered there?

Was there really a curse on the tomb of Tutankhamen and the priceless treasures that it contained? Co-author Lionel was at school in Swaffham in Norfolk, England, in the 1940s with an art and craft teacher, Harry Carter, who was a cousin of the famous Howard Carter, the man who discovered the tomb with Lord Caernarvon in 1922. Caernarvon's death a few weeks later fuelled the sensational speculation about the supposed Pharaoh's Curse protecting the boy-king and his tomb treasures. Back home on his British estate, Caernarvon's dog, Susie, was alleged to have howled desperately and fallen dead at the same moment that her master took his last breath. Conan Doyle, keenly interested in all things paranormal, expressed the idea that Caernarvon's death could have been the result of a curse.

There is some controversy about what was actually inscribed in hieroglyphs in the tomb; doubts have been cast on the famous "Death comes on swift wings to him who desecrates my tomb," but a statue of the Egyptian jackal-headed god, Anubis, in the tomb does carry the inscription "I am here to protect the dead." Howard Carter, however, lived until 1939 and was almost sixty-five when he died, and Dr D.E. Derry, who performed an autopsy on the mummy of Tutankhamen, was still alive in 1969 — nearly half a century after examining the dead king.

Whatever the reality behind the supposed curse of Tutankhamen's tomb

Pharaoh Tutankhamen.

may be, Howard Carter's brilliant discovery of it sets an example to every contemporary treasure hunter: however difficult and disappointing the early stages of a search may be, *never give up.*

Samuel de Champlain (1575–1635), known as the Father of New France, has been described as a man who combined the powers of Leonardo da Vinci and Alexander the Great. Samuel excelled as a soldier, an explorer, a navigator, a geographer, a cartographer... His talents and achievements are endless. Around such men, legends and traditions tend to gather regardless of their historicity. Money from the French king was said to have taken too long to reach Champlain, so this resourceful adventurer kitted out a privateer to attack and rob English ships — and possibly any Spanish vessels that came into range. This venture was highly successful, and Champlain was said to have acquired at least £250,000 in gold. In 1627, an English force was threatening Quebec, so Champlain and a handful of trusted companions set out to bury the treasure that his privateering activities had acquired in Mills Cove, New Brunswick, Canada.

They were in the process of filling in the trench in which they had buried the gold when a young woman appeared and accused them of piracy and murder. Before the noble Champlain could prevent him, one of the furious soldiers nearest to the girl drew his sword and decapitated her. Champlain was naturally horrified. He and his men were even more horrified when they realized that the dead girl was a young nun. They interred her with prayers alongside the treasure that had just been lowered into the trench that they were filling in. It is said that as well as being filled with sadness over the unfortunate girl's death, Champlain prayed that she would watch over their treasure.

The British took Quebec in 1629, and Champlain went to France. When peace was restored by treaty, he returned to Quebec in 1633 and died in 1635 — without attempting to recover the buried treasure in Mills Cove because of the tragedy of the young nun's death.

The legend associated with this treasure asserts that the spirit of the headless nun still guards it, and that there is a particularly dark curse hanging over it. Newcastle, on the north bank of the Miramichi River, was an independent township in Northumberland County before it became an urban neighbourhood of Miramichi City in 1995. Some farmers from Newcastle were said to have attempted to recover the Mills Cove treasure, but one of them saw the image of a blazing spectral ship — identical to the privateering vessel that Champlain's men had allegedly used — and was driven insane by the shock. Two treasure hunters from the United States attempted to dig up the cursed treasure: one was killed by a fall; the other drowned. Those who believe the legend maintain that the treasure brings only death and that the terrifying spirit of the headless nun is a very effective guardian. Legend and history are never easy to separate, but there would seem to be something well worth the modern treasure hunter's time buried at Mills Cove.

Columbia City in northwestern Oregon stands on the banks of the beautiful Columbia River just under fifty kilometres north of Portland. Ninety kilometres east of the Pacific coast, Columbia City is close to coniferous forest slopes, and the Cascade Mountains are just across the river, which is just over a kilometre wide where it reaches the city. The snow-capped peaks of Mount St. Helens, Mount Jefferson, Mount Rainier, Mount Adams, and Mount Hood are all visible from Columbia City.

The curse of the Spanish treasure ship seems out of place amidst such outstanding natural beauty, but in 1841 she anchored by the riverbank where Columbia City stands today. The ship carried a dangerous and motley crew, who had discovered that there was treasure aboard. As soon as the anchors were down, they promptly murdered the captain and carried their looted treasure ashore. Quarrels broke out among them as to who was to have what, and several of them were killed during these savage internecine struggles. Native American warriors came into view, and the surviving treasure thieves decided to bury their loot quickly in an area that was then known as Hez Copier's land. When a great many more Native Americans appeared, the Spanish mutineers beat a hasty retreat to their ship. The thieves remained on board hoping that the Native Americans would move on, but days passed and their tepees remained on the riverbank where Columbia City would one day be sited.

The Spaniards gave up and sailed away bitterly disappointed: their greed for the treasure had brought nothing but the death of the captain and many of their companions. They survived for two or three years as best they could, and then the remnant returned to the Columbia River in search of the buried treasure. The indigenous people had finally gone from the site, but the murderous mutineers could not find the exact location again. The man who had been in charge of the actual burial of the stolen treasure moved away unobserved, and the mutineers did not realize that he was missing until they gave up the search and returned to their ship.

More than forty years later, during the 1880s, a group of gifted and perceptive spiritualists were at a meeting in Columbia City during the height of interest in séances and the possibility of communicating with the spirits of the dead. One of the mediums felt certain that she had been given a psychic revelation of the exact site of the missing treasure. Treasure hunters followed her directions carefully and began to dig where she had directed. To everyone's consternation, one of the excavators suddenly fell dead. The medium felt certain that this was the work of the vengeful spirit of the murdered Spanish captain. All work ceased until 1890, when another party began excavating the site on Hez Copier's land. A layer of shattered stones was removed, and below these were skeletons that were presumed to be those of some of the dead mutineers who had killed their captain only to be killed by their companions. No one died on this occasion, but as the bones were being removed from the sinister excavation, one of the treasure hunters became wildly and dangerously insane. The search was again abandoned, as it was felt that some terrifying curse protected the dead captain's stolen treasure. The treasure would still seem to be there, waiting for a courageous treasure hunter with no fears of the paranormal — but it might be a wise precaution to take a priest along to bless the ground and neutralize the curse.

One of the most famous curses attached to a gem is the legendary curse of the Hope Diamond. It is not easy to unwind the strands of history and legend that accompany this exquisite stone. According to the popular legend, the diamond, originally taken from the Kollur mine in Golconda, was serving as one of the eyes of an Indian idol. Stolen in the 1640s by a gem dealer named Tavernier, it was sold to King Louis XIV of France in 1668. In legend, Tavernier later died of fever on another trip abroad and his body was eaten by wolves. In fact, the records show that he lived to be eighty-four.

The ill-fated Louis XVI and his wife, Marie Antoinette, were guillotined. Some said that it was because of the Hope Diamond curse — but a great many other people who had never been within a mile of the Hope Diamond were also guillotined during the Terror that accompanied the French Revolution. Having vanished during that revolution, the Hope Diamond resurfaced in London in 1823 in the possession of a jeweller named Daniel Eliason. It later seems to have become the property of King George IV (1762–1830), although there is some controversy about this. If it was one of his possessions, it seems to have been sold in 1830 to pay off a number of his debts. The diamond later passed into the possession of Henry William Hope, from whom it took its name. Various other disasters and tragedies were associated with the diamond before it passed into the safekeeping of the Smithsonian Institute in Washington, DC, where the authors inspected it. The Hope Diamond now seems to have settled down as nothing more than an interesting exhibit.

The Koh-i-Noor diamond weighs in at close to 110 carats, making it a very large and impressive diamond indeed. Its name translates as "mountain of light," and some expert gem historians believe that it has been known for five or six millennia because of a mention of it in very early Sanskrit records, where it is referred to as Syamantaka. Like the Hope Diamond, the Koh-i-Noor came from the diamond mines in Golconda in Andhra Pradesh in India. The curse on the Koh-i-Noor is reputed to be gender related: it never harms a woman, but can dethrone or otherwise damage any males who possess it. In another legend, the woman who dares to wear the Koh-i-Noor will become ruler of the entire world. Before it was taken by the British, it belonged to a number of Persian and Mughal kings and emperors who frequently fought over it with fatal consequences to the losing side.

In Hindu mythology, the stone once belonged to the mighty King of the Bears, known as Jambavantha, Jambavan, or Jamvanta; he was the first son of Brahma prior to the creation of human beings. His beautiful daughter, Jambavati, an incarnation of the goddess Parvati, became the wife of Krishna, and Jambavantha gave the Koh-i-Noor with her.

Another account of the Koh-i-Noor's history tells how it was carried away to Delhi with a great many other gems and, after passing through numerous hands, reached the thirteen-year-old Maharaja Duleep Singh, who came to Britain and presented it to Queen Victoria. It was later part of the Great Exhibition of 1851, and it became an official part of the British crown jewels when Prime Minister Benjamin Disraeli declared that Queen Victoria was empress of India in 1877. It is currently housed in the Tower of London.

Whatever legendary curse may, or may not, be attached to the Koh-i-Noor, it is interesting for modern treasure hunters to consider the psychology of such curses. Perhaps they are intended to be an additional safeguard for rare and precious stones: some criminals are notoriously superstitious, and if only a few jewel thieves are deterred by the threat of a legendary curse, that must help to increase the security of the stone.

Another famous cursed stone is the Black Orlov Diamond, also referred to as the "Eye of Brahma." Early in its history, the Orlov Diamond was one of the eyes of a statue of Brahma in Pondicherry, India. It was stolen by a temple attendant and surfaced again in 1932 when a European diamond dealer named J.W. Paris took it to the United States. Within a matter of days, he had leapt to his death from the top of a Manhattan skyscraper. Following the 1917 Russian Revolution, the families of two White Russian princesses named Leonila Galitsine-Bariatinsky and Nadia Vyegin-Orlov were living in the United States. In the 1940s both girls leapt to their deaths very much as J.W. Paris had done. Each in succession had owned the Orlov Diamond: it was, in fact, named after Princess Vyegin-Orlov.

A few years after the girls' tragic deaths, Charles F. Winson acquired the stone and re-cut it into two. This seems to have stopped the pattern of tragic suicides associated with it.

Yet another jewel with a curious curse legend attached to it is known as the Delhi Purple Sapphire. It came to prominence in the 1970s when a curator in the Natural History Museum in London, England, was working routinely among the mineral cabinets. What drew his attention to the unusual sapphire was that it was enclosed within a silver ring engraved with strange, magical-looking symbols. There was a note attached to it from a previous owner, Edward Heron-Allen (1861–1943), stating that the stone was cursed and that he had put protective symbols around it and enclosed it in seven concentric boxes before leaving it to the museum. His note ended with a warning that his advice to the new owner was to throw the stone into the sea. The museum, however, decided to keep it.

Although the scientists and professional historians in the museum do not take the legend of the curse seriously, Heron-Allen's family do. One of his grandsons refuses to touch it. According to the information that Heron-Allen passed on to the museum along with the allegedly cursed sapphire, it had been stolen from the Temple of Indra in Cawnpore (now Kanpur) and later acquired by Colonel W. Ferris, a Bengal cavalry officer. Ferris became ill and lost most of his money. Similar misfortunes overtook the colonel's son after he inherited the gem. A family friend who owned it later committed suicide. Heron-Allen said that the stone had come to him in 1890, and a great deal of trouble came with it.

Another perspective on strange, supernatural guardians of buried treasure comes from an incident in Kettering in Northamptonshire, England, in 1527 when treasure hunter John Curson approached the village priest for help. Curson was aware of the probable existence of a valuable treasure, which was said to be concealed in a mysterious ancient barrow near the town. Kettering was a settlement in Romano-British times and is mentioned in the Domesday Book. The barrow and its supposed treasures were said to be guarded by two spirits, presumably the ghosts of those interred within it — one male and one female.

The intrepid John Curson and two companions approached the barrow in the dead of night because they wanted to keep their activities secret. Curson had the idea that chanting various magical incantations before they started to dig would neutralize any negative paranormal forces in the barrow. Unfortunately for Curson and his accomplices, the movements of their feet had dislodged some insecure stones from the ceiling of the ancient burial chamber below them. The noises that they heard were almost certainly nothing more sinister than the echoing and re-echoing of the stones they had dislodged falling into the hollow chamber beneath them — but the darkness and their belief in the paranormal guardians of the barrow and its treasure terrified them. They thought they were hearing the angry warning cries of the supernatural guardians of the uncanny old tomb, and accordingly they ran for their lives. It was some time before Curson's desire for wealth overcame his fear, and he mustered a small group of determined treasure hunters to explore the ancient barrow with him. He repeated his incantations and they began to dig — then the local authorities arrived and arrested them.

Despite Curson's lack of success, it may well be that Kettering holds out good prospects for the modern treasure hunter.

Chapter Thirteen
Interesting Cases: The Seychelles, Cocos Island, and the Lost Dutchman Mine

N otorious pirate Olivier Levasseur (1680–1730) was nicknamed the Buzzard because of the alacrity with which he attacked his many victims. He was originally one of Ben Hornigold's team, but left them to ply his trade independently along the coast of West Africa. In 1719 he was working with Welsh pirate Howell Davis, but was shipwrecked in the Red Sea in 1720. Recovering from that, he raided the area around Madagascar from 1721 onwards and captured *Nossa Senhora do Cabo*, a Portuguese vessel loaded with gold, silver, and gems. This apparent success actually led to his downfall, as the French authorities were determined to put a stop to his raids. Levasseur was captured and duly hanged on Bourbon (modern Réunion) in 1730.

Just before the executioner put an end to the Buzzard, Levasseur threw some coded papers and a necklace of carved symbols into the crowd around the scaffold. He shouted derisively to them: "Find my treasure who can!" The necklace disappeared, but the coded papers survived.

In 1923 an investigator named Mrs. Savoy (rendered Savy in some versions) unearthed some very important documents apparently referring to the site of Levasseur's treasure in the Seychelles. The information that the Buzzard seemed to have left was extremely hard to decipher. There were what appeared to be a number of coordinates plus other data in characters that could not easily be understood. Savoy and her team investigated further at Mahé Island in the Seychelles group, paying particular attention to a number of curiously carved stones on Bel Ombre beach. These carvings showed a man's head, dogs and horses, snakes and turtles, and the figure of a woman. Although puzzled rather than helped by these strange carvings — but convinced that they had some bearing on the Buzzard's hidden treasure — Savoy and her team began excavating in the area. What they retrieved wasn't treasure but two long-dead corpses who appeared to have been pirates, if the gold earrings found with them were any indication.

From what Mrs. Savoy and her team could extract from the mysterious documents, Levasseur had hidden a very significant amount of treasure on an island, but the documents did not actually name it. Her friend Reginald Herbert Cruise-Wilkins came to help her on Mahé Island in the late 1940s and tried putting the coded documents and carved rocks together to solve the problem. He saw connections between Levasseur's strange ciphers and elements of Greek mythology. In particular, he got the impression that the code had something to do with the Twelve Labours of Hercules, and that certain actions had to be carried out in the same order as the famous labours. One important discovery was a statue of Andromeda buried in the sand. Other sites that Cruise-Wilkins excavated seemed to relate to clues in the cryptogram, and, thus encouraged, he continued to search. He uncovered the skeleton of a horse at one point and the bones of cattle in other places. There were also carvings representing the hoof-prints of deer. Pressing on with great determination, Cruise-Wilkins came across a carved rock showing Cerberus, the multi-headed dog of Greek mythology that guards the entrance to Hades, the Land of the Dead. It fitted in well with his theory involving Hercules, as capturing Cerberus without the use of weapons was the twelfth and final labour, thus making it the final part of Levasseur's mysterious cipher.

Cruise-Wilkins concluded that the Buzzard's vast treasure lay in a deep cavern far below the rock on which Cerberus was carved. Cruise-Wilkins had nothing like enough money to pay for the heavy-duty lifting gear that would be needed to get the rocks out of the way and reach the cave that he believed would be found below them. Sadly, he died in 1977 before completing his long search for Levasseur's treasure.

One of the strangest things that Cruise-Wilkins found during his extensive investigations on Mahé was that the elaborate subterranean system in which the treasure was said to be concealed was dangerous because Levasseur — if it was Levasseur's work — had rigged it with flood water. That was also the greatest hazard in the Oak Island Money Pit off the coast of Nova Scotia. Is it remotely possible that the Buzzard had also been responsible for the Oak Island labyrinth? Another strange similarity between the two sites was that both held curious coded clues: an engraved stone in the Money Pit and the carved rocks on Bel Ombre beach. The Seychelles treasure is well worth the attention of the contemporary treasure hunter.

Cocos Island lies in the Pacific Ocean, 550 kilometres west of Central America at 5° 31' north and 87° 04' west. It is roughly eight kilometres by three kilometres. Cocos officially became part of Costa Rica in 1949 and was incorporated into the province of Puntarenas in 1970. It was given National Park status in 1978 and World Heritage Site status in 1997. Renowned oceanographer Jacques Cousteau visited Cocos in 1994 and described it as "the most beautiful island in the world." The deep water and conflicting currents around the island encourage large numbers of hammerhead sharks, dolphins, and rays. Cocos is mountainous, composed largely of volcanic basalt, heavily forested, and riddled with caves. The heavy rainfall contributes to the island's many rivers and streams, and there are more than a hundred waterfalls on Cocos. The spaces behind such waterfalls are among the favourite places in which to conceal treasure.

The earliest and most intriguing treasure legend attached to Cocos Island concerns not only a mysterious Incan treasure but also a group of actual Inca survivors who still guard it. Within Mount Iglesias (the highest point on the island at just under two hundred metres) there is a confusing labyrinth of caves and caverns that has never been fully explored. In the depths of this underground system, there is said to be a group of surviving Inca descendants who still guard a treasure that their ancestors brought to Cocos centuries before. Bitter memories of their people's treatment at the hands of the conquistadores back on the mainland has made them so cautious that whenever strangers appear anywhere near Mount Iglesias they simply retreat deeper and deeper into the cave system until the intruders have gone.

A German treasure hunter, August Gissler, had been told by a sailor that this man's grandfather had been a pirate and had sailed with the dreaded Benito Bonito — known as Bloody Sword Bonito. Bonito began his piratical career around 1818 and continued until 1821, when he was captured by a British warship and hanged. In another version of the pirate's end, he blew his own brains out with a pistol rather than fall into British hands.

Gissler had been given clues to locations on Cocos Island by the pirate's grandson, who claimed that part of Bonito's treasure had been hidden there. Gissler first visited the island in 1889 and returned in 1891. He then stayed and hunted for Bonito's treasure for nearly twenty years, being appointed as the first governor of Cocos Island in 1897. During his lengthy, painstaking searches, Gissler did succeed in finding a few minor treasures and a handful of gold coins — but Bonito's main hoards, which Gissler had been hoping for, always eluded him.

The Bonito treasure story is complicated by the possibility that the man calling himself Benito Bonito was in actual fact a disgruntled English naval officer, Captain Bennett Grahame, who had served with Admiral Nelson at the Battle of Trafalgar. Sent to carry out naval survey work on the Pacific coast between Panama and Cape Horn, which he found boring, the adventurous Grahame decided to try piracy instead. His crew were given the option of joining him or being put ashore. Those who chose to remain honest were taken to Cocos, where Grahame promptly slaughtered them, hence his nickname "Bloody Sword." Some of the skeletons found on Cocos over the years are thought to be those of Grahame's former British warship crew who would not join him after he turned pirate. He plundered many Spanish treasure ships and raided the Mexican coast not far from Acapulco. Some reports insist that he buried all these treasures near Wafer Bay on Cocos Island.

One of his many exploits involved a running fight with five or six Spanish warships and the treasure ships they were guarding. With his own ship severely damaged, Grahame captured the *Relampago*, sailed her successfully to Cocos Island, and hid his plunder at the end of a twelve-metre tunnel. All that can be said with certainty is that many such tunnels exist among the labyrinths on Cocos. When Bonito (alias Grahame) was finally arrested and hanged, several of his crew were executed with him, while others were sent as convicts to Tasmania. One of these was his mistress, Mary Welch, whom he had picked up when she was a young girl in Panama. She is the one who maintained that the man they had captured and executed as Benito Bonito was really Bennett Grahame. Mary married on Tasmania, and she and her new husband went to San Francisco, where they organized an expedition to look for Grahame's treasure on Cocos. As far as is known they found nothing.

Before Bonito's time, however, an earlier pirate, Edward Davis — not to be confused with the Welsh buccaneer Howell Davis — was alleged to have buried no fewer than seven treasure chests on Cocos Island, having anchored in Chatham Bay.

Another vast treasure allegedly hidden on Cocos is the so-called Treasure of Lima. In 1821, a ship called the *Mary Dear* was loaded with treasure from Lima, capital of Peru, in order to safeguard it from the revolutionaries who were besieging the city. The intention was to take the entire load of valuables to Spain. The plan went astray when Captain Thompson of the *Mary Dear*, assisted and abetted by First Mate James Forbes, confiscated the treasure and sailed to Cocos Island, where they buried it. They were later captured by the authorities and taken back to Cocos to reveal the hiding place of the treasure that they had stolen. Tougher and wilier than their captors, Forbes and Thompson broke free and escaped into the jungle.

Another chapter in the Cocos Island treasure saga concerns a carpenter named Keating, who was said to have acquired information from Thompson in the mid-nineteenth century and then gone to Cocos with a partner named Captain Boag. Versions of what happened differ. In one account Boag was drowned. In another, Keating was suspected of killing him during their apparently successful search. In either event, Keating was said to have returned alone and with a large quantity of gold.

One of the treasure hunter's main problems on Cocos is that there are so many caves that it is not always possible to find one again. In the 1920s, Peter Bergmans is said to have found some of Benito's treasure in one of these myriad caves, along with a skeleton, which might have been Boag's. When Bergmans came back to Cocos later to continue his search he could never relocate the cave with the skeleton and the remaining treasure.

The Cocos treasure mystery has attracted several distinguished people. The adventurous Sir Malcolm Campbell, the fearless racing driver and world land speed record holder, visited Cocos for a few weeks during the 1920s but failed to find anything.

Just before the onset of the Second World War, James Forbes, the great-grandson of the mate of the *Mary Dear*, went to Cocos with his brother, and they searched for a few months without any success.

Of all the treasure sites in the world, Cocos is probably the most promising — the great difficulty for prospective treasure hunters, however, is its World Heritage Site status and the prohibitions on landing there. Only the Costa Rican park rangers are entitled to live on the island, and visitors are allowed ashore only with their permission.

The mystery of the Lost Dutchman Mine in the Superstition Mountains in Arizona seems to have begun with the arrival of some Jesuit missionaries in the area early in the sixteenth century. These Jesuits appear to have been successful in establishing cordial relationships with the local Apache people, who then helped the Spaniards to locate and extract gold, much of which was sent to Spain. In the eighteenth century, however, it seems that serious arguments arose between the Jesuits and the Spanish monarchy (the Bourbon Dynasty, comprising Ferdinand VI, Charles III, and Charles IV). In consequence, the Jesuits were ordered to leave America. One theory behind the so-called curse on the Lost Dutchman Mine is that the Jesuits impressed upon their Apache friends that it was of great importance to keep the locations of their gold mines a strict secret. Supposing that the area had also coincided to a greater or lesser extent with an Apache sacred site, such as a tribal burial ground, then the motive for keeping the secret would have been intensified.

The next stage in the story of the Lost Dutchman Mine involves a Mexican family called the Peraltas. In 1847 they learned of the existence of a rich gold mine somewhere in the Superstition Mountains and went out to find it. They were successful, and were returning laden with gold when they were ambushed by the Apaches and killed. In some versions of the tragedy, there were two closely linked Mexican families, the Peraltas and the Gonzales. It was the Gonzales who were massacred, while at least one of the Peraltas got safely back to Sonora with an account of the tragedy. There may be some doubt as to whether the Peraltas' mine was the same one that the Jesuits had found and worked with Apache help in the sixteenth century (and that later became known as the Lost Dutchman Mine in the 1870s after it was discovered — or rediscovered — by Jacob Walz). Walz was actually German rather than Dutch, but there was some minor linguistic confusion caused by the German word *Deutsch* being misunderstood as *Dutch*.

Another significant ingredient of the story concerns Dr. Abraham Thorne, who responded to an Apache appeal for medical help in the mid-nineteenth century. As a reward, he was blindfolded and led to a mine with a heap of gold outside it. The Apaches invited him to take as much as he could carry, blindfolded him again, and led him back to the camp where he had done the healing work that they had asked for. He remembered that the mine had been in a narrow gorge with a striking rock pinnacle nearby. This was later identified as Weaver's Needle.

In the 1930s the death toll associated with the Lost Dutchman Mine increased when Adolph Ruth was murdered somewhere along the trail through the Superstition Mountains. Ruth had acquired what were alleged to be treasure maps that had once belonged to the Peraltas or Gonzales families. Courageously, he set off alone to follow the route indicated on the maps. He was never seen again alive by his family or friends. Searchers eventually came across his body with a bullet hole in the skull.

In the early 1950s a police officer from Oregon named Travis Tumlinson and his family were coming home from a holiday in Texas. They stopped for a short rest on the road near Apache Junction in Arizona. While strolling near the car, the observant policeman noticed a protruding corner of what turned out on closer examination to be a strange map engraved on stone. The following year, the family returned and found three more of the strangely engraved stones. Years of fruitless treasure hunting passed, and when her husband died, Mrs. Tumlinson sold the stone maps. A university professor examined the engravings carefully and then gave his opinion that they were about a hundred years old. The strange markings on them *seemed* to relate to the Lost Dutchman Mine.

From the mystery of the Seychelles to the riddle of Cocos Island and the enigma of the Lost Dutchman Mine in the Superstition Mountains of Arizona, there are a great many strange and sinister treasures still waiting for contemporary treasure hunters to find them.

Chapter Fourteen
Lost Treasures in Canada

C rowland Township on the Welland River (also called the Chippawa Creek) is home to an inn that became known as White Pigeon because of the innkeeper's beautiful daughter, who always wore white. The lumberjacks who visited the inn to quench their thirst nicknamed her the White Pigeon, and the name was transferred from the girl to her father's inn. According to the story of the White Pigeon Treasure, a ship's captain who came to spend a night at the inn had a ponderous sea-chest with him. During the night, he must have slipped out of the inn unobserved and hidden it, because when he left the following morning there was no sign of the chest. The assumption was that he had buried it somewhere nearby for safety before proceeding to the next stage of his journey.

The early nineteenth century was a hazardous and uncertain time in the Niagara area because of American troops in the region who were part of the War of 1812 against the British. This war ended with the Treaty of Ghent, which left pre-war boundaries more or less unchanged and reinforced Canada's spirit of national identity. It was tragic and ironic that news of the signing of the Treaty of Ghent on December 24, 1814, reached America *after* the American victory over the British at New Orleans on January 8, 1815. During the troubles in the Niagara region, many citizens with any wealth worth concealing buried it secretly along the banks of the creek. The mysterious sea captain's treasure chest was almost certainly hidden in a similar place.

It was the American Civil War of 1861 to 1865 that generated the secret organization of southern sympathizers known both as the Knights of the Golden Circle and as Copperheads; they met in northern America and to a lesser extent in Canada. From time to time the group reorganized: they became the Order of American Knights, and then the

Order of the Sons of Liberty. Their supreme commander at this time was Clement L. Vallandigham.

By whatever name the Confederate sympathizers were known, their secret functions in Canada were of major importance to them. There were three main motives for this Canadian involvement: it provided a safe refuge north of the border for Confederate prisoners who had managed to escape from Unionist prisons; it enabled secret Confederate funds in gold to be hidden in Canada as emergency funding; and it also created an intermediate relay position for communications between Britain and the Confederacy.

From the modern treasure hunter's point of view, a detailed study of the activities of the Confederate sympathizers in Canada immediately before, during, and after the American Civil War could provide clues to the possible locations of that Confederate sympathizers' gold.

In 1858 a group of Native Canadians living in the valley of Fraser River moved down to a trading post in Hudson's Bay, where they purchased food, clothing, and other essential supplies — and paid in gold dust and flakes. Within weeks the famous Cariboo Gold Rush was on its way up the Fraser River and far beyond. Gold mining on that scale with thousands of rough, tough miners scrambling and fighting to stake their claims inevitably leads to gold being hidden for safety. Sometimes the men who hid it died before they could recover it. Its precise whereabouts were lost once that happened — but the areas around such gold rush sites are still well worth investigating.

The Seneca people (many of whom are to be found in Brantford in southwestern Ontario, Canada) played a significant role in the adventure of the lost treasure of Borie in Potter County, Pennsylvania in the United States. The history of this lost treasure — also known as the voyageurs' treasure — goes back to the closing decades of the seventeenth century when a small party of intrepid French Canadian voyageurs were making their way home to Montreal from New Orleans. They intended travelling all the way by raft up the Mississippi, then via the Ohio River and the Allegheny as far as the Conewango waterway near Warren. From there they planned to reach Lake Chautauqua and then go on to Lake Erie. Their preference for the water route was largely based on their need to avoid the redoubtable Seneca warriors.

The voyageurs were carrying kegs of gold, cleverly disguised as barrels of gunpowder. The gold coins in each keg had a layer of gunpowder on top of them, in case the party was stopped and searched en route. In Montreal the gold was to be handed to authorities representing King Louis XIV, the famous Sun King of France.

The journey began when the voyageurs prepared their rafts and canoes before venturing up the Ohio River, and all went well until it became clear that the highly proficient Seneca warriors were in the vicinity and preparing to attack the expedition. A change of plan took the dauntless voyageurs up towards the Genesee River, where they decided that the Senecas would be on them before they could reach safety. Their new plan was to bury the kegs of gold in Borie valley not far from a massive rock that would help to identify the location of the treasure when they were able to return for it later. There were two or three Jesuits with the party who identified the rock by carving a large cross on it. The party then changed direction again and went back towards the Allegheny. They eventually got safely back to Montreal, where they had the unwelcome duty of informing the French governor that the treasure was buried in the Borie valley.

Seneca traditions and the researches of a number of historians make it possible to theorize that the kegs of gold are still buried near the Borie rock. If so, at today's gold prices, those seventeenth-century coins would be well worth retrieving.

The *Le Chameau* was approaching Louisburg, Nova Scotia, during the summer of 1725 during a savage storm when she was torn to pieces on a huge reef, now called Le Chameau Reef in honour of the sailors who lost their lives in that tragedy. She was carrying an estimated three hundred thousand gold and silver coins that were lost on the seabed when *Le Chameau* met her end with the loss of more than three hundred lives. The grim destruction of *Le Chameau* came in stages. The first reef that she struck ripped her open below the waterline. She then overturned and sank in far deeper water on the other side of that first fatal reef. As ballast poured out of her and her heavy cannons and anchors were lost, she floated right way up again for a few moments before being dashed on to a second reef. This ripped away her upper deck and sides.

The fortress at Louisburg.

Finally the remains of the hull settled on the seabed beyond this second murderous reef. Gold and silver coins spread everywhere below the dying ship as she disintegrated.

A team of highly skilled Canadian experts led by Alex Storm went down in search of *Le Chameau* in 1965 and after months of gruelling work were deservedly successful in locating and salvaging a significant part of the lost treasure that she had been carrying. However, because of the wide area of seabed over which the wreck and her cargo were scattered, a great many more valuable items are still down there.

By far the best known and most intriguing of all the Canadian treasure mysteries is the secret of whatever may lie below Oak Island in Mahone Bay, Nova Scotia. This Money Pit mystery is one that the authors have investigated on site at first hand on several occasions. The modern part of the story begins in 1795 when three young men (Daniel McGinnis, Anthony Vaughan, and John Smith) were given a day off and set out to explore uninhabited Oak Island. In a clearing among the many oak trees that were there then — and from which Oak Island took its

Aerial view of Oak Island.

name — they saw a circular depression about four metres in diameter, which gave every impression of being the top of a refilled shaft. Growing beside this disturbed area of earth was a large oak tree from which a sturdy branch had been lopped at some time in the past. From the end of this branch, immediately over the centre of the circular depression, hung an old ship's block and tackle. For young men in Nova Scotia at the end of the eighteenth century, the idea of pirates and buried treasure was a relevant one. It looked to them as if pirates were responsible for the block and tackle on the oak tree.

The three lads hurried home to fetch their picks and spades to excavate the mysterious Oak Island shaft. As soon as they began to dig, it became increasingly obvious to them that they were indeed at the top of a man-made shaft. Its walls were composed of brick-hard clay in which the marks of the picks and spades of those who had originally excavated it could still plainly be seen.

Less than a metre down, the boys encountered a layer of flat stones that had *not* come from anywhere on Oak Island. The nearest location for stones of that type was at Gold River, a kilometre or two north of Oak Island. One of the strangest clues attached to the treasure mystery is that there are *two* Oak Islands in Nova Scotia — and each is close to a significantly named river. The Oak Island with the Money Pit on it is very close to Chester in Mahone Bay on the Atlantic seaboard. The other is on the far side of the peninsula not far from the Gaspareau River, but despite its name, it is no longer an island. Work was done there to counter the Great Depression of the 1930s, and this northern Oak Island was then joined to the mainland. The name Gold River has clear treasure connections: but Gaspareau is equally interesting. When spellings and pronunciations change over the years, a *G* and *C* are easily interchangeable. What if Gaspareau were originally Caspareau? It then gives the phrase *cas* (meaning a "box" or "case" that could hold treasure); *par* (meaning "via," "by," or "through"), and *eau* (meaning "water"). So a river named Gaspareau could indicate that following the course of this waterway would lead to a box of treasure.

Michael Bradley's superbly written and thoroughly researched book *Holy Grail Across the Atlantic* suggests that the two Oak Islands on either side of the Nova Scotian peninsula were intended as markers for medieval navigators crossing the Atlantic as best they could centuries ago. The secret instructions for locating a vitally important inland site in the middle of the Nova Scotian peninsula might have been to find an island covered with oak trees then sail up the river nearest to it. In the centre of the peninsula are the tantalizing remains of what *might* have been a medieval fortress, stronghold, or commandery.

Having removed the layer of flat stones that had apparently come from Gold River, the three young men continued to dig. Three metres below the surface they encountered a layer of oak logs set firmly into the brick-hard clay all around the circumference of the shaft. This, they felt certain, would be the last obstacle between them and what they had convinced themselves would be the pirates' buried treasure. Eagerly, they prised out the oak logs: nothing below them except more backfill. Overcoming their disappointment, and reasoning that whatever had been buried with such care and effort must be exceptionally valuable, they dug on again. It says a great deal for their strength, stamina, and determination that they reached the six-metre level — where a second platform of oak logs yielded no better results than the first. All the way down they had noted the pick marks of whoever had dug the mysterious shaft. Overcoming their further disappointment, the boys dug on and on until they reached the nine-metre level: here, a third platform of oak logs met their gaze. When removing these revealed nothing except more backfill, they decided that enough was enough and that whatever lay down there needed more than three men to get it out.

Life was hard and work was constant and demanding in Nova Scotia in their day, and it was some time before a larger Oak Island expedition could be mounted. It was 1803 before the Onslow Company got to work to try to retrieve the treasure. They dug steadily down into the mysterious shaft, encountering platforms of oak logs every three metres. They also extracted layers of coconut fibre, charcoal, and putty of a type used for caulking vessels to make them as watertight as possible.

At the twenty-seven-metre level they discovered a large, flat stone with an olive tinge, measuring approximately sixty centimetres by thirty centimetres and slightly less than thirty centimetres thick. It seemed to be made of finely grained granite or porphyry and was inscribed with strange symbols. It was unlike any stone found naturally in Nova Scotia. John Smith had by this time built a house on the island and was farming there. He incorporated the stone into his fireplace. In 1865 it went from there to a shop in Halifax belonging to a bookbinder named A.O. Creighton, treasurer of one of the later Oak Island search companies. He put it on display in his shop window in the hope that it might encourage people who saw it to invest in his company's treasure hunting enterprise. A witness named Jefferson MacDonald reported that he had seen the stone at close quarters and had actually been one of the team who helped to move it. In his opinion it definitely carried a coded message of some kind. Various expert cryptographers have decoded the message as "Forty feet below two million pounds are buried."

Professor Barry Fell (1917–1994) did his primary academic work in the field of invertebrate zoology but became fascinated by epigraphy after his research into Polynesian petroglyphs. Although there was considerable controversy about his work as a decoder and translator of ancient scripts, he may possibly have been right about the Oak Island Money Pit inscription. In Fell's opinion, the coded stone was actually written in an ancient Coptic dialect, and seemed to suggest that the Money Pit had been constructed by religious refugees from Egypt, who had buried their leader deep below Oak Island. If this is correct, then the elaborate system of flood tunnels connected to the Money Pit was intended to protect a sacred grave rather than to protect a treasure. In favour of Fell's argument, the type of porphyry of which the engraved Oak Island stone was made was a kind known to have been quarried by ancient Egyptians.

Whatever its real origin and whatever the true meaning of its strange inscription, when the Onslow team removed the stone and the layer of oak that lay beneath it, the diggers noticed that the foot of the shaft where they were working was becoming increasingly wet. Wisely, as it was also growing dark, they decided that they would be safer on the surface, and came up. Next morning at first light the Money Pit was flooded to a depth of at least eighteen metres. The perplexed Onslow team clustered around the top of the shaft, and one man fell in. When his companions had rescued him, his first words were, "That's *salt* water in there!" Clearly, although its hard clay sides had seemed impervious to water down to the thirty-metre level, there was a connection between the Money Pit and the Atlantic Ocean.

It appeared that the ingenious original designers of the Money Pit had rigged at least one very effective flood tunnel from Smith's Cove to the thirty-metre level in the shaft. The Onslow Company's excavations had sprung the trap that admitted the water. No amount of pumping or draining made the faintest impression on the water level in the Money Pit.

Because the clay sides were so impermeable, it occurred to the Onslow team that one way to beat the flood water would be to dig a parallel shaft and then burrow across at the thirty-three-metre level. This strategy worked perfectly until the Onslow men tried to cut across horizontally in the vain hope of being able to extract the treasure from some real or imagined storage chamber *below* the base of the flooded Money Pit: the water simply burst into their new shaft. This time they gave up.

It was more than forty years before any further attempts were made. In 1849, a new group called the Truro Company got down well over twenty-five metres before the water stopped them. Unable to get below the water, the Truro men used a pod auger on the end of their drill to try to ascertain what lay at the base of the shaft. What they found out from their drilling exercises was extremely interesting. The core samples revealed that just above the thirty-metre level there was a spruce platform. There was then a gap of half a metre or so, after which the drill bored through ten centimetres of oak. Below the oak, the drill seemed to be slipping and sliding around on what felt like almost a metre of loose metal — possibly coins — but it failed to bring any of this loose metal to the surface. Twenty centimetres of solid oak came next, followed by a further sixty centimetres of the tantalizing loose metal that stubbornly refused to come up in the pod auger. Below the loose metal the drill cut through a further ten centimetres of oak, followed by another layer of spruce. Reading from the drill samples as best they could, the Truro men thought that their drill had penetrated a treasure chamber made of spruce in which there were two oak chests full of coins stacked one above the other. Although the drill failed to raise any of the coins — if there *were* coins down there — it did bring up a few links of gold chain. Once below the spruce floor of the chamber with the oak boxes inside it, the drill continued through soft, easy backfill, indicating that the Truro men were nowhere near the true base of the shaft yet.

It was the Truro Company's misfortune to employ a drilling supervisor named James Pitblado. Thinking himself unobserved, Pitblado took *something* from the drill tip and put it in his pocket. He was, however, seen by John Gammell, a major shareholder, who asked to see what Pitblado had found. He refused to show it, and as he was a much bigger, stronger, and rougher man than Gammell there was nothing the investor could do about it at that moment. Pitblado promised to show it to everyone at the next shareholders' meeting. He never did. Leaving Oak Island in a hurry he went to see Charles Archibald of the Acadian Iron Works in Londonderry, Nova Scotia. Archibald subsequently tried unsuccessfully to buy Oak Island. When this failed, he left Nova Scotia and went to England. Pitblado has been chronicled in some reports as the first victim of the so-called Oak Island curse. He was said to have been killed shortly afterwards in either a mining accident or a railroad construction accident. The great question for the modern treasure hunter is: what did he steal from the drill tip? The Truro team came back in 1850 with better equipment and pumps. Their plan was to repeat the Onslow Company's idea of digging a parallel shaft and then going over to the treasure chamber. They would have done better to learn from the Onslow Company's mistakes. Once again all went well until they started the horizontal drive towards what they believed would prove to be the spruce treasure chamber. Once again, flood water rushed in with terrific force and filled their parallel shaft. During all the activity, a member of the company noticed that at low tide water could be seen flowing *out* of the beach at Smith's Cove. Close examination showed that about forty-five metres of that beach was artificial. During our research visits to Oak Island, we have surveyed that artificial beach carefully and marvelled at the skill and effort involved in its construction.

The people who built the Money Pit and its flood defences had constructed a fan-shaped pattern of drains deep in the beach to bring the Atlantic into the depths of the Money Pit. Each substantial drain in their pattern was filled with rocks covered with eel-grass (*Zoster marina*), which is very durable and ideal for the purpose. Coconut fibre was placed above the eel-grass, and the overall effect was to prevent the drains leading to the flood tunnels from silting up. The whole construction was highly effective.

Once they'd made this discovery, the Truro team guessed that the answer to the flooding problem was simply to cut off the water supply from the fan-shaped drainage system in the artificial beach at Smith's Cove. They attempted to build a coffer dam across the cove, destroy the beach tunnels, pump out whatever water remained in the Money Pit, and reach the treasure that way. Before their coffer dam could be completed it was wrecked by a storm. This gave them pause for thought, as did their discovery of the remains of a far older, stronger dam, which looked as if it might have been the one that the original builders used centuries before in order to construct the artificial beach and its tunnels. As the beach was too big an obstacle for them to destroy, the Truro Company's next plan was to try to intercept the tunnel that the beach drains fed. They attempted to trace its line from the beach to the Money Pit and dug down over thirty metres where they *thought* it was, but failed to find it. Their money ran out, and — very reluctantly — they abandoned their quest.

The work of exploring Oak Island and its mysterious Money Pit was taken over by the Oak Island Association in 1861. While they were working on it, the spruce treasure chamber — if that's what it was — collapsed and vanished into unknown depths. Had the cunning original builders prepared for just such an eventuality and prepared a far deeper, inaccessible chasm into which their mysterious treasure would plummet if disturbed by intruders who didn't know the secret of keeping it stable? After further unsuccessful attempts to block the flood tunnel or prevent the beach drains from working, the Oak Island Association ran out of money and gave up.

The next serious attempt to solve the mystery of the Money Pit was carried out by the Oak Island Eldorado Company in 1866. This was the group that included A.O. Creighton, who had the coded stone on display in the window of his bookbindery in Halifax. Doing their best to learn from the failures of the earlier searchers, the Eldorado group, also known as the Halifax Company, decided to concentrate on cutting off the Smith's Cove water inlet. They built another coffer dam, a very sturdy and effective one, 120 metres long and 3.6 metres high all around the artificial beach. The dam worked well at first, and it seemed to the Halifax men that they were going to succeed in draining the Money Pit at last. Then an Atlantic storm hit their dam and destroyed it. Yet again, the superior technology of the original dam builders had triumphed over nineteenth-century technology.

The Halifax team were forced to try alternative approaches. Remembering what had come up on the pod auger years before, they obtained better sampling kit for their drill tips and went down over forty-five metres. They came across more charcoal and coconut fibre as well as what seemed to be the remains of the old spruce platform on which the treasure chamber had stood before crashing down into the chasm below. Other than that, the Halifax team found nothing of any significance and gave up in 1867.

A farmer named Anthony Graves bought what had once been John Smith's land at the eastern end of Oak Island. In 1878, his daughter Sophie was ploughing there with oxen about a hundred yards from the Money Pit when the earth suddenly gave way beneath them and the oxen fell into a three-metre hole. Her husband, Henry Sellers, and his helpers rescued the oxen and filled the hole with boulders as a safety measure. When treasure hunter Fred Blair arrived in 1893, he took a keen interest in the hole. His company, the Oak Island Treasure Company, was well financed, and he and his team removed the boulders and began examining what was now referred to as the cave-in pit. Just as with the Money Pit that the three boys had discovered in 1795, the cave-in shaft had sides of brick-hard clay but was full of soft backfill that was easy to remove. The team dug down fifteen metres and then drilled for a further six metres. They encountered nothing — but in the morning the pit was flooded. Where had that mysterious water come from? Had they encountered yet another protective flood tunnel?

Blair and his team then turned their attention to blocking the flood tunnels with dynamite. They intercepted what they believed to be the main link between the drainage system on the artificial beach and the Money Pit and placed almost seventy kilograms of dynamite in the hole. The results were spectacular. Water foamed and bubbled insanely in both the cave-in pit and the Money Pit itself, but the enormous dynamite charge had had no perceptible effect on the flow from the beach. It kept on steadily filling the Money Pit as it had done since the Onslow team had triggered the flood water nearly a century earlier. Blair's men then carried out some further drilling experiments in which they encountered first an iron barrier and then what seemed to be man-made cement. The mystery deepened. They drilled again with an auger, which hit twelve centimetres of oak and then bars of soft metal — possibly gold or silver bullion. For all their prodigious efforts, Blair's team also failed to recover the treasure.

For the remainder of the nineteenth century and the whole of the twentieth, one team after another tried to solve the Oak Island mystery. During the authors' own research visits, they enjoyed the friendship of Dan Blankenship, an American war hero who lived on the island and had all the talent and determination necessary to solve the problem — but

Co-author Lionel with Dan Blankenship at the top of Borehole 10X.

even Dan has not yet succeeded. He and his co-worker, Dan Henskee, created another important shaft known as Borehole 10X. At the depths of this shaft, a remote-controlled camera revealed a human hand floating in the murky water, and later pictures showed a remarkably well-preserved corpse in the flooded labyrinth, as well as what appeared to be tools and boxes of treasure. The authors have viewed Dan's video and found it intriguing, but not absolutely definitive.

Having investigated the site at first hand for ourselves, we are convinced that there is something old, mysterious, and very, very valuable concealed beneath Oak Island. What is it and who put it there? The structure is far too elaborate for pirates. Was it a group of Coptic Egyptian religious refugees from centuries ago? Did they bury coffins rather than treasure boxes? Was it a boatload of Viking warriors? Was it the Templar fleet that escaped from Rochelle Harbour in France in 1307?

Of all the treasure sites in Canada, Oak Island is the most mysterious and the most promising.

Chapter Fifteen

The French Revolution, the Napoleonic Wars, the First World War, and the Second World War

P aris in 1791 was turbulent and seething with rumours. Were members of the nobility who still retained any power and influence planning to help Louis XVI and Marie Antoinette to escape? She wrote letters in code to her brother, the Austrian emperor, begging for help. Loyal royalist couriers tried to smuggle the letters to Austria, but there were dangerous spies within the palace and the trusted couriers were killed. The letters were intercepted by the revolutionaries and decoded.

If there was to be any hope of escape — or even of a successful counter-revolution — the king realized that a code that could not be broken must be used. He knew that he could rely absolutely on General Bouillé, a trustworthy royalist who commanded a significant and reliable army at Metz, but Metz was in the northeast of France and the king and his family were in Paris. General Bouillé had his headquarters in the fortified city of Montmédy, not far from the Austrian Netherlands, where Louis and Marie would be safe if they took refuge in the Abbey of Orval near

Marie Antoinette.

Florenville. Their loyal general did his best to plan the escape route carefully for the royal family.

In the eighteenth century — especially at times of political upheaval, unrest, and danger — people studied the writings of Nostradamus (1503–1566). De Bouillé and the king and queen knew them well. Reference to the famous, ambiguous quatrains that the strange old seer had written would serve as an unbreakable code — provided no one guessed the enciphered numbers referred to the prophet's writings. Century nine, quatrain twenty contained some enigmatic words that could be seen as referring to the royal flight. The quatrain seems to refer to night in the forest of Reims, or another interpretation of the construction may mean "queens." There are also references to a white stone (or a white butterfly, the word *Herne* appears), and there is a final grim reference to blood and slicing. Some experts on Nostradamus's early French have also claimed

Co-author Lionel Fanthorpe with a waxwork of Nostradamus in the Nostradamus Museum in Salon, France.

to find a reference to Orval as well as Varennes, and there are allusions to a black and grey monk. Is that the king in disguise? In Nostradamus's original French, the word *Vaultorte* is used, which is an imperfect anagram of Orvaulte (one *t* too many), which was the old name for Orval. In the Abbey of Orval is a white stone. The Herne reference is also interesting because the royal nurse had a cottage in that village, which was then also situated in the relative safety of the Austrian Netherlands.

What of the royal treasure during this flight? According to one tradition it was entrusted to the loyal and faithful palace hairdresser, a man named Leonard, who was believed to have taken it safely to General Bouillé. There is, however, a mystery surrounding what became of it *after* Leonard reached the general. For the modern treasure hunter who is also an historian, the fate of that royal treasure provides an interesting challenge.

In the early summer of 1798, Napoleon Bonaparte set out for Egypt with a fleet of well over three hundred ships carrying an army of more than fifty thousand men. His plan was to conquer Malta first, then Egypt, and after that to press on to capture what was then British India. One of the lasting successes of the expedition was the discovery of the famous Rosetta Stone, which subsequently enabled archaeologists to decipher Egyptian hieroglyphics.

When Napoleon's forces reached Malta, it was under the rule of the Knights of Malta, who had retreated there from Rhodes in 1522. Napoleon resorted to trickery by saying that he wished to enter harbour peacefully to take on provisions for his fleet. He then trained his naval guns on the city of Valetta, and the Knights' Grand Master Ferdinand surrendered in order to preserve lives. Within days, the rapacious Napoleon had taken everything of value that belonged to the Knights, left a strong garrison on the island, and sailed off to attack Egypt. It wasn't long before the Maltese patriots rebelled and drove the French garrison to shelter inside their fortifications. The British Navy then arrived and blockaded Malta on behalf of the citizens. The isolated French garrison surrendered in 1800.

Although Napoleon took Alexandria with little difficulty when he reached Egypt early in the July 1798, Nelson turned up with fourteen formidable British warships on August 1, and Napoleon lost the ensuing Battle of the Nile with very heavy casualties. The substantial treasure he had looted from the Knights of Malta went down with his flagship, *L'Orient.*

Franck Goddio, the celebrated underwater archaeologist, worked on many projects in the area during the twentieth century and found numerous artifacts from Napoleon's *L'Orient*. As well as cannons, hand firearms, navigational instruments, and cutlasses, Goddio's expert team found lead type from Napoleon's printing presses, which had been carried aboard his flagship prior to the start of the voyage. Coins found near the wreck included gold and silver pieces from Venice, Spain, and the Ottoman Empire, as well as Maltese coins.

Despite all their hard professional work, Goddio's team have so far recovered only a fraction of what went down with Napoleon's ill-fated fleet in 1798. Today's underwater treasure hunters would find the waters off Alexandria extremely interesting. Despite the efficiency with which Napoleon robbed the Knights of Malta, some of the priceless old Maltese treasures would certainly have been hidden from him by the islanders. The area around Valetta would, therefore, be of equal interest to treasure hunters today.

Another Napoleonic treasure can be dated back to 1812 and the Grand Army's passing through Kaunas in Lithuania on its way to invade Russia. Kaunas was founded in the eleventh century, and in the thirteenth century a wall was constructed as a defence against the continual raids on the town by the Teutonic Knights, who captured it in 1362. These earlier battles would have provided the motivation for the defenders to hide their treasure before the town was overcome. Napoleon's Grand Army inevitably carried money and treasure, and there are strong traditions that much of it was hidden in or near Kaunas. The traditions are persistent enough to make it worthwhile for the contemporary treasure hunter to work in that area in search of what was hidden from the Teutonic Knights and what Napoleon's French troops hid there as they passed through.

In the 1917 Russian Revolution, during the First World War, Colonel Ikatouroff buried a vast treasure in Armenia not far from the frontier of what was then Persia. The treasure included an octagonal golden vase, decorated with emeralds and dating from 1000 BC; more than seventy kilograms of gold and platinum; and a bag of mixed diamonds, rubies, and sapphires. The treasure had been plundered by the Turks from various Christian monasteries, and was captured from them by the Cossacks. The Cossacks in turn were surrounded by a much larger Turkish force and almost wiped out. Colonel Ikatouroff was among the dead. One of the survivors, Commander Tcherniawsky, managed to escape from the Turks carrying two kitbags filled with as much of the treasure as they could hold. At the first opportunity, he buried it in the side of a mountain.

Hearing of this event in 1933, sixteen years after the treasure was hidden, an English expedition set out to try to recover it but found nothing. In 1939, Tcherniawsky's son and a French adventurer named de Gaalon set out from Cannes to try to locate it. The outbreak of the Second World War stopped them. As far as is known, the treasure still remains hidden in its two Cossack kitbags in the side of a mountain somewhere near the frontier between Armenia and present-day Iran: not the safest or easiest hunting ground, but one that offers great prospects.

One of the most interesting treasure mysteries associated with the First World War centres on what happened to Kaiser Wilhelm II (1859–1941) in 1918. He was at the Imperial Army headquarters in Belgium when uprisings in Berlin and other centres occurred. He was particularly devastated by mutinies among his Kaiserliche Marine (Imperial Navy), whom he had believed to be unreservedly devoted to him personally. There were doubts in his mind about whether to abdicate or not, and he firmly believed that even if he gave up his German emperorship he would still remain king of Prussia. So many political and social forces were stacked against him, however, that he felt forced to abdicate, and he left Germany on a train that was loaded to capacity with his personal effects and his treasure.

Despite many appeals from the victorious Allies, Queen Wilhelmina of the Netherlands refused to extradite him, and he lived in Holland until his death twenty-three years later. Wilhelm settled first in Amerongen, but later purchased a castle called Huis Doorn. He frequently visited Corfu, where he developed a keen interest in archaeology.

A number of interesting possibilities exist regarding the fate of the ex-kaiser's treasure that came to Holland in the heavily loaded train in 1918. The first is that it was concealed in or near Huis Doorn; the second is that his growing interest in archaeology led him to conceal some of it in the ruins that he was exploring. Research at Huis Doorn — and even on Corfu — might provide pleasant surprises for the contemporary treasure hunter.

The treasure mysteries associated with the Second World War were every bit as intriguing as the contents of the ex-kaiser's train to Holland and the eventual fate of its contents. In 1945, just after the end of the Second World War, a group of German officials in Bavaria approached some American officers and offered to show them the hiding place of the Reichbank gold reserves. The Bavarians led the Americans to a cave on Klausenkopf Mountain, which is close to the city of Einsiedel. Inside the cave were piles of gold bars — more than seven hundred of them, with a value of millions. American soldiers Captain Mackenzie and Martin Borg planned to take the entire hoard: a task requiring several army trucks. The outcome was that although Mackenzie was arrested and tried, Borg got away through Switzerland in 1946 — and most of the stolen German gold vanished with him.

Another lost treasure from the Second World War — consisting of platinum and gold bars belonging to Hitler — was travelling by plane towards Salzburg in 1945 when American fighters shot it down over Lake Atter. As far as is known, the treasure on board has never been salvaged from the lake.

Numerous treasure stories associated with the Second World War are centred on the Austrian district of Salzkammergut and the Totesgebirge, which is also called Death Mountain. Another batch of Hitler's personal treasure was believed to be buried in the area close to Lake Kochel. Goering's treasure is allegedly hidden either on the bed of Lake Zeller or buried in or near Schloss Veldenstein, which was once his property. Both locations would be well worth investigating.

Whether it is a revolution, the rise of an ambitious dictator such as Napoleon Bonaparte, or the aftermath of a world war, strife, danger, and discord stimulate the concealment of treasure. It is worth any treasure hunter's time to study the history of these traumatic events in detail and to comb through the many rumours and legends of treasure associated with them. This kind of research may well provide valuable clues to the whereabouts of many such hoards that have not yet been recovered.

Chapter Sixteen
Ideas for Today's Treasure Seekers

The first essential for the contemporary treasure hunter is to know as much as possible about the laws regarding treasure hunting in the particular country in which he or she is working. As these laws are constantly changing, it is very important to check out the latest legal position regarding where searches can legally be made and what has to be done with any treasure found.

In England and Wales, for example, finders of gold, silver, and coins more than three hundred years old should report such finds in accordance with the Treasure Act of 1996. Under the law as it was modified in 2003, prehistoric base metal artifacts also count as treasure. Treasure, within the meaning of the act, includes metallic objects at least three hundred years old; two or more metallic objects of prehistoric date that have been found together; all coins from the same location; precious things that would seem to have been hidden deliberately; religious deposits such as those buried with the dead or at a shrine or other ancient religious site; anything at all that has been found *with* treasure; and anything that would once have been counted as treasure trove within the law.

The law in Scotland differs from that in England and Wales.

Treasure hunting in Austria requires an excavation permit. These are issued by the Austrian Federal Monument Authority (Bundesdenkmalamt).

In Denmark it is forbidden to use metal detectors at certain historical and archaeological sites, and the local community has the right to decide whether permission will be given to hunt over public land. On private land, there are no restrictions apart from the land-owner's permission.

In France, permission must be obtained from the appropriate administrative authority, who will want to investigate the treasure hunter's competence and experience and evaluate the scientific nature and objectives of the detection work being planned.

In the United States the treasure hunting laws vary from state to state, and in many cases the finder is allowed to retain the treasure. In some states it is necessary to obtain a permit to explore land owned by the state. The U.S. Treasury Department is the source of excavation permits applicable to public land, and the normal American income tax laws apply to treasure that has been recovered. The law covering submerged treasure is rather different. Wrecks may be legally the property of the ship's original owners, their insurers, the federal government, or the relevant state government. In cases where there is no known owner, anything found on the wreck is viewed as belonging to whoever finds it.

There are some interesting aspects of Canadian laws on treasure that apply in certain provinces and territories but not in others. In some situations the law is weighted on the side of the finder. Under Quebec's Civil Code and the common law in Ontario, the original owner of a lost object still retains a legal claim to it. The finder nevertheless has a better claim than anyone other than the rightful original owner. However, the finder has an obligation to report the finding to an appropriate public authority, who will then attempt to contact the original owner.

An important Canadian court ruling in 1993 concerned a sack containing over $10,000 that had been found by the side of the road. As the owner did not come forward to reclaim it after the finder had taken it to the police, the court ruled that the finder could keep it. However, he was told that if the original owner appeared and reclaimed his $10,000 within ten years, the finder would have to return the money.

A more substantial case took place when an off-duty police officer was walking his dog in Vancouver Park in British Columbia in 1999. The dog showed interest in a garbage bin, which, when investigated, held a bag containing nearly $100,000. Several people claimed that the loot was theirs — but none of their claims satisfied the court. The finder was told that he could keep the money, but that if the rightful owner claimed it successfully through the court within six years it would have to be returned.

Having looked briefly at the various laws regarding treasure hunting in different parts of the world — laws that every treasure hunter needs to know — a brief summary of metal detectors, the modern treasure hunter's best friend, is also relevant.

Metal detectors work on the principle of electromagnetic induction. Apart from treasure hunting, they can detect mines, weapons like knives and guns, and unwelcome foreign objects in food. Builders and repair crews are glad of them to detect wires and pipes in walls and below ground. The most basic metal detector has an oscillator that creates alternating electric current. This goes through a coil and so creates an alternating magnetic field. Because metal is electrically conductive, when a piece of metal is near this field eddy currents will be induced in that metal. The result is another alternating magnetic field coming from that piece of metal. Another coil within the metal detector measures the magnetic field and so indicates any changes in it due to the proximity of any metal objects nearby.

When transistors appeared in the 1950s and 1960s, metal detectors became a lot lighter and easier to handle. Technology advanced rapidly and benefited considerably from the use of the balanced induction system. This meant setting up two coils in an electrical equilibrium with a zero balance. When they were near metal, the equilibrium was disturbed and the tone changed. This development also enabled the machines to discriminate between different metals.

As technology has advanced further still — and it is continuing to advance exponentially — the best contemporary metal detectors allow the user to adjust factors such as discrimination between different metals, sensitivity, and volume.

The treasure hunter who knows the relevant laws and understands how to buy and operate up-to-the-minute metal detectors will be in the best position to look for treasure safely and successfully.

Bibliography

Allen, Joan. *Glittering Prospects: All You Need to Know About Treasure Hunting*. London: Elm Tree Books Ltd., 1975

Bacon, Francis. *Essays, The Wisdom of the Ancients and The New Atlantis*. London: Odhams Press Ltd, 1950.

Blashford-Snell, John. *Mysteries: Encounters with the Unexplained*. London: Bodley Head, 1983.

Bord, Janet & Colin. *Mysterious Britain*. Great Britain: Paladin, 1974.

———. *Modern Mysteries of the World*. England: Grafton Books, 1989.

Boudet, Henri. *La Vraie Langue Celtique et le Cromleck de Rennes-les-Bains*. Nice, France: Belisane, 1984.

Bradbury, Will, ed. *Into the Unknown*. United States: Readers Digest, 1988.

Bradley, Michael. *Holy Grail Across the Atlantic*. Toronto: Hounslow Press, 1988.

Briggs, Katharine M. *British Folk Tales and Legends: A Sampler*. London: Granada Publishing, 1977.

Brookesmith, Peter, ed. *Open Files*. London: Orbis Publishing, 1984.

Bruijn, J.R., F.S. Gassstra, and I. Schöffer. *Dutch-Asiatic Shipping in the 17th and 18th Centuries*. 3 vols. The Hague: Springer, 1980.

Cavendish, Richard, ed. *Encyclopaedia of the Unexplained*. London: Routledge & Kegan Paul, 1974.

Charroux, Robert. *Treasures of the World*. New York: Paul S. Erikisson, Inc., 1962.

Christie's Auction Catalogue Editorial Staff. *The Nanking Cargo, Chinese Porcelain and Gold, European Glass and Stoneware*. Amsterdam: Christie's, 1986.

Clark, Jerome, *Unexplained: Strange Sightings, Incredible Occurrences, and Puzzling Physical Phenomena*. United States: Gale Research Inc., 1993.

Clarke, Arthur C. *Chronicles of the Strange and Mysterious*. London: Guild Publishing, 1987.

Crooker, William S. *Oak Island Gold*. Canada: Nimbus Publishing Ltd., 1993.

Dyall, Valentine. *Unsolved Mysteries*. London: Hutchinson & Co. Ltd., 1954.

Encyclopaedia Britannica. Britannica Online: http://www.eb.com.

Eysenck, H.J. and Carl Sargent. *Explaining the Unexplained*. London: BCA, 1993.

Fanthorpe, Lionel & Patricia. *Secrets of Rennes le Château*. United States: Samuel Weiser Inc., 1992.

———. *The Oak Island Mystery*. Toronto: Hounslow Press, 1995.

———. *The World's Greatest Unsolved Mysteries*. Toronto: Hounslow Press, 1997.

———. *The World's Most Mysterious People*. Toronto: Hounslow Press, 1998.

———. *The World's Most Mysterious Places*. Toronto: Hounslow Press, 1999.

———. *Mysteries of the Bible*. Toronto: Hounslow Press, 1999.

———. *Death — the Final Mystery*. Toronto: Hounslow Press, 2000.

———. *The World's Most Mysterious Objects*. Toronto: Hounslow Press, 2002.

———. *The World's Most Mysterious Murders*. Toronto: Hounslow Press, 2003.

———. *Unsolved Mysteries of the Sea*. Toronto: Hounslow Press, 2004.

———. *Mysteries and Secrets of the Templars*. Toronto: Hounslow Press, 2005.

———. *The World's Most Mysterious Castles*. Toronto: Hounslow Press, 2005.

———. *Mysteries and Secrets of the Masons*. Toronto: Hounslow Press, 2006.

———. *Mysteries and Secrets of Time*. Toronto: Hounslow Press, 2007.

———. *Mysteries and Secrets of Voodoo, Santeria and Obeah*. Toronto: Hounslow Press, 2008.

Folklore, Myths and Legends of Britain. London: The Reader's Digest Association Ltd., 1973.

Fortean Times. *Various Articles*. London: John Brown Publishing Ltd., 2002–2006.

Fowke, Edith. *Canadian Folklore*. Toronto: Oxford University Press, 1988.

Furneaux, Rupert. *Buried Treasure*. England: Macdonald Educational Ltd., 1978.

Gordon, Keith. *Deep Water Gold*. New Zealand: SeaROV Technologies Ltd., 2005.

Graves, Robert, introduction. *Larousse Encyclopaedia of Mythology*. London: Paul Hamlyn, 1959.

Gribble, Leonard. *Famous Historical Mysteries*. London: Target Books, 1974.

Guerber, H.A. *Myths and Legends of the Middle Ages*. London: Studio Editions Ltd., 1994.

Haining, Peter. *The Restless Bones and Other True Mysteries*. London: Armada Books, 1970.

Hapgood, Charles. *Maps of the Ancient Sea Kings*. United States: Adventure Unlimited Press, 1996.

Harris, Graham. *Treasure and Intrigue: The Legacy of Captain Kidd*. Toronto: Hounslow Press, 2002.

Hieronimus, Robert. *America's Secret Destiny*. Vermont: Destiny Books, 1989.

Hitching, Francis. *The World Atlas of Mysteries*. London: Pan Books, 1979.

Jörg, C.J.A. *The Geldermalsen: History and Porcelain*. Groningen: Kemper Publishers, 1986.

Lacy, N.J. *The Arthurian Encyclopaedia*. Woodbridge, Suffolk: Boydell Press, 1986.

Lampitt, L.F., ed. *The World's Strangest Stories*. London: Associated Newspapers Group Ltd., 1955.

La Farge, Henry, ed. *Lost Treasures of Europe*. London: B.T. Batsford Ltd., 1946.

Lemesurier, Peter. *The Essential Nostradamus*. London: Judy Piatkus Publishers Ltd., 1999.

Melegari, Vezio. *Hidden Treasures*. Great Britain: Collins Publishers, 1973.

Phillips, E.D. *The Royal Hordes, Nomad People of the Steppes*. London: Thames and Hudson, 1965.

Pohl, Frederick J. *Prince Henry Sinclair*. Canada: Nimbus Publishing Ltd., 1967.

Pope, Frank. *Dragon Sea: A True Tale of Treasure, Archaeology and Greed off the Coast of Vietnam*. England: Harvest Books, 2007.

Pott, Mrs. Henry. *Bacon's Promus*. London: Sampson Low, Marston and Company, 1883.

———. *Francis Bacon and his Secret Society*. London: Sampson Low, Marston and Company, 1891.

Read, Paul Piers. *The Templars*. Great Britain: Weidenfeld & Nicolson, 1999.

Ritchie, Anna. *Picts*. Scotland: HMSO, 1993.

Rolleston, T.W. *Celtic Myths and Legends*. London: Studio Editions Ltd., 1994.

Russell, Eric Frank. *Great World Mysteries*. London: Mayflower, 1967.

Sinclair, Andrew. *The Sword and the Grail*. New York: Crown Publishers, Inc., 1992.

Snow, Edward Rowe. *Strange Tales from Nova Scotia to Cape Hatteras*. United States: Dodd, Mead & Company, 1946.

Spencer, John and Anne. *The Encyclopaedia of the World's Greatest Unsolved Mysteries*. London: Headline Book Publishing, 1995.

Stevens, Taff. *Ghosts of Rosevear, and the Wreck of the Nancy Packet*. Isles of Scilly: CUAU, 2008.

Strachey, Lytton. *Elizabeth and Essex*. London: Penguin Books, 1950.

Strange Stories, Amazing Facts. London: The Reader's Digest Association, Ltd., 1975.

Strong, Roy. *Lost Treasures of Britain*. New York: Viking Penguin, 1990.

Todd, Malcolm. *Everyday Life of the Barbarians*. New York: Dorset Press, 1972.

Tomas, Andrew. *Atlantis: from Legend to Discovery*. London: Sphere Books, 1974.

Von Daniken, Erich. *The Gold of the Gods*. New York: Bantam, 1974.

Whitehead, Ruth Holmes. *Stories from the Six Worlds*. Nova Scotia: Nimbus Publishing Ltd., 1988.

Williams, Neville. *Francis Drake*. London: Weidenfeld and Nicolson, 1973.

Wilson, Colin and Damon. *Unsolved Mysteries Past and Present*. London: Headline Book Publishing, 1993.

Wilson, Colin and Christopher Evans, eds. *The Book of Great Mysteries*. London: Robinson Publishing, 1986.

Wilson, Derek. *The World Atlas of Treasure*. London: Pan Books, 1982.

Young, George. *Ghosts in Nova Scctia*. Nova Scotia: George Young Publishing, 1991.

———. *Ancient Peoples and Modern Ghosts*. Nova Scotia: George Young Publishing, 1991.